12. 50N

Build a Mill, Build a City, Build a School:

Industrialization, Urbanization, and Education in Ciudad Guayana

A Publication of the Joint Center for Urban Studies of
the Massachusetts Institute of Technology and Harvard University

This book is one of a series published under the auspices of the Joint Center for Urban Studies, a cooperative venture of the Massachusetts Institute of Technology and Harvard University. The Joint Center was founded in 1959 to organize and encourage research on urban and regional problems. Participants have included scholars from the fields of anthropology, architecture, business, city planning, economics, education, engineering, history, law, philosophy, political science, and sociology.

The findings and conclusions of this book are, as with all Joint Center publications, solely the responsibility of the author.

Other books published in the Joint Center series include:

Harvard University Press

The Intellectual Versus the City: From Thomas Jefferson to Frank Lloyd Wright, Morton and Lucia White, 1962.

Streetcar Suburbs, Sam B. Warner, Jr., 1962.

City Politics, Edward C. Banfield and James Q. Wilson, 1963.

Law and Land: Anglo-American Planning Practice, Charles Haar, 1964.

Location and Land Use, William Alonso, 1964.

Poverty and Progress, Stephan Thernstrom, 1964.

Boston: The Job Ahead, Martin Meyerson and Edward C. Banfield, 1966.

The Myth and Reality of Our Urban Problems, Raymond Vernon, 1966.

Muslim Cities in the Later Middle Ages, Ira Marvin Lapidus, 1967.

The Fragmented Metropolis: Los Angeles, 1850–1930, Robert M. Fogelson, 1967.

Law and Equal Opportunity: A Study of the Massachusetts Commission Against Discrimination, Leon H. Mayhew, 1968.

Varieties of Police Behavior: The Management of Law and Order in Eight Communities, James Q. Wilson, 1968.

The Metropolitan Enigma: Inquiries into the Nature and Dimensions of America's "Urban Crisis," James Q. Wilson, 1968.

Traffic and the Police: Variations in Law-Enforcement Policy, John A. Gardiner, 1969.

The M.I.T. Press

The Image of the City, Kevin Lynch, 1960.

Housing and Economic Progress: A Study of the Housing Experiences of Boston's Middle-Income Families, Lloyd Rodwin, 1961.

The Historian and the City, Oscar Handlin and John E. Burchard, editors, 1963.

Beyond the Melting Pot: The Negroes, Puerto Ricans, Jews, Italians, and Irish of New York City, Nathan Glazer and Daniel P. Moynihan, 1963.

The Future of Old Neighborhoods: Rebuilding for a Changing Population, Bernard J. Frieden, 1964.

Man's Struggle for Shelter in an Urbanizing World, Charles Abrams, 1964.

The Federal Bulldozer: A Critical Analysis of Urban Renewal, 1949–1962, Martin Anderson, 1964.

The View from the Road, Donald Appleyard, Kevin Lynch, and John R. Meyer, 1964.

The Public Library and the City, Ralph W. Conant, 1965.

Urban Renewal: The Record and the Controversy, James Q. Wilson, editor, 1966.

Regional Development Policy: A Case Study of Venezuela, John Friedmann, 1966.

Transport Technology for Developing Regions: A Study of Road Transportation in Venezuela, Richard M. Soberman, 1966.

Computer Methods in the Analysis of Large-Scale Social Systems, James M. Beshers, editor, 1968.

Planning Urban Growth and Regional Development: The Experience of the Guayana Program of Venezuela, Lloyd Rodwin and Associates, 1969.

Build a Mill, Build a City, Build a School: Industrialization, Urbanization, and Education in Ciudad Guayana, Noel F. McGinn and Russell G. Davis, 1969.

Build a Mill, Build a City, Build a School:

Industrialization, Urbanization, and Education in Ciudad Guayana

by
Noel F. McGinn
and
Russell G. Davis

The M.I.T. Press
Cambridge, Massachusetts, and London, England

SBN 262 13052 1 (hardcover)

Library of Congress catalog card number: 78-84657

To Thomas M. McGinn
John Walsh and
Priscilla González de Walsh

Foreword

In 1961, the Joint Center for Urban Studies of M.I.T. and Harvard was given a unique opportunity to participate in the planning of a new city in the interior of Venezuela at the confluence of the Orinoco and Caroní rivers. The city, Ciudad Guayana, was being developed by the Corporación Venezolana de Guayana (CVG), a semiautonomous Venezuelan government agency charged with exploiting the great natural resources of the region—principally hydroelectric power and iron ore. The administration of President Romulo Betancourt decided not only to take advantage of these resources but in addition to provide coordinated development for the entire region around the new city so as to ensure balanced industrial growth and, above all, the creation of a metropolis that would preserve the natural beauties of the site, supply the facilities for sound community life, and minimize the hardships that inevitably attend rapid population growth in a developing country.

For five years, a group of physical planners, economists, urban designers, lawyers, anthropologists, and others recruited by the Joint Center worked as colleagues of the CVG's professional staff in meeting emergencies, assessing alternative strategies, and formulating goals and priorities. The Guayana Project staff of the Joint Center was supplemented during the summers and at other times with faculty and students from M.I.T., Harvard, and elsewhere. These scholars not only had the task of providing advice and assistance to the Project on matters of special importance but were also expected to carry out studies that would contribute to our understanding of the fundamental problems of urban and regional growth, and of the ways in which planners can and cannot cope with those problems and assist persons undertaking regional development programs elsewhere. The hope was that the Joint Center could serve not only its client but the teaching and research interests of its two parent universities as well.

Whatever success we had in meeting these dual—and occasionally conflicting —objectives was due in no small part to the imagination, competence, and forbearance of the CVG and especially of its President, General Rafael Alfonso Ravard. The work of the Joint Center in the Guayana was paid for entirely by funds of the Venezuelan government. The CVG allowed the Joint Center to set aside, out of its budget for this project, a special budget to finance scholarly studies of the project, even though some of these studies were primarily of intellectual interest to the Joint Center rather than of practical value to the CVG. We wish to record our gratitude to the CVG and to the Venezuelan government for not only permitting, but also encouraging, this experiment in combining the functions of adviser and scholar.

This book is one of a series written by men and women who participated in the Guayana Project, either as full-time members of the professional advisory staff, or as professors or graduate students who served as summer consultants to the staff, or as researchers attached to the Project. In practice, it was, of course, impossible to maintain rigid distinctions between those who were in Guayana to "advise" and those who were there to "do research." The latter group inevitably found itself drawn into discussions, and even decisions, about a wide range of issues. Happily, no researcher was so bloodless as to refuse this challenge or so weak as to lose his objectivity as a result.

This book series is not intended to be a history of the project or a record of the decisions made there. Each volume is a separate monograph on a subject of intrinsic intellectual interest, written for other scholars and practitioners working in similar fields, and published because it meets the normal requirements of scholarship by which the Joint Center and the M.I.T. and Harvard presses judge all their manuscripts. What these books have in common is that, whatever their subject, the data were drawn in whole or in part from the Venezuela project.

The first volume in this series was *Regional Development Policy: A Case Study of Venezuela,* by John Friedmann; the second volume was *Transport Technology for Developing Regions* by Richard M. Soberman. The third— *Planning Urban Growth and Regional Development*—an overview of all aspects of the project, contains contributions by some twenty specialists involved in different roles in relation to this effort. It was edited by Lloyd Rodwin who had general responsibility for the direction of the Guayana Project.

This book by Russell Davis and Noel McGinn is the fourth in the series. It sums up the experience on the educational strategy developed under the general guidance of Professor Russell Davis and his colleagues at the Center for Studies in Education and Development at Harvard University.

The book has been reviewed by both the CVG and the Joint Center, but the contents are the responsibility of the authors. Mr. Davis and Mr. McGinn were free to accept or reject any suggestions made to them by the Joint Center and the CVG as to the contents of the book.

Subsequent books in this series will include studies of migration to the region, regional economic programming, and urban design strategy.

D. P. MOYNIHAN, Director, Joint Center for Urban Studies
LLOYD RODWIN, Chairman of the Faculty Committee, Joint Center
for Urban Studies

Cambridge, Massachusetts, January 1969

Preface

To fulfill an economic development goal in Venezuela, a city was founded in the southeast and called Ciudad Guayana. To serve the people of the city, schools were established. The mine, the mill, the city, and the school: this was the sequence of events in Ciudad Guayana. Education was a consequence of urbanization, which in turn had been a consequence of industrialization. These phenomena could be observed and described in many different ways. The way we have chosen may not completely satisfy everyone, but we shall describe the contents precisely beforehand to permit skipping of material which may not be relevant or appealing.

There are three parts to the book. Part 1 describes the city of Guayana, the people, and the schools. This is the main part and it contains the essential sociological analysis. It offers a general description of the geography, demography, and economy of the city and region and then moves in for closer study of the people and the schools. Part 1 describes the Guayana schools and attempts to explain why they are as they are. Part 2 goes beyond description and explanation and attempts to design an educational system and programs for Guayana. This was necessary because the main objective was to use the study as a basis for educational planning and not as an entry in the literature of sociology. From the outset, the authors designed the research so that it would issue in plans and programs in education. Part 3 makes one march further into the dangerous world of practice when it attempts to follow the implementation of the plans and programs and to interpret the reasons for success or failure. Part 3 also highlights the fact that the research, planning, and implementation centered in a regional development agency, the Corporación Venezolana de Guayana.

This book describes an exercise in regional planning for human resource development. As it moves from research to planning to implementation, it sacrifices unity and violates conventions, if not canons, and the general reader is free to skip Part 2 or Part 3. Planners should not. It is precisely the joining of the research study to the plan to the program and its implementation which gives this book any unique character it may have in the literature of planning.

Part 1 begins with rather general descriptive material, some of which is handled in more complete and detailed fashion in other sources. Chapter 1 sketches the lineaments of the problem of rural to urban migration in Latin America and in southeastern Venezuela and Guayana. It has little new information or analysis not found elsewhere, but it is necessary if this book is to stand by itself. Chapter 2 describes the economy of the Guayana Development Zone in familiar terms, but the translation of economic facts into a human resource development program is new and necessary argument. Chapter 3 describes physical characteristics of Guayana and the surroundings, and Chapter 4 sketches the basic demographic facts of its migrant and very rapidly growing population.

Chapter 5 offers a general description of the Guayana school system, using conventional educational statistics, and Chapter 6 analyzes the primary schools for efficiency and finds it low. Chapter 7 moves deep into the problem and studies the experience of children from the barrios in the Guayana schools. Even for children from the poorest families of the barrios, this experience cannot be characterized simply. There is mixed success and failure for mixed reasons, and this is the most interesting aspect of the entire study. The study then moves on in Chapters 8 and 9 to the concomitants of school success or failure in Guayana. The family is a principal determinant of school success or failure, and family characteristics as correlates are examined in considerable detail in bivariate analysis in Chapters 8 and 9 and in multivariate perspective in Chapter 10. The bulk of the study of barrio families and their influence on education in Ciudad Guayana is covered in Chapters 7 through 10: for some, this may be all that is new and necessary; but again, we should emphasize that this book was written for educational planners and administrators, as well as for sociologists and development economists. The analysis in Part 1 suggests educational plans and programs which are presented in Part 2.

In Chapter 11, Part 2, the object is to translate the research findings into the design of an efficient school system in Guayana. This is imperfectly accomplished, but it is attempted. Chapter 12 attempts the same with informal education and training programs outside the schools. The vast need for trained people and the exiguous resources make informal education an important alternative in human resource development in Guayana. Chapter 13 describes the first and most important step to implement the educational plan for Guayana, the creation of the Guayana Center for Educational Research, Planning, and Extension Services. Chapter 13 ends in 1966 with the establishment of the Center, which was created to implement educational development plans in Guayana. The Guayana Center itself is a unique institution and merits description.

Part 3 covers activities of the Guayana Center up to 1968. Chapter 14 describes development in the Guayana schools from 1966 to 1968, compares plans and actual outcomes, and describes success or lack of it in implementing the three main Guayana Center programs in informal education, technical education, and science education. There are technical appendixes of the sampling scheme, the survey instrumentation, and a detailed description of the factor analysis, canonical correlation, multiple stepwise regression, and multiple discriminant analyses used in the sections offering multivariate perspectives on the barrio family and the schools.

The description, the analysis, and the action in human resource development in Guayana take place over a five-year period, 1963–1968. In this period, the educational problems of Ciudad Guayana are not solved. Things do change and, in most ways, for the better. The final section of Chapter 14 attempts to provide some hypotheses to account for why some plans worked and others did not. Hopefully, these hypotheses will be tested in studies during the next five years. And so it goes on.

Many friends were involved in the preparation of this book, some are mentioned here, others are thanked in silence. Brigida Hahn, Susan Vogeler, Lucia Pinedo, Mario Testa, Gustavo Herrera, José Antonio Lecuna, Helena Velarde, and others of the CVG were invaluable in many ways. The counsel of Hector Font is especially appreciated. Inspiration in Guayana was provided by the vision and sacrifices of Monseñor Zabaleta and Nicoleta Solinas. Santos Paez of the Ministry of Education provided valuable entry into schools. Among our colleagues at CSED, William Charleson, Richard Durstine, and Lawrence Wolff deserve a special vote of gratitude. Alvis Martinez prepared the manuscript. In addition to the sponsorship of the CVG and the Joint Center for Urban Studies, we were assisted by the Ford Foundation.

NOEL F. MCGINN
RUSSELL G. DAVIS

Cambridge, Massachusetts
November 1968

Contents

Tables

Illustrations

Abbreviations

Bs.	bolivares, monetary unit of Venezuela 1 bolívar = U.S. $0.22 (1968)
CSED	Center for Studies in Education and Development, Harvard University
CVG	Corporación Venezolana de Guayana
DARINCO	Dirección de Educación Artesanal, Industrial, y Comercial Department of Artisanal, Industrial, and Commercial Education in the Ministry of Education
EDUPLAN	Oficina de Planificación Integral de la Educación Office of Educational Planning in the Ministry of Education
ETI	Escuela Técnica Industrial Technical-Industrial School in Ciudad Guayana (public secondary school)
INCE	Instituto Nacional de Cooperación Educativa National Institute of Educational Cooperation
ODEA	Oficina de Educación de Adultos Office of Adult Education in the Ministry of Education
OECD	Organization for Economic Cooperation and Development (Common Market)
SIDOR	Siderúrgica del Orinoco (Venezuelan government-owned steel mill in Ciudad Guayana)

Part One

Guayana:
Its Future and
the Schools

1
Social Consequences
of Urbanization

Blessing or curse, the linked phenomena of urbanization and industrialization are strongly with Latin America, and the subject of this book, Ciudad Guayana, will typify some but not all of the gains and losses that come with such changes. Ciudad Guayana is an industrial city in southeastern Venezuela. In Ciudad Guayana the pace of urbanization and industrialization is as brisk as anywhere in Latin America, but it differs from other, older cities—the tenth birthday of the city will be celebrated in 1971—in that expansion is deliberate and also better controlled and planned.

Urbanization is outstripping industrialization in Latin America, although the exact relationship that should be maintained between the two is difficult to specify.[1] Certainly, urban populations are increasing much faster than employment opportunities in industry and the sectors of the economy that support it; and the result in some countries is urban unemployment that runs from 10 to 20 percent of the eligible work force. If there is not unemployment outright, there is underemployment masked by the absorption of rural migrants into sporadic and petty trading and services. In Ciudad Guayana there is a deliberate policy to control and minimize this, but still 10 to 15 percent of the work force may be unemployed between construction activity peaks.

Presently about half of the population of Latin America lives in cities and, at present growth rates, in ten years almost 75 percent of the population may be urban. Caracas, Venezuela's capital, has increased in population almost 7 percent a year in the decade 1950–1960. Ciudad Guayana is increasing in population at almost twice this rate. Twenty-five years ago, Venezuela had slightly less than 20 percent of its population living in cities of more than 20,000 inhabitants. Now almost 50 percent live in cities of 20,000 or more. In 1930, there was one city of more than a million in Latin America; in 1940, there were four; and now there are ten. Montevideo, the capital of Uruguay, has about 46 percent of the total population of the country.

There is no question where the population is coming from. First, there is the general population increase. Natural increase rates in Latin America are high, averaging 2.8 percent per annum over-all and exceeding 3.5 percent in Central America. Birth rates in all except five countries of Latin America are over 4 percent and in some countries in Central America, over 5. Meanwhile, mortality rates are declining, although they are still high in some Caribbean countries. There is migration, but it is mostly internal. Except for Venezuela and Argentina, external migration has had only a slight effect in the past twenty years, and even in these countries external migration has slowed to a trickle. Still, the urban populations grow. The root cause is the vast in-migration from rural areas and small provincial towns and cities.

There is general agreement that the chief cause of rural to urban migration in Latin America is economic. Flinn in Colombia, Matos Mar in Peru, and Germani in Argentina have all found the same prime cause.[2] People come to the city seeking steadier and better paying employment. There is excess population in the rural regions of Venezuela as elsewhere in Latin America. Natural increase of the population has been high and employment opportunities have diminished markedly either because of rises in productivity in export agriculture or the disappearance of marginal farms in the subsistence sector. In Venezuela, it has been the latter cause largely, as men have left the low-yield *conucos* of eastern Venezuela.

Before 1958 the economic lot of the rural dweller in eastern Venezuela was hard indeed. Usually a *conuquero* without title to his land planted corn, yucca, and bananas, and in some places beans and yams, and produced an average family income of 100 bolivares (U.S. $22) a month, sufficient to meet basic needs of survival, if illness or accident did not exhaust even those meager resources. Before 1959, when many of the workers had already started their exodus from the rural areas to the oil fields and construction sites, there were no IAN (Instituto Agrario Nacional) or MAC (Ministerio de Agricultura y Cria) programs to assist the farmers. After the election of AD (Acción Democrática) in 1958 and the formation by the Federación Campesina of rural *sindicatos*, the farmers had some means of pressing the government for credit, technical assistance, and relief; but before that there was nothing. Even the low average earnings of service workers and menials in the urban areas was double that of the campesinos. In the beginning, then, it took no very glowing prospect to attract the campesinos of eastern Venezuela in to the labor camps and the towns.

By no means all of the motives for rural to urban migration have been economic, although the social and political reasons have been entwined in economics. Central governments have failed to bring basic services, let alone amenities, to rural areas. The studies by Flinn, Matos Mar, and Germani already cited show remarkable agreement on the other causes for rural to urban migration. Migrants come in to the cities seeking education, health, and housing Often a catchall reason which may be described as "social" stimulated the migration. Social covers the physical and cultural amenities of the city, as well as the pull in to community life for those who have been living in brute isolation. All studies also show the influence that family connections have. One member goes in and the others follow, sometimes this spreads through in-law and *compadrazgo* connections to many families, and the chain of attraction stretches out over several generations. In Venezuela, as in the rest of Latin America, those who sought anything more than the most rudimentary and empty pretense at education were forced to come in from the rural regions.

On every measurable indicator of educational service, quantitative and qualitative, rural schools in Latin America suffer by comparison with even the worst urban schools. Highly centralized federal systems, managed from remote ministries in the capital city, have failed to translate even the most meager benefits of education to rural regions. The problem is compounded in the case of rural regions with non-Spanish speaking indigenous populations. The ratio of primary school teachers classified as *empiricos*, a euphemism which means mostly untrained and uneducated, is four times as high in rural as in urban regions in some of the countries. Countries, from Argentina to Costa Rica, show an excess of trained primary school teachers who wait years for teaching appointments in the urban schools rather than go out into the rural schools.

Rural facilities are rudimentary and the cost for a rural classroom in Central America is a fourth that of an urban classroom. In the countries that distribute textbooks, Mexico and lately Venezuela being exceptions, vast rural regions receive none, although hundreds of thousands of books may molder in warehouses in central cities. The service of supply in most rural regions consists of an annual distribution of chalk, pencils, and notebooks. In one Central American country the rural schools had not received such a distribution for more than two years, and the only supply was what parents brought back from their trading trips to provincial towns.

Most serious of all deficiencies is the fact that no effective school system really exists in the interior. The common pattern is to appoint a provincial chief education officer. In Central America the officer may not be an educator at all, merely a provincial lawyer who takes on a host of government jobs to supplement his income. Even if he were a dedicated and able educator, there are rarely travel funds, and the provincial education officer may never in his entire career visit the schools which he presumably supervises. The provincial or state officer spends such time as he spends supervising the compilation of statistics—most of them inaccurate—for transmittal to the Ministry.

In addition, there is sometimes a group of rural school supervisors or inspectors, again without sufficient funds to travel and with vast territories dotted with small one- or two-room schools that are never visited. Although they may be called "supervisors," they often exercise no supervisory functions and are in fact immobile inspectors. The magnitude of their responsibilities is so great that many in desperation content themselves with filling out reports in the capital. In Guatemala fewer than fifty supervisors try to cover the entire rural area of the country, in Nicaragua it is common to have two years pass without a visit, and in rural Venezuela the situation is as bad.

In Latin America it was not uncommon to have one supervisor with responsibility for a hundred schools. The pattern of organization is like an army in which there are a few general officers and staff back at headquarters and no intervening command links right down to the firing line, in this case the individual school. This total lack of direction and supervision with untrained teachers and no books has made a farce of rural education in Latin America.

Prior to 1958 there were almost no schools in the rural regions of eastern Venezuela and when schools existed there was no supervision or control. Schools were, more often than not, one-room, one-teacher affairs which either ended at the second or third grade or made a pretense of offering education in all the grades. There were no textbooks or supplementary materials; teachers were badly trained or not trained at all and had no qualifications beyond a shaky grip on fundamental literacy.

It is not now possible to state whether rural parents realized the deplorable state of education in eastern Venezuela, but if experience in other similar Latin American settings is any guide,[3] it is probable that the parents divided into the usual groups. There were those who knew and cared, who either helped to improve education locally, or sent their children or moved their families elsewhere to get adequate schooling. There were those who knew the education was useless but did not care because they had a low opinion of the usefulness of education generally. These parents sent their children sporadically and never let schooling interfere with farm or household chores for the children. There was also a large group who cared, but either did not know because they had no basis for judgment and were themselves illiterate, or felt powerless to do anything about conditions in the schools. The majority of migrants came from the first two groups.

The bane of rural education has been the incomplete or unitary schools. The central government yields to pressure from rural people who wish schools on any terms; rural people are powerless to secure an educational benefit of any consequence. Instead the central government provides them with a one- or two-room building that is a school in name only. The building may house one, two, three, or four grades, but there is no path through this school to a complete primary education or even to sufficient education to ensure functional literacy. The unit is completely dead-end.

There is no bus service to more complete primary schools, and the central boarding school has never been as common in Latin America as it has in Africa. Children enter the incomplete school, spend a few years of desultory squinting toward the blackboard, and drop out before they attain any benefit from the experience. For this reason the wastage rates are enormously high in rural areas, even in Argentina. In rural Latin America only 5 or 10 percent of the entering cohort may survive to complete primary education. This has to be so, for except in a few of the larger towns or in areas where rural feeder schools are tied into a central nuclear establishment, there is no possible way to complete primary school. In addition to being an educational farce, the rural education system represents an enormous waste of scarce resources. If one calculates the average number of years to produce a graduate, instead of the legally prescribed six years, it may take ten or even fifteen years of education for every graduate of primary school produced. In Alta Vera Paz in Guatemala, it takes twenty-one years of education to produce a sixth-grade graduate. Even at very low per-pupil annual costs the bill for primary education comes high.

A description of rural educational services is appropriate and has relevance to Ciudad Guayana. Presently, Ciudad Guayana is just growing out of a classic rural educational pattern. Even up to 1965 there were dozens of *unitaria* (one-room) schools scattered around the edges and sometimes in the middle of the older parts of the city. These schools had almost no yield in primary graduates for it was often more difficult to transfer to complete primary schools than it would have been to enter the complete school in grade one. The unitarias were a sop thrown to neighborhoods that demanded education under any terms. In the past two years some unitarias have been suppressed, either by abandoning them and routing the children to larger and complete schools or by combining them to make a complete primary school.

The unitary school in Ciudad Guayana is usually in or near a shanty *barrio*. That education in the shanty barrio follows a rural model is not so surprising because the barrio is urban only in the sense that it is near, although not necessarily effectively connected to, an urban area. This is a peculiarity of many so-called barrios on the outskirts of Latin American cities. They are urban only in name. The people are so recently in from the country that they live, or attempt to live, almost the same rural life. They may even follow about the same work rhythm as they did in the subsistence agriculture from which they came. The conquero directly in from the rural regions of eastern Venezuela, when living in a shanty barrio of Ciudad Guayana, may keep a few chickens and a pig or two, maintain a garden in which he grows yucca and plátanos, work season-ally or sporadically, and pay about as much attention to environmental sanita-tion as he would in the *llanos*. He is not so much a city dweller as a displaced farmer.

The tragic farce of rural primary education has relevance to Ciudad Guayana also because the vast majority of migrants coming in from the rural regions of eastern Venezuela come from areas where such schools and schooling are common. Ciudad Guayana must offer the first opportunity for a complete primary schooling to people who never have had such an opportunity. As the central study will show, parents, especially the mothers, are well aware of this opportunity and eager that their children take advantage of it.

If primary school service is deficient in rural Latin America, middle and higher education are almost completely lacking. There are middle schools in the larger provincial cities but they do not serve the wide surrounding rural regions in any adequate way. In rural Latin America in the past years, educational service has stopped just beyond the second or third grade of primary school.

Medical and health services historically have been almost as bad as education in rural Latin America, although some progress has occurred in recent years. For example, mass immunization and inoculation programs have been initi-ated. Children and adults are now regularly vaccinated against smallpox, sometimes tested for tuberculosis, and, in the event of outbreaks of typhoid or typhus, assistance is rushed into even the most remote areas. Extensive malaria control programs have operated in rural areas, and measures against yellow fever have had success. Rural problems of nutritional deficiencies have also had some effective measures applied. For example, goiter has been controlled in rural Guatemala and Incaparina (a protein-rich corn meal) developed as a cheap nutritional aid. Rudimentary school lunch programs operate in many areas, and certainly in those areas surrounding Ciudad Guayana in eastern Venezuela.

But in most of Latin America doctors are almost unobtainable outside of the capital and a few provincial centers, and there are no hospital facilities. The local druggist, if there is a drugstore, prescribes and sometimes administers general medicines. The midwife, usually with no formal training, handles births. The *inyector* wields the needle. In some countries he doubles as a tailor, which has a certain amount of sense to it. In rural Mexico, Central America, the Caribbean, and in parts of Venezuela, the *curandero* or local medicine man still operates and sometimes his remedies for snakebite work well. But people who have lived where medical service is available, and who are then condemned to a rural area where it is not, may live in fear. If they are seriously injured or sick, the chances of getting adequate assistance are small. Ciudad Guayana was served in the early days by a company hospital available only to the employees of the Orinoco Mining Company. Later, a Social Security hospital was built on the opposite side of the river. This inadequate facility will now be supplemented by a central hospital perched on a commanding height on the San Félix side of the city. At least the possibility of medical assistance is visible.

The opening up of rural areas to radio and in some cases television and the occasional movie has made rural people aware of the virtues of medical assistance, although the result is often blind faith in the curative powers of pills, ointments, and injections. As yet effective education on the importance of environmental sanitation and prevention has not kept pace with the spread of faith in modern medical cures. Rural people will buy and eat pills like popcorn when amoebic infections flare up, but they will be less concerned about digging and positioning a latrine, about the removal of garbage and waste from the house yard, and the maintenance of clean sources of drinking, cooking, and bathing water. The only advantage they do have in rural areas is that space is not lacking; when they come into more cramped urban settings, they will often pay as little attention to the disposal of waste and rubbish as they did out in the empty spaces from whence they came. This was, and still is, observable in

Ciudad Guayana, especially in the less organized neighborhoods of newly
arrived migrants. Ciudad Guayana is not a clean city—at least in some neighborhoods—and municipal sanitation services often seem to be fighting a losing
battle against general indifference and lack of urban discipline.

If medical and educational services are lacking, the services of agencies that
would contribute to increased agricultural productivity are just as bad. There
are in Latin America few well-run national agricultural extension services.
IBRA, in Brazil, comes as close to being one as any other, but most are poor.
Agricultural experts are concentrated at the ministry; there are a few in the
provincial cities, and the service to remote farm stations is sporadic and badly
supported. With the low literacy that prevails, the use of printed material
circulated through the mails, when the mail service functions at all in rural
regions, is not a feasible alternative. Radio and television have not yet been
fully exploited, although in Central America, Brazil, Colombia, and Mexico
there have been some attempts to incorporate useful information on agriculture
into programs in basic and adult education which run nights at the schools or
sometimes on regular radio broadcasts. There is little assistance in rural credit.
The agricultural banks are in the capital cities and they lend to people who live
there and own their land outside. The rural citizen gets his credit, if he can get
it, from moneylenders, and it comes high. There is no assistance in many areas
in marketing, although cooperatives have been started in almost all of Latin
America. Adult education, when it runs at all, still has not spread out of the
cities.

With vast new highway systems and the beginning of concern for secondary
and access roads, the rural regions are not as isolated as they were even fifteen
years ago. Air travel for rural people is common enough so the airplane is no
novelty, particularly in Venezuela. The radio is everywhere, although music and
commercials, both loud, absorb the major portion of the program time. Television has not come to the rural regions, but movies get out into the provincial
cities and towns and are generally available on weekends and holidays when the
rural people go in. There are no libraries even in the larger provincial towns,
and magazines and newspapers do not reach areas on a current or regular basis.
The rural people, apart from the large landowner who lives on his property, are
not book owners or readers.

Because the rural areas are not isolated, all of the image of the good life of
the city (with some blurring in transmission) comes through to the remotest
regions and acts as a powerful attraction. There is no living to be made in the

rural region; there is no chance for improvement through education; there is no medical assistance; there are no cultural amenities; goods are scarce and poor; and entertainment must be self-generated. There is not even any chance to feel important or involved, or to get one's voice and vote to matter. Except for occasional pre-election barnstorming, all the action is elsewhere. Local government has no power or funds or importance.

When the score is reckoned, the *campesino* feels that he cannot possibly be any worse off in the city. His only loss in the city will be living space; and he faces the fact that his housing will not improve. If he cannot buy goods in the city, he can at least see them. If he cannot get the best medical attention in the city, at least he is assured of a minimal service. He will not be left to die on the street, particularly if he has an infectious disease. Such social assistance as there is can be found in the city. In the city, he will be at least heard. He knows nothing about industry except that it pays better. Perhaps he will be given a chance to learn, and if he has had any experience with agricultural machinery or if he has worked in a small garage or shop, the chances are good that he will get a job and learn something. Above all, there is a better chance for his children. The schools may be poor in the city, but they are infinitely better than in the country. There is just the chance that children, getting a start in the city schools, may do better someday.

With nothing to lose, the campesino comes into the city. Thousands are pouring into Ciudad Guayana, without education or skills or experience of urban industrial living. They come with the prevailing opinion that they have nothing to lose, and in large measure they are right. Less apparent to them is that they have very little to offer but their hands, arms, and backs. In a complex industrial setting there is little demand for unskilled labor. In Ciudad Guayana there is even the problem of single migrant women with families who have even less possibility of finding employment in heavy industry. The result can be frustration, fear, and apathy. But even in the case where the adjustment is made and employment sought and found, there are frustrations. The city offers promise but it exacts a toll by limiting freedom to live as one pleases. Land may be there and be unoccupied, but it is not for the taking. The Corporación Venezolana de Guayana (CVG), the autonomous government agency charged with development of the region, has its long-range plans for the city. Migrants are posted off land that is reserved for highways and parks and industrial centers, and if they squat there the bulldozer will someday move them.

Often new migrants are forced to live in enormously crowded little slums and in flimsy and makeshift hutments with neighbor piled on top of neighbor. Water is scarce and despite enormous potential reserves of electric power, there is for the moment a heavily overtaxed distribution system in the barrio areas. Sanitation services do not operate in such areas and the migrants discover that they cannot merely use the open surroundings as a dump or the nearby street as a sewer. Public transportation is overtaxed and relatively expensive and it is a long walk from the barrios to the center: the city covers twenty-five kilometers from west to east.

But frustrations are not limited merely to living. Work in industries requires new forms of discipline and irksome regulation. There is the need to be punctual and regular in attendance. A melt at the steel mill cannot be postponed from one day to the other as some forms of subsistence agriculture permit. There can be less visiting and strolling. There are safety regulations to observe, fewer holidays, large amounts of time spent being bussed to the plant, and always a full-shift load of work to perform. The experience of country living has not fitted the conuquero for the new discipline demanded by work in industry. Nor has his wife been prepared for managing a house and raising a family in the middle of crowded barrios and in the face of overtaxed services. And the schools themselves, the great new opportunity, impose their own demands on parents and children. There are forms to be filled out, conventions of dress and behavior, and above all the need for regular attendance. So the city is not an unmixed blessing.

2
The Economy of the Guayana Development Zone and Its Educational Consequences

In 1950 the collection of riverine villages later joined to form Ciudad Guayana had a population of slightly less than 4,000. As the vast and rich iron deposits of the Cerro Bolívar were opened in the early fifties, population began to collect at the junction of the Orinoco and the Caroní. On one side of the Caroní River, the Orinoco Mining Company built its loading docks, administrative head-quarters, and housing for its professionals, technicians, and some workers: this was Puerto Ordaz. On the other side of the Caroní basin, around the nucleus of the small old town of San Félix, the houses of the workers began to spread into the empty spaces. In the early sixties, the government steel mill, La Planta Siderúrgica del Orinoco, was completed, with an investment of U.S. $360 million and an installed capacity of 750,000 ingot tons. The first phase of a hydroelectric complex that is to have a generating capacity of eight million kilowatts was completed at Macagua and now has an installed capacity of 350,000 kilowatts.

Also taking form was the concept of a development zone that would include the major resources of the region and center at the confluence of the Orinoco and Caroní. To plan the development of this region, as yet not precisely defined in geography but roughly describable in terms of supporting resources, the Corporación Venezolana de Guayana (CVG) was established in 1960. The CVG took over the two major development enterprises, the steel plant and the hydro-electric complex, and prepared to plan the long-range development of the region. Along with the mandate to plan the total economic development of the region grew the realization that its central city had also to be planned. Puerto

Ordaz, San Félix, and other smaller clusters of settlements on both sides of the river were to be linked together in one city. The physical linkage was to be provided by a bridge across the Caroní; the social linkage was to be established by creating a name for the city—Santo Tomé de Guayana, or Ciudad Guayana.[1]

The Economy

Investment and Output Goals. From the outset the goals of the Guayana venture were couched in economic terms.[2] CVG planners estimated that a total investment of U.S. $1,762 million would be required during the period 1963–1975. This would launch the necessary infrastructural services, develop the heavy industry linkage, exploit the mineral deposits, provide the hydroelectric power and the gas transmission lines from the oil fields of eastern Venezuela, and stimulate the medium and light industries that would be ancillary to the heavy central industrial base. As a return on the vast investment contemplated, it was envisaged that by 1975 the Guayana development zone would produce goods and services valued at $1,500 million, which would represent more than 9 percent of the gross domestic product of Venezuela.

The very magnitude of the investment and output targets and the income to be generated in the Guayana zone imply a demand for the establishment and support of extensive educational services. And most important in its implication for the educational and training systems of Guayana, the output of the region was to represent 20 percent of the total industrial product of Venezuela. The Guayana was not planned as a center for medium and light industries producing goods for import substitution. The bulk of the Guayana product was to come from the formidable industrial linkage system depicted in Figure 2.1. Quite clearly an ignorant and untrained work force could not operate the complex industrial machine planned for Guayana in 1975.

Heavy Industry Link-ge System. Figure 2.1 sketches the industrial linkage system planned for the Guayana and throws into sharp relief the necessity for a highly trained work force. The aluminum plant and the steel plant—scheduled

---

Figure 2.1   Industrial flow diagram, Ciudad Guayana, 1975.

Industry Key

1. Basic metals industry
2. Machinery-metals fabrication industry
3. Construction materials industry
4. Chemical inputs and industry
5. Other inputs and industry
6. Forest resources and related industries

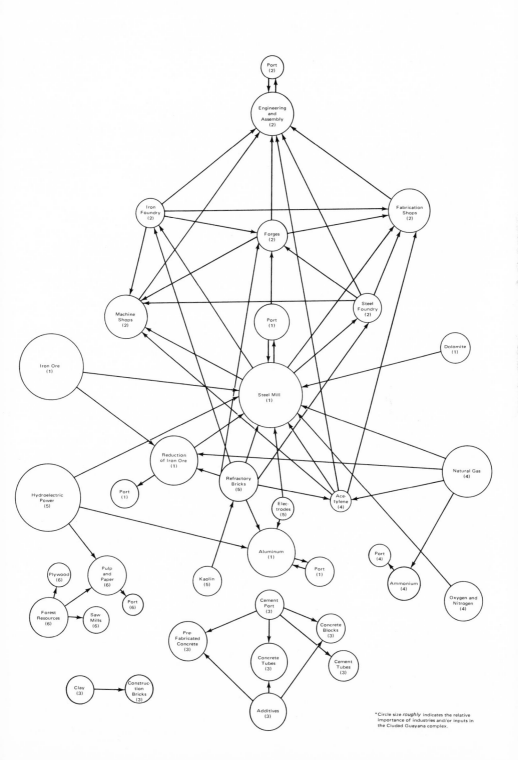

*Circle size *roughly* indicates the relative importance of industries and/or inputs in the Ciudad Guayana complex.

to raise its capacity, through oxygen injection, to 2.6 million tons in 1975—form
the central axes of the electromechanical complex. Linked are the vast reserves
of natural gas, the processing of nitric acid, ammonium nitrate, and ammonium
phosphate, and the plants for reducing and enriching the iron ores of the region.
Enriched iron ore and sponge iron will be major products of the heavy industry
complex. Tied in directly from the steel plant is a heavy machinery complex. A
pulp and paper industry will draw on the vast forest reserves of the region.
Cement will be shipped in to supply a concrete and construction materials
industry. Coal is available from the mines at Naricuál, and abundant and cheap
power will come from the Guri Dam which, when completed, will be one of the
largest in the Western Hemisphere. Not shown in the diagram, but planned as a
Guayana regional project to be closely linked to supplying the demands of the
population of Guayana, is the development of highly productive and intensive
agriculture in the Delta Amacuro region.

Around the central core of heavy industry there will be medium industries set
up to supply and support the heavy industries and to absorb inputs from them.
With a population that will almost triple by 1975, the demand for construction
activity and services will grow enormously. About 25,000 new housing units will
have to be built by 1975, and at least half that many will have to be extensively
remodeled. The entire range of health, education, and public and private
services must be made available in the Guayana. Professionals and technicians
to man industry and provide services must be imported in vast numbers, or
educated and trained within the zone itself. The educational and training burden
that falls to the schools and training institutions of the Guayana is truly vast.

Export and Trade. If the complexity of the industry planned for the Guayana
implies a highly trained work force, so too does the planners' expectation that
by 1975 Guayana will be producing a quarter of the total value of Venezuelan
exports. This implies that the industry of Guayana will produce at costs and sell
at prices that will be competitive in world and regional markets. With Venezuelan lábor costs high in Latin America, the implication is high output per
worker, and this level of productivity implies very high managerial skill and
technical competence in the work force.

Much of the impetus for the enormous industrial investment in the Guayana
grew out of a study of Venezuela's future in world trade. In 1962 Venezuela was
the leading export country of Latin America, exporting over \$2.5 billion, almost
30 percent of the export value of the region. But 91 percent of the export
value of Latin America came from exports of raw commodities, in the case of

Venezuela, petroleum and iron ore. With vast new oil reserves opening in North Africa and the Middle East and with the poor prospects for world petroleum prices, the Guayana investment in heavy industry was necessary forethought. With an export balance of $1.5 billion, Venezuela could afford the venture; and, in fact, with the prospects of petroleum prices as they were, the country could scarcely afford to do otherwise.[3]

The significance of export industry goals in the development strategy of Guayana is highlighted by one of the economic advisers who played a central role in planning the development strategy of the region:

The fundamental concept has been the necessity of making certain that the design of the industries, as to technology and scale, maximizes the region's potential competitive position in the export market as well as insuring a supply of basic and intermediate inputs to Venezuelan industry at competitive prices. Hence, as a basic policy Guayana industries must be efficient, modern and competitive in order to compensate for production costs and exchange that are typically high in the country.[4]

Economic Goals and Educational Development Strategy of Guayana

Primary and secondary schools enrolling over 15,000 students, and training programs which accommodate another 2,000, have been established to serve the city of Guayana. Ciudad Guayana in turn serves the industrial development of Venezuela. This latter fact has profoundly influenced the strategy for the development of education and training in Guayana.

Education and training are provided and paid for largely out of public funds in Venezuela, and in the case of Guayana almost the total burden has been borne by the federal government. The principal support for education has come from the Ministry of Public Education, but the CVG has contributed substantial amounts through capital grants and subsidies to private schools and in support of selected national school programs. There can be sundry motives for such provision, but in the case of Guayana there were three principal ones.

First, there is provision of education because the Venezuelan Constitution from 1870 on has stated that children of primary school age have a right to free, complete public education. This motive, laudable in its social aim, has not guaranteed provision of universal, free, public education in Venezuela. In the Guayana, which is more amply provided for than many regions, 20 percent of school-age children were not accommodated in the schools in 1965.

Second, education in Guayana has been provided to satisfy the demands of professionals, technicians, and skilled workers who must be attracted to the region to work in its industry and who demand adequate educational provision for their dependents. On this basis, in the early days of the Guayana development, heavy capital grants and program subsidies were given to private educational agencies in order to attract them to Ciudad Guayana.

Third, and this is the dominating strategy in later Guayana development planning, education and training are provided so that workers and technicians may be prepared for productive employment in the industrial complex of Guayana.

The third motive stems from the assumption that education and training contribute materially to enhancing productivity. The complexity of the industrial linkage system planned for Guayana and the requirement that Guayana industry have high productivity to compete in world markets demand a highly skilled labor force. Yet Guayana cannot hope to attract all of its workers fully educated and trained. In the general population pool of Venezuela, from which Guayana must draw, a third of the adults in the prime working ages thirty to fifty have insufficient formal education to guarantee functional literacy. The mass of migrants to Guayana are either rural people or oil field laborers from eastern Venezuela. They lack industrial experience and average less than four complete years of formal education. The very numbers of skilled and technical workers required in Guayana industry make it unreasonable to expect that they can be recruited fully trained from other areas. Vast numbers must be educated and trained in Guayana, and the education and training must be relevant to the complex industrial tasks that workers will perform.

Methods for Relating Education and Economic Development

Education is presumed to increase production and enhance consumption. This has been the view of economists for many years. The proposition, seemingly obvious, is not so easily proved. There is indirect evidence galore that in the aggregate output per worker varies positively with the educational attainment of workers and that income rises with educational level attained; but it is less easy to prove cause and effect or attribute increase in output and income uniquely to education rather than to other common factors. Building on the work of Von Thunen, who stated that knowledge and skills generated by education and training enhanced the capital value of an individual, Marshall provided a formula for calculating the productive return that education makes in the individual's work life;[5] Schultz and his followers advanced the methodology for calculating net benefits to education;[6] Mincer calculated returns on training;[7]

and Becker used the internal rate of return on net benefits to education to rank education as an investment in human capital.[8] Out of this line of development came the rate-of-return or investment-in-human-capital approach in which education, at least in its contributions to increased earnings and returns, could be ranked and compared with investments in more conventional forms of physical capital. None of the economists cited minimized the difficulties, conceptual and arithmetical, in calculating benefits and returns to education, and none of them views education as either solely responsible for increased returns or solely limited to providing increased returns. However, there is an overwhelming indication that education and training do increase output and income.

If this approach were taken to estimate the returns on education in Guayana, one possible formula for making the calculation might be

$$\sum_{t=0}^{L} \frac{X^1}{(1 + r)^{t+1}} - \sum_{t=0}^{L} \frac{X^0}{(1 + r)^{t+1}} = 0 \qquad (2.1)$$

where

X^1 = net benefits (earnings less costs) on completion of the next higher educational level above X^0.

r = rate of return which reduces the difference of the two net benefits streams to zero.

Differences in income would be calculated over the work life of the graduates of the two respective programs, and the internal rate of return to educational level X^1 would indicate the net benefit of the investment. Presumably if these calculations could be made in Guayana, the return on successive levels of education could be computed and compared, as an investment, to any other investment. Shoup has computed rates of return on successive levels of Venezuelan education in 1959 and estimates that the rate of return on primary education varied from 80 to 130 percent; return on secondary education was 17 percent; and return on higher education was 23 percent.[9]

For application in the practical planning situation there are more serious problems than the conceptual ones of attributing earning differentials to education solely, rather than to native intelligence and connections, and the difficulties of by-guess-and-by-God calculations necessary when one works with bad cost and earning data. The absolute cumulative levels of education and their payoff is of less significance to the planner than the kinds of education offered within the levels. For example, it could very well be that sufficient numbers of secondary school graduates could be produced but that they would be produced in the wrong kinds of programs, that is, general preparatory rather than vocational or technical. If this were the case, the earnings would soon adjust to the surplus and the rate of return used to make the estimate would not last very long into the earning life of the graduate.

A second attempt to relate educational investment to production comes in the so-called residual factor approach, the advocates being Solow[10] and Kendrick[11] and the critics being legion. Solow tried to trace output per head over time and attribute part of the per-head increase in output to technical change rather than increase in capital. One of the major components of technical change in his scheme was education. The approach has no ready route for calculation and for ranking with respect to other investment possibilities, although it is conceptually off the same base as the first approach. Untangling the part of technical progress that is uniquely attributable to education rather than other forms of organization makes the approach unfeasible for planning.

There is a third approach possible for relating investment in education and training in Guayana to the economic development goals of the region. This is the so-called manpower education approach, originally given a full-dress tryout in Puerto Rico in the middle fifties, applied in a more general way by the Ashby Commission in Nigeria, and brought to a state of greater systematization and, superficially, more precision and accuracy by Parnes[12] and the OECD economists who applied the techniques in the Mediterranean Regional Project.[13] The essentials of the method are that a given economy has or will have a given mix of industries in its major sectors. In the case of Guayana the heavy industry system has been portrayed in Figure 2.1. The other sectors, the medium and light industry, transportation, gas and electric, mining, services, and even agriculture, can be built up around the heavy industrial core and thus describe the present and future economy of the region. Within the sectors and the industries there is a given occupational structure and for the occupations a given pattern of education and training. Hence the method works through industries to occupations to education and training; and given the present and future pattern of industries, the demand for educated and trained people in the work force can be estimated.

It can be roughly estimated, that is, for there is slippage and lack of precision between industry and occupation and between occupation and education. The occupational requirements may vary considerably according to the scale of the industry, the investment, and the technology employed. Educational fit to occupation is also notably loose, and different educational and training backgrounds can prepare a man, sometimes with experience and brief training added on, to fill various occupational classes. Nevertheless, there is an over-all fit. And, as with the rate of return and ranking of investment in human capital, there is, despite problems conceptual and arithmetical, some utility in using manpower planning to estimate the demand on education or training, or at least to set minimal targets for the education and training establishments.

Demand for Education in Ciudad Guayana According to Work Force Requirements

The strategy and plan for educational development in Ciudad Guayana was prepared for the Human Development Section of the Corporación Venezolana de Guayana. As has been stated, CVG is an autonomous regional development agency funded on a multi-year basis by the federal government of Venezuela, but with authority to borrow on short and long term from Venezuelan and international credit sources.

From the outset, social development, insofar as it can be separated from economic development, had a lesser priority for the planners and administrators of CVG. Their mandate was to develop the economic resources of the region. The first plan for educational development emphasized the contribution that education and training make to increasing productivity. The social consequences of education—vital in the case of poor and uneducated country people moving into an urban and industrial setting—were given much less attention.[14] This lack of balance will be addressed in the body of this work, but first the lineaments of an educational development strategy based on manpower requirements should be sketched in.

To relate educational attainment to increased productivity of the Guayana work force, the population, work force, and economic characteristics of the region had to be assessed for the base year and output projected for the target date. The base year chosen was 1966, and the target year, 1975. There is no need to detail the technics nor to present the data used to make the projections. Tables 2.1 and 2.2 show the results of one setting for the target year.

In Table 2.1 the 1975 target year labor force is projected by sectors and educational levels within sector. The essential methodology is simple. For the central core of heavy and medium industries, the method consisted of

1. Projecting the output from the base year 1966 to the target year 1975.
2. Projecting the output per worker for the same period.

TABLE 2.1
Distribution of 1975 Employed Labor Force by Educational Level and Industrial Sector

Educational Levels	Industrial Sectors										
	Agriculture, Forestry, Fishing	Mining	Pulp, Paper	Energy Generation and Distribution	Basic Metals	Heavy Machinery	Chemicals	Wood and Wood Products	Construction Materials	Food and Beverages	Clothing and Footwear, Textiles
Graduate Studies	11	32	7	99	34	7	4	—	10	2	—
Sci., Arch., Eng.	8	97	5	145	305	63	24	1	40	19	5
Lib. Arts, Law, Econ.	5	137	8	10	45	7	15	11	25	43	50
Med., Dentistry, Phar.	—	5	—	1	6	—	—	—	—	—	—
Vet., Agron.	35	—	16	—	—	—	—	—	—	—	—
Inst. Pedagógico	—	—	—	—	—	—	—	—	—	—	—
Politécnico	4	58	2	72	180	34	21	6	31	6	5
Tech.-Artisanal	133	891	145	229	3,497	734	87	224	244	192	356
Commercial	21	261	29	110	1,117	210	79	51	144	168	149
General Secondary	14	131	14	32	1,084	113	47	19	46	110	152
Normal	—	—	—	—	—	—	—	—	—	—	—
Agricultural	131	—	51	—	—	—	—	—	—	—	—
Nursing	—	15	—	2	6	—	—	—	—	—	—
Primary Graduates	744	1,946	295	202	3,554	728	222	417	663	645	992
4–5 Years, Primary	1,602	1,368	138	80	1,455	293	75	225	539	334	546
0–3 Years, Primary	655	20	30	9	—	68	12	54	192	80	119
Totals	3,363	4,961	740	991	11,283	2,257	586	1,008	1,934	1,599	2,374

TABLE 2.1 (continued)

Educational Levels	Industrial Sectors										
	Other Industry	Construction	Commerce	Government and Communication	Transportation	Medical Services	Educational Services	Services to Business	Domestic Services	Other Services	Totals
Graduate Studies	—	41	9	30	4	47	16	19	—	2	374
Sci., Arch., Eng.	65	315	173	123	20	24	207	97	—	12	1,748
Lib. Arts, Law, Econ.	61	108	233	221	31	6	109	165	7	51	1,348
Med., Dentistry, Phar.	—	—	—	—	—	277	4	—	—	—	293
Vet., Agron.	—	—	—	—	—	—	5	—	—	—	56
Inst. Pedagógico	—	—	—	—	—	—	626	—	—	12	638
Politécnico	16	66	25	76	22	63	49	27	—	2	765
Tech.-Artisanal	642	1,913	180	272	313	63	62	41	—	333	10,551
Commercial	334	265	1,429	772	226	110	217	140	27	327	6,186
General Secondary	148	66	1,376	277	191	79	—	76	19	226	4,220
Normal	—	—	—	—	—	—	1,356	—	—	20	1,376
Agricultural	—	—	—	9	—	—	9	—	—	—	191
Nursing	—	—	—	—	—	434	—	—	—	—	466
Primary Graduates	1,258	2,385	2,810	1,069	1,980	231	48	48	524	1,455	22,216
4–5 Years, Primary	780	2,037	765	214	1,109	142	110	23	913	1,140	13,888
0–3 Years, Primary	200	1,085	675	148	157	98	—	—	1,981	374	5,957
Totals	3,504	8,281	7,675	3,211	4,053	1,574	2,818	636	3,471	3,954	70,273

Note: The 21 sectors of Table 2.1 are aggregated from a list of 40 subsectors.

3. Dividing output per worker into projected output to get number of workers or employment.
4. Distributing employment by occupation.
5. Relating occupation to education for employed persons.
6. Estimating unemployment and adding it to employment to get the work force classified by education.
7. Establishing the so-called demand for education in the work force by subtracting the base year numbers from the target year numbers and adding to this result the estimated number of those who will die or leave the work force (wastage).

The outline of the procedure masks a great deal of complexity and considerable imprecision. For existing industries in Guayana, there are data on present capacity and technology and fair estimates of future investment, expansion of capacity contemplated, changes in technology, and the resulting likely increases in output and output per worker. For industries in plan, there are detailed feasibility studies that provide fair estimates of the same characteristics. Output and output per worker under varying assumptions of market, capacity, and technology can be estimated. Employment will follow, and occupational and educational distributions can be set. For the industries that will be linked to the central core, there are also some bases for estimates, that is, oxygen from steel, caustic soda and chloride from pulp and paper, reduction of magnesium from aluminum. There are also ways of linking industrial and private consumer demand to output in the supporting sectors of electricity, water, and gas. And for light industries, services, government and private, and transportation, estimations can be derived from the work force, population, and income levels. The method is full of circularity, sometimes recognized and controlled, sometimes not. Work force can be used to estimate population and population may feed back to determine work force in services and commerce.

There are notorious ambiguities and problems in relating output to occupational distribution, and occupation to educational attainment. Educational attainment is both a cause and a result of increased output. There is a great deal of loose definition in occupational and educational attainment categories. Various occupational and educational distributions are possible with different combinations of factors of production and permutations of technology. But the method provides at least rough and minimal targets. The significant point here is the rationale of the strategy for an educational plan, rather than the precision or accuracy of the first round of target setting.

In Table 2.2 appear data on the so-called final demand on education in the Guayana in 1975. The final demand data come from a comparison of the stock

370.987   M175 b

C. 1

TABLE 2.2
Estimated Demand on Education in Zone Work Force in 1975

University	Targets[b]		Final Demand	
			(Target Minus 1966 Work Force Wasted)	
Graduate Studies	374		332	
Science (professional)[a]	1,748		1,455	
General (liberal arts, economics, law)	1,348		1,111	
Medical	293		254	
Veterinary, Agronomy	56		56	
Instituto Pedagógico	638		568	
Politécnico	765		755	
		5,222		4,531
Secondary				
Technical-Artisanal	10,551		10,190	
Commercial	6,186		6,036	
General Secondary	4,220		3,120	
Normal	1,376		1,220	
Agricultural	191		191	
Nursing	466		442	
		22,990		21,199
Primary graduates	22,216		17,215	
Finished grades 4 and 5	13,888		10,427	
Less than 3 grades	5,957		−8,384[c]	

[a] The split between science and general is flexible.
[b] No significance in last two digits.
[c] Expressed as a negative quantity because fewer workers with this educational level will be needed in the labor force in 1975 than are present now. Either these men will have to be upgraded or face chronic unemployment.

of educated people in the work force in the base year and the stock of educated and trained people that would be necessary, according to the plan, in the work force of the target year. Because the estimate runs over a ten-year period during which people in the original stock will die, retire, or migrate, the base year stock must be wasted. The wastage is added to the deficit on which the final demand figures are based. Furthermore, because educational levels successively feed each other, that is, a secondary school graduate must also be a primary school

TABLE 2.3
Supply of Education Projected for the Schools of Ciudad Guayana Compared with Labor Force Demand

	Educational Level	1975 Labor Force Demand[a]	Education Provided in Cd. Guayana 1966–1975	Difference Demand-Supply
University Level	1. Graduate Studies	332		332
	2. Sciences, Arch., Eng.	1,455		1,455
	3. General (liberal arts, law, economics)	1,111		1,111
	4. Medicine, Dentistry, Pharmacy	254		254
	5. Veterinary, Agronomy	56		56
	6. Instituto Pedagógico	568		568
	7. Politécnico	755		755
High School Level	8. Technical-Artisanal	10,190	6,475[c]	3,715
	9. Commercial	6,036	3,280[d]	2,756
	10. General Secondary	3,120	3,104[e]	16
	11. Normal	1,220		1,220
	12. Agricultural	191		191
	13. Nursing	442		442
	14. Primary Graduates	17,215 (38,412)[b]	17,462 (30,321)[b]	−247
	15. 4–5 Years, Primary	10,427 (48,839)[b]	12,626 (42,947)[b]	−2,199[f]
	16. 0–3 Years, Primary	−8,384	7,834 (50,781)[b]	−16,218[g]

[a] With 1966 labor force wasted out, that is, subtracting numbers of persons present in 1966 labor force who will not have died or retired.
[b] Those terminating at this level and those feeding higher levels.
[c] All students finishing 3 or more years in technical or artisanal schools.
[d] All students finishing 3 or more years in commercial schools.
[e] Liceo graduates.
[f] Negative numbers indicate that the total number of people "leaving" school at this level exceeds the minimal number required by the labor force. The apparent oversupply is deceptive, as many people educated by the schools will never contribute to the labor force, although they may contribute to the society (for example, women who become housewives). At the lower levels the apparent oversupply represents persons who in future years will not be the feed for higher levels of education.
[g] Includes the 7,834 persons who will not go beyond the third grade in this period (most of whom will still be in school in 1975), and the 8,384 persons currently in the labor force with less than 4 years of education who will probably be unemployed.

graduate, the demand targets must be cumulated upward to provide for terminal demand at the specified level (primary graduates who enter work force) and also feed to the next higher level (primary graduates who enter middle school; see Table 2.3).

With output targets for schools and training establishments set, part of the education and training task for the future can be laid out. That it is only part of the task is obvious. The targets are expressed in terms of the work force (persons who seek gainful employment or are employed), but the schools serve the total population without respect to present or even likely participation of the individual in the work force. Education will be given to many who will never join the work force. In Venezuela, employed persons represent about 88 percent of the work force, and the work force in turn represents about 33 percent of the population. Education to satisfy the general population demand will also have to be given, and it will later become apparent that this so-called social demand may be as important as the economic demand.

Lineaments of an Educational Development Strategy in the Guayana

At the outset it is clear that Guayana with a population of 85,000 and a work force of about 28,000 in 1966 cannot even reach the requirement targets for 1975 in mere numbers of workers, without respect to their education and training, unless there is heavy migration into the city and the region. Hence, the region must first attract migrants to man its industry. Presumably the employment opportunities in Guayana will provide this attraction. The experience between 1960 and 1965 demonstrates that in number terms alone the industrial development in Guayana was providing sufficient attraction to migrants. In fact, migration in the early half of the sixties was outstripping employment opportunity—not surprising when in the country as a whole unemployment varied between 12 and 15 percent. For certain periods in 1965 unemployment in the Guayana region ran as high as 20 percent. Thus, Guayana was demonstrating that the problem was not one of merely attracting worker bodies.

More significant is the need for Guayana to recruit selectively and attract migrants with capacities and skills already formed by previous education, training, and work experience. In 1965 there was no institution of higher learning in Guayana, and so professional, technical, and managerial personnel who require postsecondary education must be educated outside the region, then attracted to Guayana through selective recruitment. Although there is a plan for establishing a postsecondary technological institute, the start-up time and the course of study would make it impossible to guarantee any significant output of graduates before the target year.

Educational targets in the Guayana, then, are limited to the output of primary and secondary school graduates, as well as participants in shorter and more specialized training programs in the training centers of INCE (Instituto Nacional de Cooperación Educativa), in schools, and in school-industry combinations. The output of these institutions, when projected under the most optimal assumptions, is still insufficient to meet the economic demand targets.

In bare quantitative terms a strategy for education and training in Guayana can be summarized as follows:

1. Expand to the maximum possible primary education so that sufficient feed of students is assured to middle level schools and so that workers have sufficient basic education to profit by shorter special training courses that must be given to cover the education and training deficit among middle level workers, that is, operators and semiskilled workers.
2. Expand to the maximum the middle-level school facilities (bachiller, vocational, commercial, and technical programs) so that sufficient numbers of graduates will be available for meeting the terminal demand and also for feeding the higher levels of education. The expansion can come in the present specialized middle schools or in large comprehensive schools with, in one establishment, programs in preparatory, commercial, vocational, and technical education.
3. In the time that remains before the target year, the major portion of post-secondary graduates must be recruited from outside the zone. This does not obviate the necessity of establishing and expanding a technological institute which would prepare technicians in subprofessional specialties for industry. It also implies that the primary and middle schools must not only be expanded but improved in order to offer the educational opportunities that the professionals recruited from outside the zone are certain to demand for their children.
4. Inasmuch as even the quantitative targets cannot be met, there must be massive programs of training within industry, training in INCE centers, and training in school-industry courses. Informal education through correspondence, night, weekend, summer, and home training through radio and television must also be tried.

Primary Education. The targets call for 38,000 primary school graduates by 1975. This is the number necessary to satisfy the final demand for primary graduates in the work force and to provide the primary school feed to secondary and postsecondary education. Even under the most optimistic forecasts the output of the Guayana primary schools will be insufficient to meet this target (see Table 2.4).

TABLE 2.4
Primary School Enrollments and Graduates in Ciudad Guayana, 1961–1975
(Assumes Model System)[a]

Actual								
				Grade Level				
Data	TE[b]	1	2	3	4	5	6	G[c]
1961–1962	7,339	1,932	1,605	1,584	1,054	816	348	292
1962–1963	9,032	2,491	1,888	1,583	1,455	966	649	610
1963–1964	10,242	2,796	2,098	1,810	1,513	1,231	794	746
1964–1965	11,536	2,970	2,317	2,047	1,764	1,472	966	908
1965–1966	13,538	3,435	2,774	2,473	2,024	1,600	1,232	1,158
Projected								
Data	TE	1	2	3	4	5	6	G
1966–1967	16,235	4,132	3,374	2,722	2,410	2,041	1,556	1,463
1967–1968	19,365	4,957	4,021	3,326	2,712	2,379	1,970	1,852
1968–1969	23,033	5,813	4,756	4,049	3,307	2,777	2,331	2,214
1969–1970	27,069	6,712	5,520	4,722	4,102	3,372	2,741	2,604
1970–1971	31,705	7,568	6,499	5,404	4,757	4,036	3,341	3,174
1971–1972	36,231	8,476	7,257	6,419	5,406	4,693	3,980	3,821
1972–1973	40,777	9,440	7,975	6,880	6,435	5,499	4,548	4,364
1973–1974	45,417	10,384	9,013	7,520	6,868	6,268	5,364	5,149
1974–1975	50,248	11,408	9,758	8,800	6,815	6,815	5,917	5,680
1975–1976	55,770	12,326	10,966	9,539	7,539	7,539	6,705	6,437

Total Primary School Graduates 1966–1975 = 30,321

[a] Projected enrollments were calculated on the basis of assumptions about the population pyramid, percentage of total enrollments in each grade, and age distribution by grade. The resultant is thought to be more reliable than a linear application of prosecution rates, although it can be seen that the method does not produce smoothly descending diagonals.
[b] Total Enrollment. Held to same level as shown in Table 5.1 to facilitate comparison.
[c] Graduates.

Middle Level Education. Venezuelan middle schools are organized in special program areas rather than in a comprehensive pattern. The liceos grant the *bachiller* degree; commercial and technical schools are separate and distinct in programs.

LICEOS. The output of *bachilleres* from the liceos of Guayana will just meet the minimal requirements for the labor force in 1975, if the programed improvement in liceos is realized. However, some number of the bachilleres will

TABLE 2.5
Liceo Enrollments and Graduates, 1961–1975, in Ciudad Guayana

				Grade Level			
Actual Data	TE[a]	1	2	3	4	5	G[b]
1961–1962	461	232	129	70	30	0	
1962–1963	694	285	200	150	49	10	
1963–1964	1,015	487	243	151	105	29	
1964–1965	1,060	395	281	220	100	64	58
1965–1966	1,292	493	309	243	185	62	56
Projected Data	TE	1	2	3	4	5	G
1966–1967	1,701	646	391	323	238	102	92
1967–1968	2,074	767	477	394	290	145	132
1968–1969	2,848	1,430	506	418	308	176	160
1969–1970	2,910	844	1,054	458	337	217	200
1970–1971	3,424	1,028	665	975	454	302	278
1971–1972	4,098	1,303	936	584	870	405	377
1972–1973	4,931	1,614	1,141	851	525	800	752
1973–1974	5,695	1,965	1,453	1,025	811	440	414
1974–1975	6,683	2,005	1,770	1,203	969	736	699

Total Liceo Graduates 1966–1975 = 3,104

[a] TE = Total Enrollment.
[b] G = Graduates.

not directly enter the labor force—female graduates will marry, others will continue on in the university—so that migration will have to supply some liceo graduates (see Table 2.5).

TECHNICAL AND ARTISANAL SCHOOLS. The combined output of technical and artisanal schools would satisfy about 60 percent of the requirements for skilled craftsmen. This would mean accepting the graduates of three-year artisanal and technical programs as trained up to entry-level standard, with the presumption that experience and further training would fit them to perform in the work force as highly skilled workers in industry and as individual craftsmen in light industry and services (see Table 2.6).

COMMERCIAL SCHOOLS. About 80 percent of the requirements for commercial school graduates would be filled by the output of the Guayana schools if all graduates entered the labor force. The bulk of the output would be secretarial assistants and secretaries with two or three years of postprimary training (see Table 2.7).

Middle school targets appear formidable indeed when it is reckoned that about a third of the migrants coming into Guayana, largely from surrounding rural regions, are illiterate; and fewer than 10 percent have had secondary education.

Specifications for Education and Training Programs in the Guayana

Based on the general strategy that has been outlined, detailed programs were written (in December 1964 and again in August 1966) for formal and informal education in the Guayana. The programs covered,

TABLE 2.6
Technical and Artisanal School Enrollments and Graduates, 1964–1975, in Ciudad Guayana

Actual Data	Technical TE[a]	Artisanal TE	Technical						Artisanal		
			1	2	3	4	5	6	1	2	3
1964–1965	442	15	442						15		
1965–1966	548	42	362	151			35		32	10	
Projected Data											
1966–1967	790	63	430	190	100		40	30	35	20	8
1967–1968	1,271	122	778	205	127	75	51	35	82	26	14
1968–1969	1,583	212	843	398	191	77	38	36	134	60	18
1969–1970	2,193	339	985	654	317	151	57	29	203	95	41
1970–1971	2,868	514	1,241	642	603	235	102	45	288	149	77
1971–1972	3,557	734	1,478	814	456	561	163	85	382	220	132
1972–1973	4,218	1,010	1,596	980	627	353	535	127	485	313	212
1973–1974	5,096	1,349	1,770	1,247	863	432	288	496	614	432	303
1974–1975	5,628	1,758	2,026	1,463	1,069	563	338	169	761	580	417
Graduates 1966–1975					2,206	1,100	895	1,052			1,222

[a] TE = Total Enrollment.

TABLE 2.7
Commercial School Enrollments and Graduates, 1961–1975, in Ciudad Guayana

Actual Data	TE[a]	1	2	3	4	5
1961–1962	332					
1962–1963	473					
1963–1964	667					
1964–1965	661	421	140	81	19	
1965–1966	578	341	130	82	25	
Projected Data						
1966–1967	600	336	132	84	42	6
1967–1968	600	318	132	90	48	12
1968–1969	953	550	219	100	56	28
1969–1970	1,624	887	433	199	72	33
1970–1971	2,054	883	614	349	165	43
1971–1972	2,417	943	670	435	266	103
1972–1973	2,781	973	746	528	334	200
1973–1974	3,147	1,007	847	629	410	254
1974–1975	3,497	1,020	914	703	504	356
Graduates 1966–1975				1,339	906	1,035

[a] TE = Total Enrollment.

1. Organization and administration of formal and informal education in the Guayana, from primary through postsecondary, including school and within-industry courses.

2. The courses of study required at the various levels and in the various kinds of programs and the textbooks, library holdings, teaching materials, and equipment necessary to implement the curricula and programs.

3. The physical requirements in buildings and equipment to carry out the programs.

4. The personnel requirements for classrooms, teachers, special teachers, supervisors, administrators, and supporting staff.

5. The costs, capital and current, of carrying out a program of the size and specified quality level, and the share of this outlay that should fall to the CVG in order to supplement and stimulate Ministry of Education efforts in Guayana.

Implementation of the Projects: Center for Educational Research, Planning, and Extension Services

To implement the educational projects which came out of the strategy for educational development in Guayana, a unique center was proposed. This center for educational research, planning, and extension services would be established in Ciudad Guayana and have responsibility for developing and implementing education and training programs from primary through postsecondary. It would be a joint venture of the Ministry of Education and the CVG. A detailed description of the Guayana Center appears in Part 2. Implementation of the plan through activities of the Guayana Center will be described in Part 3.

Presently, education in Venezuela suffers from the same deficiencies found in most Latin American countries. Although by law both municipal and state governments are permitted and encouraged to operate schools, in fact the burden is borne by the federal government and the national Ministry of Education. There is little contact between the Ministry in Caracas and outlying schools; the only Ministry officer in Guayana is a district supervisor of primary schools. The district supervisor has neither the time, resources, nor authority to manage the local schools, and the result is that there is only sporadic and ineffectual contact between the Ministry and the individual schools. There is no long-range planning, or even any short-range program planning; there is no coordination of programs among different schools and no articulation between different levels and programs. There is only minimal supervision of instructional personnel. There is no coordination of services. In the matter of supply, each school buys at retail prices whatever minimal supplies it is allowed. Once a year, a budget, based on minimal provision for the number of children estimated, is submitted to Caracas. The budget exercise is the only direction or control which Guayana schools receive. The purpose of the Guayana Educational Research, Planning, and Extension Services Center is to make an educational system out of a clutter of individual schools that happen to be concentrated in and around Ciudad Guayana.

Behind the Quantitative Façade

To this point it seems that educational development in Ciudad Guayana has been planned and programed by the numbers. First, the numbers and kinds of workers that would be required in the future were estimated. These numbers were associated with education and training and the work force demand for educated and trained people was established. According to the kind of education and training required, program specifications were written. According to the number of persons in the various kinds of programs, educational targets were set. Program standards expressed in quantitative terms (curriculum, pupil/teacher ratios) furnished a basis for estimating unit costs in the various education and training programs. Unit costs multiplied by the numbers set in educational targets furnished estimates of future capital and current expenditures.

There is an air of spurious precision and accuracy about the whole procedure. The education and training that is proposed must take place in a setting with unique physical, cultural, social, and political characteristics. These characteristics make Ciudad Guayana what it is, distinct and different from other cities, even in Venezuela. The educational development strategy and program plans were based almost entirely on the technology and economy, present and future, of Ciudad Guayana. The physical aspect of the city and region, the political setting, and the cultural, social, and psychosocial characteristics of the people in Ciudad Guayana have to this point been almost ignored. In the following chapters it is fitting, in fact necessary, to move in to a closer observation of the city and its people.

3
The City
and Surroundings

Guayana as It Was

Ciudad Guayana is at the junction of two very different rivers. The Orinoco is big and slow-moving and runs along the southern edge of the Guayana llanos. The Caroní bursts down from the mountains over rapids and falls. It drops thirty meters at the falls of the Caroní, runs through a narrowing basin, and gouges deeply into the bed of the Orinoco, pushing the larger and more sluggish river north. From the junction the Orinoco runs northeast 130 miles to the Caribbean.

The original settlements that were combined to form Ciudad Guayana were on both sides of the Caroní basin. Puerto Ordaz is to the west on an outthrust of land around which the Caroní loops. San Félix is east of the basin and bounded on the north by the Orinoco. The Orinoco is a wide river and a likely northern bound to the city; the Caroní is narrower and is bridged at the basin. On both sides of the basin there are headlands that fall gradually away toward the riverbank, and both are prominent features of the river-riven city. The climate is hot year round, the temperature staying around eighty-five degrees Fahrenheit during the day, but the heat is tempered by a constant northeast breeze which makes life on the higher ground pleasant.

Alta Vista, the mesa on the west bank, has an altitude of about five hundred feet. It overlooks the town of Puerto Ordaz, built to house the workers and facilities of the Orinoco Mining Company. Puerto Ordaz was planned as an open city, rather than as a company camp; the central plaza of the town was located up on a meseta; housing for the technicians was provided on the slopes

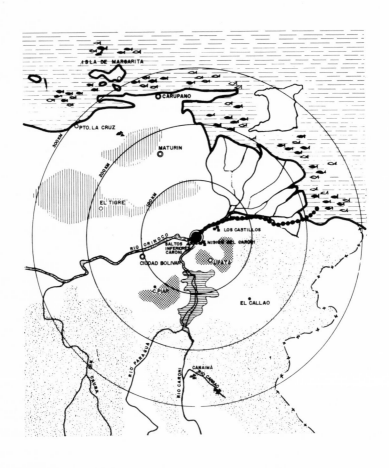

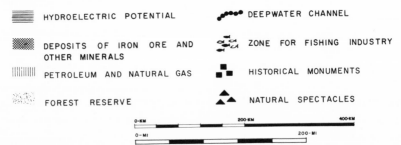

and housing for higher officials was laid out to the northwest. Docks and company facilities were built along the basin. Among the Orinoco Mining Company facilities, open land was left for housing and commercial enterprises not directly connected with the company. Until early 1960 Puerto Ordaz may have been open, but it was a company-dominated town.

From the outset, the officials of the CVG have insisted that Ciudad Guayana become an open city and not a camp or company-dominated enclave. The camp, with privileges and facilities limited to company employees and often with manifest discrimination against Venezuelans from surrounding areas, was a feature of many of the petroleum and construction centers of an earlier day. Inasmuch as all services and facilities must be open to all residents, the city is a much more ambitious undertaking than a camp. Labor contracts, in effect although not through intent, often encouraged the building of camps rather than cities by specifying the services, health, education, housing that the company must guarantee the workers. From the outset the CVG-operated steel mill has had to move rapidly to ensure that facilities will be adequate to cover not only its employees but others, without being able to control the matter as precisely as would be the case in a company camp.

On the east bank, the *casco* or old central section of San Félix lay beyond the main ridge and toward the banks of the Orinoco that bound the village on the north. The main port and market of the area were on the Orinoco. A main road ran from San Félix to the banks of the Caroní at Dalla Costa, where there was a ferry. When the mines and the mill began to attract workers, settlements appeared along the road and off in surrounding barrios, and the ferry terminal became a low-grade commercial center with a gaggle of bars and shops. As the pace of migration quickened, barrios spread west and east of the casco and began to fill in solidly between San Félix and the Caroní basin. Across the river in Puerto Ordaz shantytowns grew up between the main commercial street which ran below the mesa and the basin of the Caroní. The predominant characteristics of the settlement on the west bank, before the bridge was built, were company housing, industrial installations, and a modern plaza and shopping district. The prevailing environment was upper middle class and slightly foreign. In the eastern settlement the center was a gridiron pattern built out from a plaza, and the form of the casco was not different from other sixteenth-century Spanish colonial towns. Away from the casco, sometimes connected by continuous building and sometimes separated by natural breaks formed by swamps, barrancas, and lagoons, were the barrios. Some began as shantytowns and moved toward stable lower-class communities as workers improved their housing and began to build with concrete blocks. The prevailing appearance of the east bank settlement was old-fashioned, *latino*, and working class.

The City as It Will Be[1]

This was the situation before the joining of the east and west settlements by the bridge, and the creation of the city in 1961. The disparateness of the two main communities, each with a different history and *ambiente* made it no easy task to create the concept of one city. The very distance worked against urban unity. From the steel mill on the west it is twenty-five kilometers to San Félix on the extreme east. To this day the idea of one city has not completely taken hold in the minds of older residents of isolated barrios. This is hardly surprising when during the days of the ferry it could take hours or even a half day to travel from one end of the city to the other. And indeed, there was no visible city, but rather two different centers on opposite sides of the Caroní basin.

With the building of the bridge and the running of the Avenida Guayana, the lineaments of one city are appearing. Avenida Guayana, which is laid out to run parallel to the Orinoco from the steel mill in Matanzas to San Félix, has provided the backbone around which the structure of the city can be seen to be shaping. Major metropolitan institutions will be built along Avenida Guayana. The avenue will connect the communities, and within the communities, neighborhoods and subneighborhoods will be laid out. For the medium term the city is planned for a population of 300,000, although a population of 500,000 could be accommodated in the area without a basic restructuring of the city. The city population will be concentrated in communities which may vary from thirty to fifty thousand. The community would center on a secondary school, sports and recreation center, a cultural or educational center, and perhaps a regional shopping center. The communities will be made up of neighborhoods centering on an elementary school of about 1,000 students with police, fire, health, and recreation centers appropriate to the size of the area and population.

The center of the metropolitan area, that is, Ciudad Guayana, is planned to be Alta Vista, the mesa on the western bank of the Caroní. Alta Vista has an area of 900 hectares (2,286 acres) formed by two widening plateaus, one east and one west, with a narrowing waist in the middle. On the eastern plateau will be the principal metropolitan service and government centers as well as concentrated urban dwelling units. In the narrower waist will be the sports center. The western shelf will be the location for light industry and commercial areas

Ciudad Guayana as Planned for 300,000 Inhabitants.

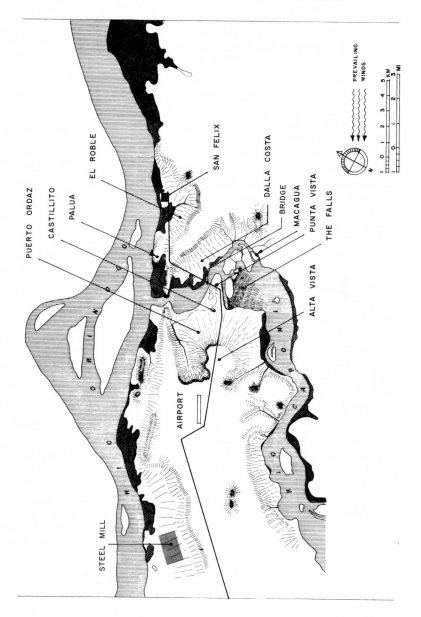

and the transportation terminals, including the airport. The main feature of the
Alta Vista area, however, will be the social, cultural, and government center on
the eastern bluff which will dominate the city and give it its unique identity and
tone. The Alta Vista area will be linked to the rest of the city with modern
highways that will give access to 9,000 vehicles an hour. Alta Vista will probably
also be the site of the first center for postsecondary education. The plan is for a
technological institute that may eventually be expanded into a full-fledged
university.

The communities will also be served by a central artery and feeder roads from
the neighborhoods. The dominating educational institution of the community
will be the middle or secondary school. Hopefully these schools will be comprehensive, housing preparatory, technical, and commercial programs, although
the economic differences and the demographic characteristics of the communities will probably ensure special qualities for each of the schools. Some
may be more heavily technical than preparatory, and presumably open enrollment will be permitted to allow children to come from other communities in
the city.

Ciudad Guayana should be a city of considerable beauty when plans are at
last realized. Avenida Guayana and the principal avenues of the communities
will be spacious, tree-shaded, and lined with handsome buildings. The Alta
Vista center will be on an imposing height with a fine view of the basin and the
river and the distant hills of the old Guayana range. The loop of the Caroní that
lies to the southeast of the western community is the river at its wildest and
most spectacular with the Caroní falls, rapids, gorges, rocks, islands, and
whirlpools. The riverbanks are lush with tropical growth and bridges wind
through the jungle and around the rocks and afford spectacular views of the
river. Punta Vista park at the bridge-crossing will be a handsome place of
greenery and riverscape. On the San Félix side the Orinoco riverfront will be
provided with a *malecón*—a shorefront park and drive—that will give a view of
the river and the plains beyond. Throughout the city the plan is for green space
and open land for views.

The City as It Is

Ciudad Guayana is not what it was in the 1950's, and a long way from what it
will be in the 1970's. Gradually the spine of a single city is showing through
and, from Matanzas on the western edge to the bridge, one can see at least how
the city will lie. The layout of Alta Vista is taking shape. Where many of the

handsome buildings and the commercial center will stand there is raw, red earth, but survey stakes are in the ground and the form is there. The urban housing on the Puerto Ordaz side is gradually filling in along the skirts of the meseta, and entire housing developments, such as Los Olivos, are being completed. The festering slums of Castillitos are withering away along the shore of the Orinoco basin, but there is still a hodgepodge of shanties and open drains down in the heavy growth behind the commercial street. Punta Vista and the riverscape park are there, as always, but not as visible or accessible as they will be.

On the San Félix side the route where Avenida Guayana will swing to the northwest has been marked out, although the old road from Dalla Costa is still in use. The new hospital building is already up on the ridge but not in operation. The Dalla Costa and El Roble neighborhoods are changing. Houses are being improved and the streets and services regularized. Scattered along the edges of the older settlements, new housing developments are underway and the eastern terminus of the highway system is appearing. The San Félix casco is relatively unchanged. The waterfront and the industrial area near the port have nothing attractive about them. The new neighborhoods grow, some as shanty-towns, but some are rapidly improving through self-help housing.

A few of the major institutional buildings are already up and in service. The new industrial technical school on the San Félix side is open and operating; the artisanal school is open; the INCE training center is functioning; the new public liceo is open; two handsome private secondary schools for girls are finished, and a private residential school for boys is approaching completion. Six new public primary schools have recently been opened, and the old unitary schools in the barrios are disappearing. In the detailed section on education it will become clear that there is still a great deal left to do, but the start has been made.

Guayana is no longer a conglomerate of company town, old Spanish town, and slum barrios, as it was less than ten years ago. Neither is it the completely modern and unified city that the plans show ten years from now. It is a place in transition. It is a place of ferment, activity, rawness, and thrusting growth, with deep and stagnant pools in certain of its poorer areas. The first impression is one of raw earth and bulldozers. The next impression is of disorder and even confusion and frustration. Shantytowns are put to the blade and people must move up to better housing or find other areas to squat. Traffic patterns are changed as old roads are ripped out and new ones are run. There are excavations everywhere, sometimes caved in and crumbling when the heavy rains flood down through old channels that are blocked. In places there are row on row of concrete slabs for house foundations, and buildings in every stage of completion. In places it looks like a new city. In other places it looks like a battlefield. And in the quiet and dark places it looks like a slum, as though the shanties had been there since the beginning of time.

Urban services exist, but they are irregular and differ greatly from neighborhood to neighborhood. In the condemned slum areas there are no collection or sanitation services and neighborhoods are dirty and cluttered. Water is abundant in potential but scarce in fact in some areas. Electric power is superabundant in potential, but the distribution system is constantly being changed and overtaxed. The sports and community centers are in, but not the parks and green spaces, except along the Caroní, where they always existed. Along the completed stretch of the Avenida the traffic flows fast and smoothly, but in the areas where building is heavy and changes frequent there are jams of rickety buses, *por puesto* cabs, trucks, and private cars.

For some there are amenities, but they are the "few" who would have them anywhere. There is still the Orinoco golf course and club, open to many more now but beyond the ambitions of 95 percent of the families. There are movie houses of varying comfort and quality. There is a so-called tourist hotel on the Puerto Ordaz meseta.

The tourist hotel has little importance for most local citizens, but it sits up on the meseta and is something to point to. There are restaurants for all purses although it is not common to dine out, especially for the poor. One good restaurant left Ciudad Guayana. The proprietor felt that he had arrived ten years before the proper time. There are beaches along the Caroní and children of the poor swim in the basin and lagoon. There are sports fields and open fields where there is room to play; there are cock pits and *bolas criollas* pits, places to fish, and shade to sit under. Sitting seems to be the most frequent form of leisure for the local poor. There are bars ranging from the most rustic table under a tree to rather elaborate establishments. There are whorehouses, but fewer than in the early boom days of the fifties. There are more churches, but it is not a city of churches. There are a few small libraries in the community centers and lately in the schools. There has been at least one small newspaper; there are radio stations, and television antennas to catch broadcasts from Caracas and Trinidad. At all levels there is a lot of home and family entertainment featuring food, talk, and drink.

In Guayana there is expectation and hope. Some things have come to some people. There is also a great deal of frustration and muted anger because the things have not come nearly as fast and as fully as people expected they would, or could have, come. CVG, which plays a complex role of landlord, employer, provider of services, governor, regulator, and sometimes benefactor and father surrogate, is not always popular among large numbers of people at all social class levels. This is scarcely surprising for a government agency that has to be so many things to so many people.

Regional Development and Local Government: A Note

The problem of regional development and local government is treated more fully in Chapter 14, but a brief statement is appropriate here. If funds mean control and control means power, then the federal government is the power in Venezuela. By constitutional provision and law, states, districts, and municipalities are supposed to govern and provide public services in Venezuela, but capital and current budgets by government agencies clearly show that the national government controls the purse and dominates the action. In 1960 the federal government of Venezuela received Bs. 6,140.2 million in revenues and disbursed 136.9 million in Estado Bolívar, the state in which Ciudad Guayana is located. Estado Bolívar collected and disbursed Bs. 19.2 million in 1964–1965. Contrast this with national investments in the Guayana development zone. In 1963, the Corporación Venezolana de Guayana was created and took over an investment of 1,500 million Bs., of which the steel mill represented 300 million alone; 60 million had been invested in urban services. The Guayana plan called for an investment of Bs. 13,000 million between 1963 and 1975, of which 31 percent would come in direct investment from the national government and about the same amount would come in foreign loans which the federal government would repay. The contrast between national investment and local expenditures is staggering, and it is scarcely surprising that the national government, principally through its regional autonomous development agency, CVG, and its other ministries, dwarfs local governmental action in Guayana.

Below the state level the constitution of Venezuela indicates that the principal and basic unit of government is the *municipio*. The municipio is governed by a *junta communal*. Actually, however, the junta communal is appointed by the *concejo* of the district. The district concejo is elected at the same time and for the same term as the President of Venezuela, the national legislature, and the state legislature. In each district, in addition to the concejo, there is a prefect appointed by the governor of the state. The prefect of the district, in turn, appoints the prefects of the municipios.

Prior to 1961 the chief officer of local government was a municipal prefect residing in San Félix. There was also a junta communal in San Félix. In 1961 the state legislature of Bolívar created the Caroní District. The district is governed by a prefect and a municipal district concejo. Local government has never functioned well. At their best local officials try hard but are poorly prepared. For example, the concejo spent several years without bothering to collect taxes on the Puerto Ordaz side of the Caroní.

In addition to lack of training in administration, the local government is limited by its ignorance of future plans for Ciudad Guayana. There has been constant friction between the CVG and other conventional ministries at the federal level. But there has been even less effective communication between CVG and the local governments. First, CVG is too rich and powerful to be much loved by undermanned and fundless local administrators. Second, CVG has had long-range developmental responsibilities which do not always fit the short-range demand for local favors and services. CVG has had to bar squatters from public lands designated for other uses and forcibly evict when necessary. CVG has also had to pay squatters' relocation costs when the occupants held and improved the land for a long period. Third, CVG has had autonomy and acces₅ to the highest councils of federal government. No local chieftain could compete with CVG in Caracas. Also, CVG officials have lived and worked remote from the zone.

The CVG central office and the locus of its activities and decisions are in Caracas. This has worked well in some situations, not so well in others. Being remote CVG could be more objective and take the longer view of development. However, the separation also cut CVG off from intimate contact with the daily frictions and problems in the zone. Somebody has had to face the daily and weekly complaints and usually this has been the local authorities. The inaccessibility of CVG officials and the length of time required for decisions in Caracas has created resentment among local people and local officials. CVG has been accused of being high-handed and unresponsive to pleas from local people for help in resolving local problems. In some cases this has been unavoidable, but in other cases it would seem that CVG could have made a greater effort to explain its reasons and justify its actions.

There is one further relevant characteristic of CVG's mandate and manner of operating. CVG was not created to take on the entire expense of the Ciudad

Guayana development program. CVG was created to stimulate and coordinate effort and initiative from private, local, and other national ministry sources, as well as foreign investment and assistance. CVG had no mandate to use its own resources as a substitute for those that would normally be expected from other ministries.[2] For example, public education is presumably the responsibility of the Ministry of Education and both state and local authorities are supposed to contribute, but there has been much feinting and maneuvering between the Ministry of Education and CVG. This is described in more detail in Chapter 14. The same backing and starting has taken place in housing and health. National ministries have maneuvered to get CVG to commit its resources in place of their own, and the result has been that services sometimes have come slowly and haltingly; the local government has had to live with the criticism and there has been resentment. Resentment in Ciudad Guayana is chronic but it never seems to rise to an explosive level. The common belief is that it is kept down by the promise of the future. And this may well be the truth of it.

4
The People of
Ciudad Guayana

City of Migrants

In 1954 the population was about 4,000 in the component towns that were formed into Ciudad Guayana. Twelve years later the population was close to 100,000, and since 1960 the growth has been an annual average rate of 13 percent. Guayana is a receiving area of heavy migration and the bulk of its population are migrants from eastern Venezuela.[1]

People have come into Guayana for the same reasons they have moved from rural to urban areas in the rest of Latin America. As mentioned in Chapter 1, the principal attraction is economic opportunity, the same motivation reported by Flinn in Colombia, Matos Mar in Peru, Germani in Argentina, and de Camargo in Brazil.[2] The Guayana migration has some differences, however.

De Camargo reports that in Brazil high natural increase in the rural population and increased productivity in agriculture have created surplus populations which must move on to other areas or to the major cities. This is somewhat the case in Venezuela and Guayana. Certainly, there is high natural increase in eastern Venezuela—demographers report one of the highest population growths in the world. However, most of the Guayana migrants have not been recently crowded off farms by increased productivity. In most cases they left low-yield conucos many years ago to work in oil exploration and construction, and as these activities have slackened, they have moved on to Ciudad Guayana.

Security—flight from *la violencia*—has been a strong motive for migration in Colombia, but has not been markedly present in eastern Venezuela where guerrilla activity has been minimal. The Colombians and Peruvians who migrate

to the city for health, housing, and educational opportunity find their counterparts in Guayana. In Peru, Colombia, and Venezuela these reasons have been
less powerful than work opportunities, but they have had influence. Word-of-
mouth reports of brisk economic activity in Guayana have had a pronounced
effect. Throughout eastern Venezuela common talk has it that things are
booming and jobs are plentiful in Guayana. Migrants who once followed
construction and oil sometimes do not realize that the educational and skill
demands of Guayana industrial jobs are higher than the traditional ones in
eastern Venezuelan camps. Workers come and find this out, often remaining
unemployed for lengthy periods after their first arrival.

The migrants arriving currently in Guayana are like migrants arriving in
urban areas in other parts of Latin America, but there are some differences. Not
such a high percentage of Guayana migrants are female, although lately large
numbers of women have been arriving. In age, migrants are overwhelmingly
under forty. In education they are slightly above the average in eastern Venezuela, but not above the average in Venezuela as a whole. Eastern Venezuela
traditionally has been a low educational attainment area compared with the
rest of the country. Large numbers of the arrivals are unmarried, or at least they
migrate without their families and form liaisons after their arrival. This holds
both for women and men. The women often bring their children with them and
this has made the Guayana age structure appear somewhat different from a
typical migrant area.

Other Demographic Characteristics

If the population growth in absolute terms shows heavy migration, the
steadily normalizing age structure shows, among other things, that over the past
fifteen years the birth rate in Ciudad Guayana has been very high. Sources of
data for adequate demographic analysis are either lacking or incomplete in
Ciudad Guayana. There is no population register or adequate record of births
and deaths. Nonetheless, the evidence is that fertility for both recent migrants
and longer-term resident women is as high as anywhere in Latin America, or
perhaps the world. This would put the birth rate over fifty per thousand.

CVG demographers point out that the age structure of the population of
Ciudad Guayana runs counter to the contention that a population pyramid fed
by migration grows with an irregular distribution unless migrants are drawn
from a cross section of a "normal" population forced to migrate by some
overwhelming external pressure.[3] In the case of Guayana the expectation would

have been that male migrants in prime working ages drawn by employment opportunities would have given the age and sex distributions a special cast that would have lasted perhaps two decades. The prime opportunities in Guayana have been in construction and more recently heavy industry. This feature would seem to attract a population of male migrants between the ages of twenty-five and fifty. Yet, as the demographers point out, the age-sex pyramid in Guayana has gained a "normal" smooth shape in a very short period. So Ciudad Guayana is a community with a balance of women and children and not a city of male adults as the earlier oil and construction sites sometimes were, and as the diamond and gold camps in the Guayana hinterlands still are.

The age frequency distribution of the Ciudad Guayana population compared for various time periods over the past fifteen years is shown in Figures 4.1 and 4.2.

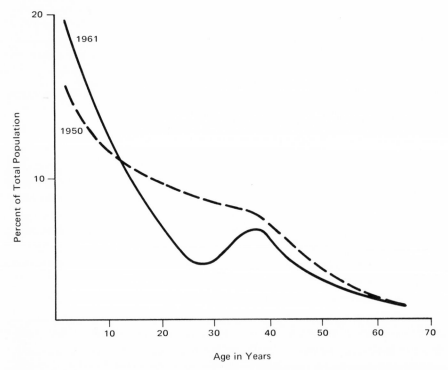

Figure 4.1   Age frequency distributions for the population of Ciudad Guayana, 1950 and 1961.

Source: Censo Nacional, 1950 and 1961. This and other figures in this chapter were designed by Richard M. Durstine of CSED.

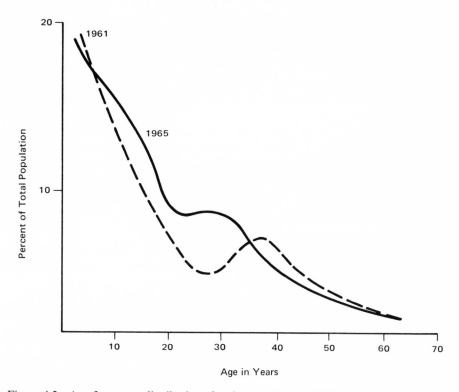

Figure 4.2   Age frequency distributions for the population of Ciudad Guayana, 1961 and 1965.
Source: Censo Nacional 1961; 1965 data from survey by Banco Central de Venezuela.

In 1950, before the boom came, the population showed high frequencies in all the younger age groups and a relatively smooth descent down through to the higher age groups where the mortality conditions that prevailed historically in rural Venezuela ensured small surviving cohorts. In 1961, there is a definite bump up in the prime working age groups, although there are also high percentages in the younger groups. The workers were coming in large enough numbers to distort the distribution, but they were not coming alone. First, men were bringing in their wives and children. Second, because males and females were grouped in these distributions, large numbers of women were migrating in, without husbands but with children. Once arriving in Guayana, they were forming new relationships and maintaining high fertility. This is not shown in the figures but it has later become obvious to the demographers through sample

surveys of households. In the 1961–1965 comparison, the distribution is already
beginning to smooth out and there are even larger numbers of young children
and young adults just below the modal age of skilled workers and technical and
professional employees.

CVG demographers state

In Ciudad Guayana the age-sex pyramid has been smoothed by family migration, by lone male migration, by migration of women with children but no
husbands and by the high fertility of women after arrival in the city, regardless
of their marital status.[4]

The reasons for high numbers of young dependents in the Guayana are many,
and the consequences for educational, health, and other services patent.

Households form rapidly in eastern Venezuela. Given the warm, even climate
and the amount of open land in eastern Venezuela, it is no difficult matter for
the male to move his entire household with him. An empty piece of land and the
simplest of building materials are all that is necessary to build a shack rancho.
In Ciudad Guayana it might seem to be more difficult, inasmuch as CVG
controls the land and building materials are expensive. It has not been difficult
in fact, however. First, there have been unused areas into which squatters could
move and remain unmolested long enough to get some kind of claim on the
land. If they remain five years in uncontested possession the CVG has to
resettle them elsewhere. Second, the construction and heavy industry boom in
Ciudad Guayana has generated much waste material that can be used as a start
in the simplest construction. Without engaging in actual pilferage, although this
has existed on the usual scale that prevails in a situation of extreme inequality
and real and/or fancied inequity, there has been plenty of waste and scrap
lumber, tin (sometimes in sheets but often formed from hammered-out tin cans),
cement, and even steel. Mud and poles are available everywhere. So the basic
ingredients for establishing a house have been on hand in Guayana.

Third, the conditions for rapid formation of informal liaisons have been
present. Among the poor, unmarried motherhood may or may not be a mis-
fortune, but it is almost never a disgrace. There is even some evidence to suggest
that fertility is higher in informal liaisons than in formal marriages, but this is
by no means clearly shown in the Guayana. There are large numbers of women
who, after being abandoned elsewhere by nomadic mates, trek into Guayana
with their children. In the region, women are abandoned, but children are not,
except indirectly. The women apparently find no great difficulty in locating
another mate who takes on, as part of the arrangement, the existing brood.

Curiously, the male who abandons his own children takes on someone else's; he would not expect his new mate to abandon her children any more than he expected his old mate to abandon his. Large numbers of women without husbands and with children remain unattached, and as the study of parental attitudes toward education will show, these women have very high aspirations for the educational achievement of their children. Ciudad Guayana is an area of high marital mobility, if such a term may be used. There is a kaleidoscopic pattern of formation, shifting, and disintegration of households among the poor. The demographic consequences are high fertility and the social consequences are that women perforce assume a large share of family responsibility and a major role in raising the children.

The origin of the poor mass of migrants is eastern Venezuela. Except in the oil fields around El Tigre and the area around Barcelona, economic development has been slow or stagnant. Fertility rates have always been very high. Fertility rates continue to be high among the migrants. Demographers find no evidence that they are going down as a result of urbanization. They find no evidence that the example of the middle classes in the urbanized sections of the city is influencing the fertility of the women in the barrios. Women in the *urbanizaciones* (housing developments) have just as high fertility as the women in the barrios, and even if they did not, social distance and poor communication would probably prevent much of an exchange of information or change of attitude.

MacDonald finds no reason to believe that fertility will go down in the near future. Although middle-class barrio females who wait for formal marriage and housing show slightly lower fertility because of a later start, as fast as these women move into stable homes, new migrants pour into the shacks. There are no existing birth control programs operating in Ciudad Guayana and fairly slim prospects that assistance in family planning is contemplated. Whether or not family planning assistance would be acceptable, and whether or not it would be acceptable at some class levels and not others, has not been investigated.

Origins of the Migrants

Overwhelmingly the population of Guayana is either migrant or the dependents of migrants who have come into the city within the past ten years. The bulk of the migrant population comes from the eastern region of Venezuela, and more specifically from rural areas west of the Caroní, although they may have moved farther away, spent some time in the oil fields or cities to the north and

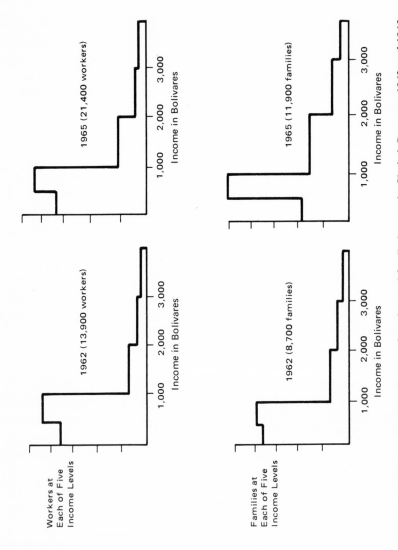

Figure 4.3   Frequency distribution of worker and family income in Ciudad Guayana, 1962 and 1965.
Source: Surveys by Banco Central de Venezuela.

then returned. By origin they are mainly from cities of less than 20,000 and even when they have lived in larger cities they have lived in barrios that were by no means thoroughly urbanized, that is, made up of regularly patterned streets and urban facilities and provided with urban services in education, health, and sanitation. The eastern region is one of the most backward and underdeveloped of Venezuela when measured in conventional economic, political, social, and cultural terms.

Some migrants have also come in from Caracas and the cities of northern and western Venezuela. In general these migrants were sent or recruited into Guayana to occupy specific technical jobs. Many were transferred in to open company branches and agencies; many are assigned by the central government; others are highly skilled technicians brought in to occupy a specific post in industry. There are also foreigners. Americans were present in large numbers in the early days of the Orinoco Mining Company but are gradually phasing out. Italians came during the building of the steel mill, and there is a scattering of Spaniards and other Europeans.

The Trinidadians are rather different from most of the foreigners and northern Venezuelans and they occupy positions that are no higher and sometimes lower than the eastern Venezuelans. The dark-skinned migrants from Trinidad, the West Indies, and Guyana (formerly British Guiana) have often lived in other places in Venezuela before coming to Ciudad Guayana.[5] In some cases they have passed several generations in Venezuela. There is color bias in eastern Venezuela although it manifests itself more in economic discrimination and class distinctions than in racial segregation. Poor Negroes, Indians, and Latinos have mixed considerably in the region.

Economic Characteristics

Migrants for the most part came seeking either employment in Ciudad Guayana or assistance from friends and relatives employed there. The migrants from the West Indies and eastern Venezuela occupy the lowest economic and social positions in the city. They swell the lists of the unemployed and when employed occupy the lowest positions. Although some have taken advantage of the economic opportunity through employment in industry, in the main they work as day laborers on an occasional basis or, in the case of women, eke out an existence in petty trade or domestic services.

Figure 4.3 shows average earnings of workers and average income of families in Ciudad Guayana. The average worker earns between Bs. 500 and 750 a month ($115 to $170). Family income is slightly higher, being between Bs. 750 and 1,000 ($170–$225). The average figures tend to cover the fact that large proportions earn incomes that put them at minimal subsistence levels, given costs of equivalent goods and services equal to or higher than cost in the United States. A third of the workers earn $100 a month or less and almost a fifth of the families have a total monthly income in this range. Furthermore, these data are for employed persons. Unemployment in Ciudad Guayana is high.

Employment opportunity fluctuates in Guayana, not only according to peaks of construction activity, but also according to the recency of the arrival of the migrant. The over-all unemployment rate varies between 10 and 15 percent but it may rise to 20 percent in slack times. However, at its worst, Ciudad Guayana unemployment is not as serious as it was for the migrant before he came there. Data indicate that about half the migrants were unemployed before arriving in Guayana. After arriving in Guayana, about two thirds fail to find employment in the first month, a third are unemployed for over a month, and after six months one tenth are still unemployed.

Public assistance services are not lavish in Guayana, and there is the usual irony that those who need assistance most get the least. This is so because most benefits are tied to employment and guaranteed through union contracts. Until the worker can get employment he has almost no official protection or assistance. The paradoxical nature of welfare assistance in the Guayana has been pointed out in reports and publications to the officials of CVG.[6]

CVG officials state that they are not indifferent to social welfare but point out that their mandate is the economic development of Guayana and that this can only come with employed, productive people. There is an unvoiced fear that if welfare assistance were more ample in the Guayana, it would attract large numbers who would come to live on the bounty of the region rather than to add to it. CVG planners not only hope that outright loafers will not come to Ciudad Guayana, they also hope—but cannot ensure—that petty traders and service workers will not form a large part of the work force of the future.

One would expect that the dire consequences of being separated from employment would lead to low turnover in industry, but this is not the case. The high turnover in the steel mill and in all other jobs indicates that workers are undeterred by the bleak possibilities for public assistance.

Punctuality and responsibility are not said to be characteristics of Guayana workers, although there are no adequate data on residents' expressed attitudes toward work. Some part of the turnover may be involuntary. The workers have no skills or even aptitude to acquire them. Activity falls off and work rolls are cut. There is some favoritism for family and friends but, in any case, unskilled workers get chopped first. Still, the turnover is so high and frustrating to managers that it cannot be completely explained by involuntary separations. Some workers lack the discipline for punctuality and constancy that industrial employment demands. They have had seasonal work all their lives and when the vacation cycle comes they go. They may only later find out that the job is not waiting for them as patiently as did the field and plow.

It may even be that the rapidity with which households form and disintegrate and re-form with new participants influences the matter. Having a stable income cannot be seen as an important responsibility by the husband who will move on to a new mate as rapidly as does the Guayana male. In some way the matter evens out. He later goes back to work and takes on a new mate and her children, and meanwhile, hopefully, mother works or makes a new connection. The reasons underlying instability in the job are perhaps a mixture of voluntary and involuntary causes. Among some classes there seems to be no more stigma to being unemployed than there is to being unwed and pregnant, and this being so, the men fall into the pattern without pondering the matter deeply. Perhaps even the boom-town mentality prevails, and eastern Venezuelan workers hope to move on to better things, just as the "boomers" did in the North American West.

If government welfare services are deficient, there can be little expectation by Ciudad Guayana residents that they will be taken care of by organized, private charity. The resources of organized charity in Guayana are scarce. Such as there are are mainly Catholic, and the Guayana poor are not formally religious. Further, the Catholic enterprises also are oriented toward development rather than subsistence charity, and most of their resources go into education and training.

The prevailing source of charity and support is informal and comes from family and friends.[7] Observers in the barrios report that unsystematic assistance is so vast and pervasive as to appear almost formal and systematic. Peattie has observed that inasmuch as the only hope of soliciting aid is to seek out friends and to pass the time of day with them, it is small wonder that many men spend long hours drinking and conversing with friends. This is merely a way of working at the one job likely to yield something, that is, the friendly touch. This would be one of the pleasantest ways of satisfying one's wants if it really worked that well. One could see it working in a neighborhood of mixed prosperity

where there are employed workers who have earnings to lend to their less
fortunate friends. How it works in barrios where large numbers are unemployed
and without earnings is difficult to imagine. Some earnings must take place
before the lending and hand-out cycle can start.

One would expect that because it is so obvious that all good things come from
employment there would be competition for jobs and despair in the face of
unemployment. Jobs are sought, but failure to find them is not a sufficient cause
for despair in Guayana. One could also expect that because lack of education
and training is so often the bar to attractive employment there would be keen
competition for training. Again this is not manifest. At least adult males do not
always see the connection in their own case. The study of parental attitudes will
show, however, that they often see it for the next generation; and that women,
particularly those bereft of spouses and breadwinners, realize even more
poignantly how important education is for their children.

Educational Attainment of the Population

Lack of formal education, training, and industrial experience are the great
bars to employment in Ciudad Guayana. No one doubts this, either in upper- or
lower-class families. Ultimately, the bar is lack of education and training, for
this precludes even getting the job from which experience can be obtained.

It is widely asserted that education is a primary and absolute precondition to
employment in the city, but this precondition has not always existed. The
educational attainment level in the steel mill work force averaged about four
years in 1964, and in the mines it was lower. This of course reflected the situation as it was, and not as it should have been, for no one would claim that the
steel mill workers were ideally educated. Turnover was high and output per
worker fairly low, although this latter fact had other antecedents besides the
general educational level of the workers. Management problems had at least as
much influence on output at the steel mill. The newness of the operation and the
scale of operation during start-up affected the matter, and some claim that the
main problem was and still is technological, that is, the process used. Still the
low level of educational attainment among workers already employed does
demonstrate that education was not the insuperable bar in the earlier days of the
city that some claimed. More recently, given a larger pool from which to select
and increased recognition of the value of an educated worker, the steel mill and
the Orinoco Mining Company have refused to accept applications for employment from men with less than six years of education.

Many migrants coming into Ciudad Guayana have had very little formal education. Although only 10 percent are classified "illiterate," this seems too low. Almost 40 percent have less than four years of primary school education, which would be one standard for determining literacy. On functional grounds it appears that about half with four years or less of formal education can read and write. Functional literacy among adults in the total population is now about 65 percent, and in the work force it probably runs about 10 percent higher.

Figure 4.4 shows the cumulated educational levels and indicates that slightly less than 40 percent have insufficient primary education to ensure functional literacy. Some of these may be able to write well enough to fill out an application form, if someone reads and interprets it for them and gives them some assistance with the writing. They might also be able to decipher simple printed directions but it is unlikely that they could read sustained printed text, even a newspaper.

The close relationship between educational attainment and prosperity is apparent in Figure 4.5, which plots the education of the head of the family against family income. Few families where the head of the household is in the lowest education category have incomes of more than $275 a month, and the average is about $130. By contrast, families where the head of household has more than a complete primary education have almost three times the average income of the most poorly educated group. These differences are not lost on even the poorest barrio dwellers, although the resolve is usually to make it up in the next generation by educating the children.

Migrants have come in various waves to the Guayana and level of education of the migrants varies with time of arrival in the area. Figure 4.6 shows a steady increase in education level according to recency of arrival. Those who arrived before 1948 have the lowest educational level of all. These people were residents of the zone when it was thoroughly rural and typical of the low level of educational development in eastern Venezuela. Education was bad throughout Venezuela in those days, but worst of all in the rural regions. As the boom began in the fifties and the mines and construction industry opened new opportunities and attracted new people, the level of educational attainment of migrants began to rise. The average was almost a complete primary education— note that these are employed heads of households—and substantial numbers had secondary and higher education. This could be accounted for by migration of professional and skilled workers attracted through selective recruitment. However, in the last two-year period, 1964–1965, a noticeably larger number of

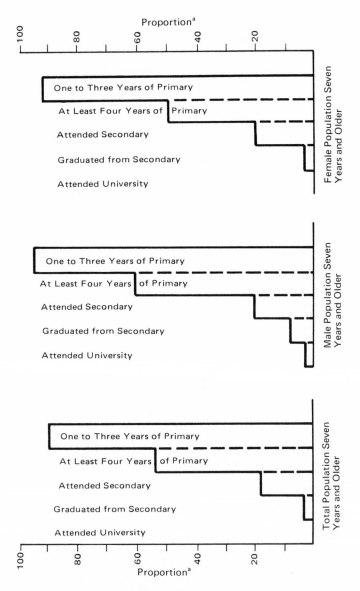

Figure 4.4   Levels of education in Ciudad Guayana in 1965.

[a] The figures are cumulative, so that each group to the right includes those who have gone on to higher levels, that is, those with university attendance are also included in the group of secondary graduates, both are included in the group attending secondary, and so on.
Source: Survey of Banco Central de Venezuela, 1965.

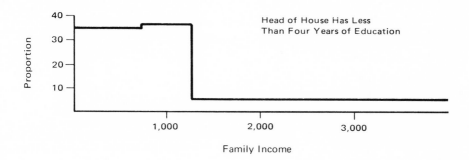

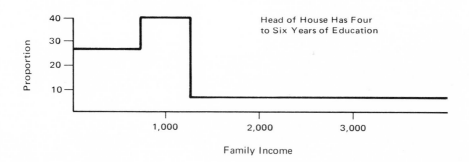

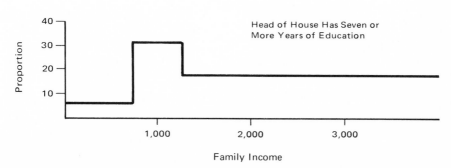

Figure 4.5   Family income in bolivares in Ciudad Guayana in 1965 according to education of head of household.
Source: Migration survey carried out by John MacDonald in 1965, sponsored by the Joint Center for Urban Studies.

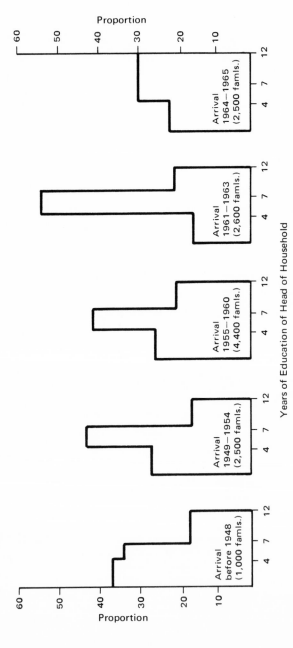

Figure 4.6   Education level of head of household according to time of arrival in Ciudad Guayana.
Source: Joint Center for Urban Studies Migration Survey, 1965.

migrants with very little education came in to Ciudad Guayana. In this most recent wave of migration there began to appear a number of badly educated rural people who poured into the shack areas and replaced those who were moving up into the more developed neighborhoods.

Income distribution shows a similar pattern according to time of arrival. The number of recent arrivals with low incomes is even more pronounced than would be expected, given education levels. At the same time, recent arrivals who are recruited for specific jobs have high incomes and hence there is a tendency toward a bimodal distribution with the larger hump toward the low end.

Neighborhood Differences

There are, of course, pronounced differences among neighborhoods in Ciudad Guayana. The largest difference is between residents of the new housing developments, the urbanizaciones, and residents of the shack rancho barrios. But there are also finer differences that grade all the way from the poorest end of a poor rancho settlement to the housing for Orinoco Mining Company executives in the country club area of Puerto Ordaz. Figure 4.7 compares average family income in the more affluent sections, Puerto Ordaz and company settlements, with that of the barrios. All except one barrio, Castillitos, are on the San Félix side of the Caroní basin. Although income is higher in Puerto Ordaz and the company settlements in both 1962 and 1965, the income distribution in the barrios has moved higher during the years 1962 to 1965. Still the difference is pronounced and remains.

Inasmuch as education of the household head is highly correlated with family income, one would expect differences in average education level among the neighborhoods; and there are. These differences reflect education attained outside of Ciudad Guayana, for the head of household generally would not have been educated in the area. However, it will become apparent that the neighborhoods also differ a great deal in terms of educational facilities available for future household heads. Of course the direction of this difference is markedly in favor of Puerto Ordaz and the company settlements. The same difference would appear with respect to possession of facilities and amenities, and access to water, electricity, sewer and sanitation services.

Growth and Improvement of Urban Housing and Amenities

Despite the grim picture of the shack barrios, the problems of unemployment and the lack of services, and the heavy turnover among workers in the steel mill

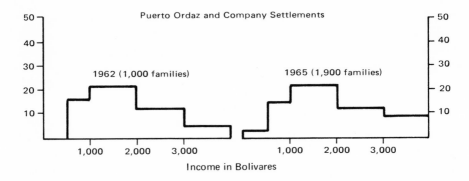

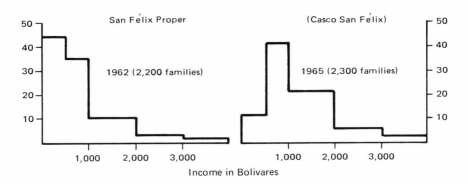

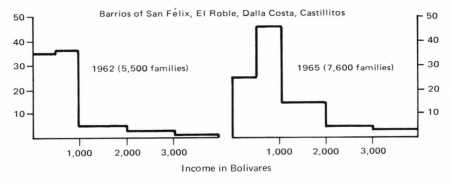

Figure 4.7   Family income in Ciudad Guayana in 1962 and 1965 according to neighborhood.
Source: Surveys of Banco Central de Venezuela, 1962 and 1965.

and other industries, the MacDonald data suggest that remigration from Ciudad Guayana is relatively small and that many residents plan to stay. This is in contrast to previous unsupported opinions that there were large numbers arriving in Guayana only to become discouraged and remigrate. The migrant survey would suggest not only that relatively few leave but that few plan to leave.

The signs are that migrants are steadily improving their houses and making them more permanent. This does not mean that Ciudad Guayana is a city in which contentment prevails. Things are too raw, too unsettled and unsettling, too isolated and too dependent on decisions that are made in Caracas, or even in the United States, to make Ciudad Guayana every man's favorite city. Gossip, rumor, griping, and petty intrigue are high by any standards. But migrants continue to pour in, sometimes at a rate of 1,000 a month, and apparently most come to stay.

One reason for the holding power of Ciudad Guayana is that it has promise. Often the very inconvenience demonstrates the promise, as old roads are torn up to make way for sewer and utility lines or for larger new roads. There is dust and mud because the bulldozers are always at work excavating sites for new housing. Urbanization is taking shape. The population in the urbanizaciones doubled in three years. The urbanizaciones are growing faster than the shack barrios in the ratio of three to two, and that is a sign of progress that even those who are not privy to the economic development plans can see and understand. The housing of many is improving, and, in increasing numbers, people are moving out of the barrios and into the urbanizaciones.

Development housing was more plentiful for the higher and middle income groups but it is now beginning to open to the lower income groups. Not for the very low, and not for the unemployed, but for the wage earners just below average, there is beginning to be housing. The lower wage earners had previously been bumped out of housing by a squeeze that came progressively down from the top, as high income groups took middle income housing and middle income people squeezed out the lower groups. This demand is at last beginning to be saturated and the likelihood is that there will be much more low-cost housing open in the coming years than previously. With urbanización living comes enormous improvement in services and much better access to schools.

For the whole city, improvement in services and conveniences has not been spectacular and in some situations it has even suffered slightly in relative terms. This is so because of the recent wave of poorer and less well-trained migrants.

Over-all the direction is up. New migrants arrive and go into shacks which are gradually transferred into more stable lower-class houses: the final step in the transition may be that they sell the house in the barrio and move into the urbanización. There are aided self-help programs in which barrio owners can get assistance in improving their houses and, although credit is not easy, it is better than in most other areas of Latin America. The housing scene brightened considerably after the opening of the large low-rent urbanizaciones in 1966. Rental costs are felt to be fairly high but at least rentals are available. The majority of Ciudad Guayana residents own their own homes, mean though they may be, so the rental problem is not acute. It is likely that ownership of homes and real estate in Ciudad Guayana will also act as a force to hold people in the city.

Social Integration

The people of Ciudad Guayana are migrants, but they are not transients. The likelihood is that they will stay and tie their future closer to the development of the zone. Hopefully, they will show interest in institutions that will have significance in the development of Ciudad Guayana. This would include educational and cultural, medical and health, political, religious, and economic organizations and institutions.

At present interest and involvement is limited, and is restricted to organizations that can promise immediate, concrete rewards. There has been little tradition of local government and political activity, and interest is relatively slight at this time. Political activity and participation is also low, although some may think it too high as it is.[8] On the economic side, workers are interested in new industrial enterprises and employment possibilities as sources of homes and household possessions. As expected, interest and sympathies are with the unions and the benefits they ensure. Unions are fairly strong in Ciudad Guayana, and reasonably effective in comparison to other areas of Latin America. Guayana has not had a great deal of labor strife. In 1959, strikes in the Orinoco Mining Company idled large numbers and caused hardships in worker families, but did not provoke outright violence. The Venezuelan political terror of the sixties did not come to the surface violently in Guayana, perhaps because the llanos are not ideal terrain for guerrilla activity. In general, political or economic turbulence has not affected Guayana.

In Guayana there is high interest in medical service, although more concern with the curative aspects than the preventative. Religious interest as measured by formal association with churches is fairly low, at least among the poor. In part this also comes from the past. In eastern Venezuela a strong and effective church has not been present. The spread of a strong press has perhaps been hampered by the level of literacy and education. Radio has a high and constant following in Ciudad Guayana.

The one institution that does elicit very strong interest from people at all levels is the school. It is perceived as a key to wider economic opportunity, more stable civic and political action, and enhanced social and cultural development. Attitudes toward education are surprisingly similar among all classes and levels in Guayana, from those who plan and direct the development of the zone to the poorest citizens. Education is perceived as having many benefits, but the prime one is its power to open economic opportunity for all.

5
The Educational System

The future of Ciudad Guayana depends on the people who live in it, who man its factories, run its businesses, govern its activities. The heavy industry complex which is the backbone of the city's future economy demands men with skills and discipline; the mushrooming size of the city requires a populace capable of coping with the complexities of urban life; looming poverty and misery and sickness can be eliminated only by determination, imagination, and effort.

However, most of the people who have flocked to Ciudad Guayana, and those who will continue to come in the future, are badly prepared to meet the demands of the city. What is more, their low level of education and training argues against their ability to overcome this lack of preparation on their own. To the schools of the city falls the sizable task of not only educating the children of Ciudad Guayana, but also helping to prepare and motivate adults present and coming to meet the challenges the new city poses.

To meet their responsibility to an expanding economy, the educational institutions of Ciudad Guayana must be able to graduate a high proportion of the students they enroll. To meet their responsibility to the citizens they have a mandate to serve, they must guarantee them that education necessary to get work. Schools can no longer be content with giving children an opportunity to enroll, for more and more of the industries which locate in the region will demand a minimum educational level of sixth grade.[1] Men who once considered themselves educated because the school carried them to the third grade now recognize that modern industry demands ever higher standards of formal education for its workers. The new city with its complex net of transportation facilities, industries, and businesses needs people educated to understand a world in which science and technology play a dominant role, and in which men live in close contiguity with their neighbors. The new city demands citizens fully aware of their mutual interdependence in work and play. Men and women must be willing and able to use legal means to resolve their grievances, willing to exchange the apparent freedom of anarchy for the individual and societal development which can only be brought about through organization.[2]

However, it is doubtful that the educational system of Ciudad Guayana, any more than that of the rest of Venezuela, can now educate most of its "clients" to a level which ensures individual development and prosperity in the urban environment. The schools do not enroll all those children who are eligible. The primary schools graduate less than half of those who enter. The education provided students who do graduate poorly equips them for dealing with the industrial metropolis of the future.

The implications for the development of the city, given no improvement in the city's schools, are easily demonstrated, and they are grave. At its present level of operation, the school system of the city is not capable of supplying more than half of the number of primary school graduates needed for the labor force by 1975. Table 5.1 shows how many sixth-grade graduates Ciudad Guayana could expect from its schools by 1975, assuming current rates of efficiency and a growth rate of the enrolled student population of 14 percent per year. The schools could graduate about 24,000 children from the sixth grade, but at least 38,000 primary school graduates will be needed to meet production targets in the industry-business complex (and this assumes that all graduates enter the labor force).

The shortfall of primary school graduates is a serious problem, for the history of migration into the city indicates that those who will continue to come in the future will lack the industrial skills and urban attitudes necessary for the social development and economic growth of Guayana. Migrants do not arrive with modern work skills or urban experiences and, unless the schools of the city can be improved to the point where they make up for these deficiencies, the dreams of Venezuela's leaders, planners, and people are in jeopardy.

In this and the chapters that follow, we set out to answer these questions:

1. Is it reasonable to expect that maximal enrollment in the city's schools can be obtained over the next ten years? What factors currently operate against achieving full enrollments? How can they be overcome?

TABLE 5.1
Numbers of Graduates that will be Produced by the Primary Schools of Ciudad Guayana if No
Qualitative Improvements are Made

Actual Data

	Total Enrollment[a]	1	2	3	4	5	6	Graduates
1961–1962	7,339	1,932	1,605	1,584	1,054	816	348	292
1962–1963	9,032	2,491	1,888	1,583	1,455	966	649	610
1963–1964	10,242	2,796	2,098	1,810	1,513	1,231	794	746
1964–1965	11,536	2,970	2,317	2,047	1,764	1,472	966	908
1965–1966	13,538	3,435	2,774	2,473	2,024	1,600	1,232	1,158
Projection of Current Promotion Rates								
1966–1967	16,235	4,887	3,074	2,766	2,372	1,842	1,294	1,216
1967–1968	19,365	5,624	4,374	3,065	2,653	2,159	1,490	1,401
1968–1969	23,033	6,540	5,033	4,361	2,939	2,414	1,746	1,641
1969–1970	27,069	7,389	5,853	5,018	4,182	2,674	1,953	1,836
1970–1971	31,705	8,476	6,613	5,835	4,812	3,806	2,163	2,033
1971–1972	36,231	8,998	7,586	6,593	5,596	4,379	3,079	2,894
1972–1973	40,777	10,200	8,055	7,563	6,323	5,092	3,544	3,330
1973–1974	45,417	11,131	9,129	8,031	7,253	5,754	4,119	3,872
1974–1975	50,248	12,225	9,962	9,102	7,703	6,602	4,654	4,373
1975–1976	55,770	13,816	10,941	9,932	8,730	7,011	5,340	5,018

Total Graduates 1966–1975 = 23,754

[a] Held to same level as shown in Table 2.4 in order to facilitate comparison.

2. What factors influence school attendance or desertion? What role can the school play in reducing or eliminating the tremendous waste of human potential represented by current nonenrollment, desertion, and failure rates?

3. What factors are relevant for achievement within the school system? Can the school improve its ability to develop students who meet its requirements? Can this be done while at the same time raising demands made on students?

4. What programs can be developed, and implemented, to make the school a more effective instrument for the development of human resources, both socially and economically, in Ciudad Guayana?

To begin to answer these questions, it was necessary to collect a great deal of information about the city, its people, and its schools and training institutions. Among the kinds of information gathered, and presented in this book, are the following (a detailed description of procedures is contained in Appendix A):

a. Information on the composition of the student and teacher populations collected by the Ministry of Education's Office of Statistics.

b. Descriptions of each of the schools and institutions in the city. Assessment of the capacity and condition of educational facilities.

c. A census of households in the city enumerating all children between the ages of six and fourteen to determine attendance rates and to provide a base for further sample surveys.

d. An analysis of data contained on school enrollment cards to provide information on the location of students attending the various schools.

e. A sample survey of mothers of school-age children to investigate attitudes toward education, levels of motivation, socioeconomic factors related to attendance and achievement, and to provide more definite information on the academic history of children now in schools.

The Ciudad Guayana School System: General Characteristics

Figure 5.1 outlines the varieties of educational institutions of Ciudad Guayana. For the reader unfamiliar with Latin American education, it should be noted that whereas Ciudad Guayana has several kinds of schools offering programs in different levels and kinds of education, it has no school system. This is not peculiar to Ciudad Guayana but applies equally to education throughout Venezuela and most of Latin America.[3] The various primary schools of the city are oriented mainly toward the Ministry of Education in Caracas; local decision making is limited and seldom carried out jointly. There is no relationship or communication between primary and secondary schools. The various kinds of middle-level schools share teachers but do not cooperate in programs or use of materials.

Preprimary Education

Venezuela has not yet had a strong development in preprimary education. In the country as a whole, less than 2 percent of the total primary enrollments are found in preprimary classes. The reluctance to expand preprimary education is hardly surprising; Venezuela has not yet attained universal enrollments of age groups in the regular primary grades. Almost all the preprimary enrollments are in urban schools; in fact, almost all the enrollments are in Caracas schools. Most enrollments are in private schools and the children are from upper-middle-class families.

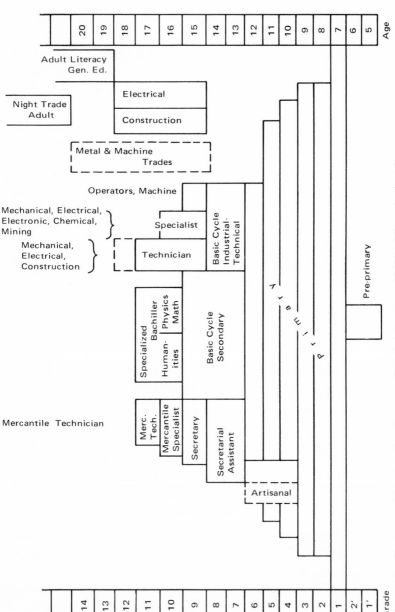

Figure 5.1   Structure of the educational system of Ciudad Guayana, 1965 (public and private).

Artisanal is dotted because it is supposed to exist at La Salle School but in fact may not. Horizontal distance is only roughly proportional to enrollments. INCE programs are not an integral part of the school system; age but not grade levels determines entrants. There is no normal school in Ciudad Guayana; it would run from grades 7–10 or 7–11.
Source: CSED, Harvard University.

There were approximately 1,000 children enrolled in some kind of program serving children of preschool age in Ciudad Guayana in February 1967. This is about 7 percent of the total primary enrollment, and 6 percent of the total population of children two to six years of age. However, only one hundred of the thousand children attended a free public educational center. The rest attended private kindergartens (which charge fees) or public "child breakfast" programs. These latter have no educational content. The majority of the staff in the public institutions had not completed primary school and the average client-to-staff ratio in the public facilities was thirty-four to one.[4]

It is difficult to evaluate the worth of preprimary education in Venezuela. It is dismissed by some educators as a baby-sitting operation, and is definitely peripheral in present educational planning. Yet, for several reasons, preprimary education should not be rejected as an extra frill in Ciudad Guayana. First, there are pedagogical reasons. For children of illiterate rural parents living in homes deprived of all cultural stimulation, the preprimary educational experience, appropriately designed and supported, could prove invaluable in promoting readiness to learn in the primary grades and in enriching the experience of children from deprived homes. It is precisely the shack rancho children who need whatever head start the preprimary schools might provide to compensate for their bleak home backgrounds. There is every reason to believe that an appropriate preprimary experience would eventually cut wastage in the first few grades of primary school and have a measurable effect on achievement. The children in the ranchos live in a culture of poverty and deprivation, and the preprimary schools are important in leading them out of it.

If resources were available and a program were launched in preprimary, it could be as inadequately supported and as inflexible as the present primary level program. Until a well-developed readiness and enrichment program is devised and until teachers are trained, educational materials designed and developed, and suitable physical surroundings provided, the program would perhaps be only a baby-sitting operation. Even so, the possibility should be examined for social and economic reasons.

Large numbers of women with children and no husbands must leave the house for such work as they can find. Even a poor program of day care of children would be helpful to these already overburdened mothers. It would also be beneficial for older siblings who are now forced to stay home to mind the young children and thereby lose continuous learning experience in the primary grades. There are some centers in the city where this is done, but they are inadequate in staffing and programing. The participation rate of women in full-time employment in the work force will rise as Guayana industrializes more, and the provision of child-care centers and preprimary schooling would have a reasonable economic payoff as well as cultural and social advantages. Women could leave their children in preprimary schools while attending industrial training programs and, later, while working.

In summary, preprimary education is conducted on a very small scale in Ciudad Guayana and in Venezuela generally, but the establishment of programs might have important economic, cultural, and social benefits in the future. When and if such programs are established they should be planned to ready children from culturally deprived homes for regular primary school attendance.

Primary Schools: General Characteristics

Just as there is no general educational system in Ciudad Guayana, so there is no primary school system. Of the twenty complete primary schools operating in 1965, eight were run by the federal government, nine were under private auspices, mostly Catholic, and three were run by the state of Bolívar. Formal communication among these three educational groups was limited to sporadic directors' meetings; the schools ran quite independently of one another.

There was at least a titular head in the person of a "supervisor" who was assigned and stationed in Ciudad Guayana, responsible for primary schools. He had meager resources and was not a highly trained specialist in supervision or administration, but was willing to help in the few cases where help was within his means and limitations. He installed weekly teachers' meetings and there was some discussion of program content and methods.

Curriculum for the primary schools is fairly clearly prescribed in Ministry regulations, which have at one time or another been communicated to the teachers.[5] Presumably state, local, and private schools conform to Ministry of Education programs and standards. At least the *ley orgánica de educación* specifies that this should be so. The supervisor has been fairly successful in enlisting the support of both public and private schools in attempts to improve instruction. In the event of a gross departure from norms that might reach the proportions of a "public case," the district supervisor would probably not intervene in private schools. The reason is obvious. He is a low-level member of the educational establishment and could easily be by-passed; he might very well be reprimanded if he took on a high-ranking ecclesiastic in public dispute. There have been cases, however, in which private schools in Guayana have been intervened and forced to close or make changes. One school was closed in 1965 because it did not meet safety or sanitation standards. In this case the action was taken by highly placed officials in Caracas, rather than by the district supervisor.

Each private school operates independently within its own group except, for example, when the same order of nuns runs more than one school. There is no effective church coordinator of education in Ciudad Guayana, although there is a vicar who has titular jurisdiction over all Catholic educational activities in the district. He is a dedicated and saintly man, much respected for his good works. In confrontation with state authorities he has proved extremely courageous and in fact has been marked down somewhat as an agitator. He admits, however, that he would be extremely reluctant to engage in combat with some of the formidable Mother Superiors who run the better Catholic schools. The Monsignor has complained to them in some cases, but it is doubtful that he has any effective authority over them. Each school is run by "Mother" and she brooks no interference from any man.

The schools run by the state of Bolívar are also largely independent, the only difference from other schools being the source of their funds. If state authorities visited them at all in 1965–1966, it was on a sporadic basis; what direction and supervision there was, was provided by the Ministry's supervisor. In general, federal schools are autonomous even to the point of buying their few supplies from local stores at retail prices. All schools are required by law to furnish periodic reports and enrollment and promotion statistics. No one checks the accuracy of these statistics, and until the advent of the CVG-assisted school census the true state of primary education in Ciudad Guayana was largely unknown. Even at this date the exact locations of some small unitaria and dame schools are not known. In some cases the unitarias move around neighborhoods like an old, established, permanent floating crap game; and they are pretty difficult to find at times.

If schools within the primary level operate independently from one another, it goes without saying that they are completely detached from the preprimary level below and the secondary level above, except in the circumstances when one private teaching order operates schools at more than one level. This is the case in three of the Catholic schools, Nazareth, Fatima, and La Salle, which operate at both the primary and secondary level. Here there may possibly be articulation between levels, but in the general case the primary and secondary worlds are separate, both in Ciudad Guayana and in Venezuela generally.

Primary School Facilities. In September 1965, about 13,500 students enrolled in primary schools in Ciudad Guayana. This was about 90 percent of the eligible population. Most of the students (9,300) were enrolled in eleven public schools, and 2,700 were enrolled in the city's nine private schools. Another 1,500 were enrolled in twenty-eight unitaria schools, controlled by the Ministry of Education, the state government, or the municipality.

Enrollments in primary schools have increased at a rate parallel to that of the growth of the city (see Table 5.2), about 13 percent a year over the past five years. Enrollments in unitarias declined until September 1965, as some of them were absorbed into the six-year schools and others coalesced and formed into

TABLE 5.2
Enrollments in Schools in Ciudad Guayana, 1961–1965, by Levels

Primary	1961–1962	1962–1963	1963–1964	1964–1965	1965–1966
Public	4,815	6,213	7,026	8,378	9,297
Private	1,351	1,825	2,274	2,435	2,682
Unitaria	1,173	994	941	723	1,559
Total	7,339	9,032	10,241	11,536	13,538
Secondary					
Liceos	461	694	1,015	1,060	1.292
Public	378	470	756	776	976
Private	83	224	259	284	316
Commercial	322	473	667	661	578
Industrial	—	—	—	442	549
Total	783	1,167	1,682	2,163	2,419

escuelas concentradas and received status as six-year schools. In September 1965, the supervisor decided to maximize school enrollment and created more unitarias.

In 1965, seven of the eleven public primary schools were located in buildings designed as schools, and three in rented buildings; the other school was housed in a tin shack built by the people of the neighborhood who could not wait for the Ministry of Education or the CVG to deliver on their promises. The newest school building had been constructed in 1963, but there were seven new schools under construction in 1966.

The older public schools, Antonio de Berrio, San Félix, Puerto Ayacucho, Tumeremo and José Angel Ruiz, were built for a cooler region; ventilation is bad and classrooms receive little natural light. These schools were built between 1958 and 1962, when the haste to erect buildings did not allow time to develop designs suited to the region. But the schools built with a more "tropical" plan, Mercedes Prospert and Felipe Hernández, suffer from too much exposure to the elements during rainstorms, when the noise on the tin roofs drowns out even the most strident teacher and water driven by wind pours through the ventilating spaces. These are technical problems which would have been corrected immediately if architects and builders had been accessible to local school people.

The pressing need for new school buildings is illustrated by a description of four facilities operating in 1965. José Félix Ribas was housed in an old residence, with first and second grades in the living room, the principal in the kitchen, and other grades in the back bedrooms. The roof was collapsing in several of the rooms. There were no toilet facilities, but the river was near—too near according to the teachers, who complained that some students never came back to class. Silvana de Irady was in an old *pensión*. The patio served as a classroom too. José L. Guzmán had adequate classrooms, for the rented property was built to serve as a school, but the play area was low ground which received deposits from several open sewers. The worst school in the city was no doubt Consuelo Navas, at least in terms of physical comforts. The community which built this school with little money and no guarantee that the government would provide teachers had to settle for a chicken house kind of arrangement. The school had to be closed when it rained because of noise on the tin roof and walls, and when the sun came out interior temperatures would soar over one hundred degrees Fahrenheit.

The unitarias are not housed in school buildings. Teachers usually receive about $9 a month to rent space for their classes; the living room in their own home is a frequent option. Chairs and blackboard are begged, borrowed, or improvised. The front door on the street remains open to let in light, but with that also comes dust, noise, and the flies that congregate near the open sewers in the barrios. Forty, fifty, or sixty children may be crammed into the room, at the beginning of the year anyway. If children are lost during the year those that remain have more space and attention, and perhaps everyone is grateful.

Until September 1965, none of the schools provided free textbooks for their children. There are lists of approved books, but teachers seldom required any one book and students made do with what their parents could afford to buy, or used the hand-me-down of an older brother or sister. All schools had some teaching materials, such as maps, globes, and visual displays, but in the public primary schools these were in short supply and in an advanced state of de-composition. None of the schools had basic materials for science demonstrations.

The private schools were much more fortunate. All but one of the nine were located in buildings designed as schools, and five of the schools were built within the past three years (by the CVG). They were well stocked with materials and parents could buy the best textbooks. The only inadequate private school was located in a slum area in Castillito, where it served the indigent poor. Two schools accepted only children of employees of the Orinoco Mining Company (U.S. Steel) or the Iron Mines Company of Venezuela (Bethlehem Steel). Six of the other seven were run by Catholic religious and charged fees, but accepted all applicants. There was one small school run by a Baptist congregation in San Félix.

Construction costs for the private schools, operated at similar capacities to the new public schools but better built, were four times as high as those for public schools.

Primary Teachers.[6] The 250 primary school teachers and principals in Ciudad Guayana in 1964 were all certified by the Ministry of Education. Sixty-nine percent were graduates of normal schools, that is, they had received four years of teacher education following primary school. A few were graduates of other secondary school programs. About 27 percent were sixth-grade graduates who obtained their teaching certificates through Ministry of Education summer courses. About a quarter of the primary school teachers were men. In the unitarias, which pay lower salaries, only 6 percent were men. Seventy percent, or 180, of the teachers were less than thirty years old at the time the information was collected; 41 or 16 percent were over forty. Some 65 percent of the teachers had less than six years' experience in teaching. Only 10 percent had more than ten years' experience.

Most of the teachers received less than $155 a month for their services (see Table 5.3). Lowest salaries were paid in the unitarias and the free private schools. Not all of the teachers are listed in the Tables here because the religious do not receive a regular salary. Basic pay for a full-time primary school teacher in Venezuela in 1965 was Bs. 600 ($132) a month: teachers in Ciudad Guayana received an extra Bs. 100 for living in a hardship area. Pay increases are tied to time in grade, and to number of dependents. Women teachers get twelve weeks maternity leave plus an extra Bs. 80 for each child. There are no pay increases for further study or for participating in the refresher courses offered by the

TABLE 5.3
Salaries Paid Teachers and Principals in Ciudad Guayana, 1963–1964

Median monthly salary in bolivares and dollars	Type of School			Total number of teachers	Percent of total
	Public	Private	Unitaria		
Bs. 500 ($110)					
Percent of teachers	1.2	22.8	16.7	—	—
Number of teachers	2	13	3	18	7.6
Bs. 700 ($154)					
Percent of teachers	60.2	21.1	22.2	—	—
Number of teachers	97	12	4	113	47.9
Bs. 950 ($209)					
Percent of teachers	20.5	14.0	44.4	—	—
Number of teachers	33	8	8	49	20.8
Bs. 1,250 ($275)					
Percent of teachers	13.7	38.6	16.7	—	—
Number of teachers	22	22	3	47	19.9
Bs. 1,550 ($341)					
Percent of teachers	3.7	1.8	—	—	—
Number of teachers	6	1	—	7	3.0
Bs. 1,700 ($354)					
Percent of teachers	0.6	1.8	—	—	—
Number of teachers	1	1	—	2	0.8
Total number of teachers	161	57	18	236	—
Percent of total	68.2	24.2	7.6	—	100.0

Ministry during the summer. A new education law was proposed, and defeated, in 1966 which would have changed this policy. School principals receive a base salary of Bs. 1,200 or $264 a month.[7]

Primary school staffs are skeletal. There are no school psychologists, no "visiting teachers," and no truant officers. School principals often do double duty as substitute teachers.

Secondary Education

At the secondary level, called "middle school" in Venezuela and most of Latin America, there are no "comprehensive" schools, although the Ministry of

Education has declared that this will be the pattern of secondary education in the future. The merits and problems of comprehensive secondary schools have been extensively studied by Venezuelan planners; several pilot schools have been established. However, Ministry of Education planners cannot now estimate when the comprehensive pattern is likely to be introduced generally to Venezuela, and middle schools are still planned to serve specific programs rather than to house several tracks in a comprehensive establishment. At the middle level there are *liceos*, which prepare students for entrance to the university; normal schools, which prepare students for primary school teaching; agricultural schools; industrial and artisanal schools; and commercial schools. Most of these schools have a basic cycle which students must complete before they begin their specialized studies.

The Basic Cycle. Students in Ciudad Guayana, as in Venezuela generally, enter the basic cycle directly after completing six years of primary school. The length of the cycle varies according to the kind of school. The enrollments shown in Table 5.2 do not separate the basic cycle from the specialized level. The basic cycle in the liceos, or university preparatory schools, lasts three years. On completing the three years, students receive a certificate of secondary education which entitles them to enter bachiller level studies. The basic cycle in industrial schools lasts two years. When students complete the two years they go into special vocational studies which vary in length. In normal schools the basic cycle is also two years, after which students take up their "professional" studies. In commercial schools there is no basic cycle. Agricultural schools vary. In the schools of practical agriculture there is a three-year first cycle that prepares agricultural specialists who have the equivalent of a certificate of secondary education. Students may then go on to take a bachiller or agricultural technical degree by finishing two more years. There are a variety of other special schools which need not be described because they have no local representation in Ciudad Guayana.

The Specialized Cycle: Commercial School. Students enter directly into specialized studies in the commercial schools; there is no basic studies cycle. There is one public commercial school in Ciudad Guayana which accommodates about 600 students. The building was designed to be a house of prostitution but, on the fall of the dictator Pérez Jiménez in 1958, local residents were successful in driving their neighbors out, and the building took on a different function. Most of the students in commercial school are girls, though boys failing the liceo sometimes enroll in order to get some kind of secondary education. The school has been recently remodeled and is now an excellent facility. Commercial programs vary in length: a secretarial assistant receives two years of training; a secretary, three; a commercial specialist, four; and a commercial technician, five. The vast majority of students leave before the fourth year.

Employment opportunities for office workers in Ciudad Guayana are good and will be better. Commercial education should have a high priority in educational development in the city but by tradition Latin American governments have left commercial education to private schools. This may yet be the pattern in Ciudad Guayana. By 1975 there will be an effective demand for commercial facilities that house six times the present enrollments. Whether these enrollments will be accommodated in separate commercial schools or in the commercial track of a comprehensive high school depends on how rapidly the pattern changes at middle school level. By 1975, the city should provide minimally four commercial school facilities instead of the one that presently exists.

Liceos. Preparation for entrance to the university is provided by the liceos. There are presently five liceos in Ciudad Guayana, four private and one public. The newest three, private, were built by the CVG. The public liceo, which in 1965 enrolled three times as many students as the private ones combined, has recently (January 1967) been installed in a new building. Three of the private liceos have new and, in fact, elaborate facilities which serve both primary and secondary levels. This includes a facility that was supposed to have been built as an artisanal school, which may evolve into a regular liceo with some shop courses included. In the liceos the three-year basic cycle is followed by a two-year bachiller program. There are two tracks in the bachiller program, humanities and sciences. In addition to the existing liceos, construction has begun on a large and elaborate private residential secondary school.

Liceo enrollments have nearly tripled in the last five years, even though the number of graduates from primary schools has not yet doubled. As more space has been made available in secondary schools, primary school graduates who had previously been denied admission have gone back to school. Many of these young people returned to school after unsuccessfully looking for work.

By law secondary school teachers should be graduates of a pedagogical institute, a university-level teachers' college. In fact, less than 20 percent of the liceo professors are, as the institutes have not turned out enough graduates to meet demand. In Ciudad Guayana, as in the rest of Venezuela, most secondary teachers are university graduates in some field other than education. Most teach part-time and are paid on the basis of class hours taught. By teaching in various liceos, "riding the circuit," a liceo professor may earn up to about Bs. 3,000 a month, but Bs. 2,200 is an average salary.

Secondary education in Ciudad Guayana has been badly planned. There are too many places in the private schools because the middle class population who can pay fees will not reach capacity numbers until after 1970. One of the schools built by the CVG required a subsidy for a period of time in order to meet expenses. The problem is the opposite on the public side. Despite rapidly increasing enrollments, ground for a building was not broken until 1965, and classes were held in a primary school building.

Instruction at the secondary level in Ciudad Guayana, public or private, suffers from the classic ailments of secondary education in Latin America.[8] Teaching features rote memorization, whatever the subject matter. Science and mathematics programs are poor and, except for the private facilities, there are inadequate laboratories and a shortage of laboratory equipment. Reforms in curriculum and instructional methods are being planned in Caracas but may take a long time to reach Ciudad Guayana. Although physical science programs are most obviously weak, programs in the social sciences are no better. History and geography are exercises in memorization of place names and dates. Language instruction is an outmoded exercise in etymology and formal grammar; literature, although largely confined to Spanish language classics, is usually the best taught program in the curriculum. Physical education, music, and graphic arts are sometimes good when the teacher is good. Courses in morality and religion loom large in the church-run schools, although generally some form of moral philosophy is taught in the public schools. This moral philosophy lays out the rules of conduct in the best legalistic form. Good textbooks have not yet appeared; libraries are inadequate and there is no standardization of teacher quality.

Industrial Education. An industrial school was opened in Ciudad Guayana in 1964. It is large, reasonably well designed and provided with space for shops and laboratories, but still somewhat incompletely equipped and stocked. It could accommodate 800 to 1,000 students, 1,600 if shifts were established. In 1965–1966, it offered a two-year basic cycle followed by a one-year program for semiskilled workers, and a four-year program for certain technical specialties. No students had reached the technician level of studies. The fields covered are the conventional ones of automechanics, electrical, carpentry and cabinet-making, machine operation, sheet metal forging, and refrigeration.

As yet the industrial school programs have not been closely articulated with the industries of Ciudad Guayana, but there have been attempts to design programs of cooperation between the school and industry. Before 1975 three more industrial school facilities of equal capacity should be built; if comprehensive high schools are attempted, industrial tracks should be established in two of them. Facilities which presently exist are not used to capacity, the major problem being lack of instructors, stock, and even students with sufficient preparation to enter the programs. The programs and instructional methods are typical of vocational schools of twenty years ago in the industrialized countries.

Venezuela and Ciudad Guayana suffer from an enormous shortage of trained vocational school teachers and shop supervisors. Because of this, it is likely that expansion of industrial education in Ciudad Guayana will be hampered. Industries will pick off those capable men who are available. This may help industry in the short run but it will hurt over time. With more flexibility in the educational establishment, it is possible that industry could also contribute some of its better technicians and mechanics to help take on the instructional burden at the industrial school.

Artisanal. The Colegio La Salle was founded as an artisanal school which by plan would take students at the fourth grade and give them prevocational and later some specialized vocational training. It now seems to be evolving into a regular secondary liceo that offers some shop training. It is doubtful that the artisanal school has anything to offer to Ciudad Guayana, the training being insufficient to furnish entry-level skills for workers in the more highly complex industries that will be founded.

Other Secondary Level Programs. There is no normal school in Ciudad Guayana, and it does not seem necessary to establish one. Venezuela was able to overproduce primary school teachers between 1959 and 1964, and the Ministry of Education is now closing public normal schools. There are unemployed primary school teachers in Ciudad Guayana, waiting for new schools to be built. Similarly it does not seem necessary to build a middle-level school to train people for agriculture. The Universidad del Oriente has an agriculture school in Jusepín, which could well serve the eastern region.

Summary. The increase in secondary-level enrollments in Ciudad Guayana offers promise for the future, but in 1965 only ninety students were graduated from all secondary schools together. With the completion of the new public liceo there will be sufficient capacity for the next several years to enroll all graduates from primary schools, but numbers of graduates from primary schools must increase sharply if the secondary schools are to have sufficient feed

to fulfill their targets in supplying a trained labor force for 1975. Chapter 6
focuses more sharply on the city's primary schools.

Postsecondary Education

There is no postsecondary education in Ciudad Guayana. There will be a
technological institute established, but this is still a few years away. Previously
there was an insufficient feed of students from the secondary schools to open
such a facility, but presently this is sufficient to provide the first year of enrollment for such an institute. The nearest postsecondary facility is the branch of
Oriente University at Ciudad Bolívar. Oriente is a government-run university
specializing in practical arts and engineering programs. Eventually it will have
campuses scattered in the major cities of eastern Venezuela. At Ciudad Bolívar
mining, geological engineering, and medicine were the first specialties established. Mining has been running for three years. The idea of Oriente is sound
but a great deal of difficulty has been experienced in implementing programs.
Shortage of university professors has been the main problem.

Ciudad Guayana could support a postsecondary technical institute and such
a facility will be established soon.

Existing Informal Education and Training Programs

The Ministry of Education runs programs in basic education and literacy
under ODEA (Oficina de Educación de Adultos). Ministry activity in basic
education goes back to 1958 and again reflects the problem of attempting to
satisfy demand that has been dammed up over many years. The first pilot
project was launched in Venezuela in 1958 and in the face of an overwhelming
response the program was expanded with great rapidity, so that by 1960 the
Ministry was operating basic education programs in six states. The program
continued to expand rapidly during the sixties—far too rapidly to maintain any
quality control. Reportedly, by the end of 1960, the program had produced
200,000 new literates.

In early 1967 ODEA was operating night literacy and basic education programs for about 1,500 adults in the Guayana. (The details of ODEA and INCE,
Instituto Nacional de Cooperación Educativa, programs are shown in Table
5.4). ODEA operates three kinds of programs: literacy, cultural expansion in
which adults are given the equivalent of a complete primary education, and
women's courses which train for both domestic and vocational skills. ODEA
courses are of fairly low quality and have a high wastage rate. Thirty-five to

fifty percent of those who enroll fail to finish the course. Unit costs per student enrolled are low, about $25 for 450 hours of instruction. But with wastage as high as it is, the per graduate costs are almost doubled. ODEA programs in Guayana, as elsewhere in Venezuela, are high cost-low yield. The low quality of informal education reflects a history of frustrated demand and very rapid expansion without plan or control. ODEA programs are of lower quality than corresponding courses offered by INCE, but neither organization runs quality programs in literacy and basic education.

The history is considerably different in informal, technical education. Here the problem was that of beginning *tabula rasa*, for there had been no such organization as INCE before 1960. Before 1955 Venezuela not only had little industrial training, it had little industry to train for. Despite the size of its total national product, industry has been late developing in Venezuela. Prior to 1950 product was chiefly generated by petroleum and the construction and services that supported petroleum or fattened on its profits. Manufacturing, modern agriculture, and construction grew rapidly in the early sixties and all competed for workers out of a very tight pool of skilled people. Tables 5.5 and 5.6 show the changes in product in selected years from the early fifties through 1966.

In the years 1930 to 1950, Venezuela was moving from a predominantly rural and agrarian society to a more heavily urban, but not wholly industrialized, one. The activities of petroleum, mining, and construction could have generated cadres of skilled workers who would have been retrainable later for industry, had not individuals and circumstances connived to foist an incredibly short-sighted human resource development policy on Venezuela. Foreign business-men, largely North American, and their Venezuelan counterparts were mainly influenced by two factors: profit as demonstrated by analysis of short-term cash flow, and the availability of Italian migrants and North American and other expatriates who were already trained and experienced and willing to come to Venezuela to fill the skilled jobs in petroleum exploration and production, construction, and nascent industry.

In the short run, and given the no-tomorrow view of the foreign conces-sionaires, it was cheaper to bring in North American and Italian skilled workers than to train Venezuelans who had no basic education or life experience with modern industry or technology. In 1959 in Guayana, Orinoco Mining Com-pany, one of the most enlightened of the foreign companies, was still bringing in locomotive engineers and firemen from "the Pennsy" to run its ore trains down the mountain from Cerro Bolívar. After 1959 the Venezuelan government began

TABLE 5.4
General Information: Adult Basic Education Programs, Ciudad Guayana (March 1967)

Various Characteristics	Programs and Sponsoring Organizations					
	ODEA Literacy (Radio Instruction)	ODEA Literacy (Mobile Teachers)	INCE Literacy	ODEA Cultural Extension	INCE Cultural Extension	ODEA Feminine Specialties
Level	Literacy	Literacy	Literacy	Complete primary education	Complete primary education	Domestic and vocational skills
Duration in hours	350 hours	Varies, by teacher	80	1,050	480	Varies, 36 to 108 hours
Hours per day	2	Varies, by teacher	1	2	2	1 or 2 hours
Hours per week	10	Varies	5	10	10	1 to 3 hours
Calendar time required to complete program	9 months	Normally 5 months	4 months	34 months	12 months	9 months
Time in year when program begins	October 1	October 1 and March 15	Varies, at all times of year	October 1	Varies, at all times of year	October 1
Time in year when program terminates	July 24	February 1 and July 15	Varies, at all times of year	July 24	Varies, at all times of year	July 1
Time of day when classes are held	Night	Varies by teacher	Late afternoon and evening	Night	Mostly late afternoon and evening	Varies, but mostly late afternoon
Programs which precede this one in sequence	None	None	None	ODEA Literacy	INCE Literacy	None
Programs which follow this one in sequence	ODEA Cultural Extension	ODEA Cultural Extension	INCE Cultural Extension	None	None	None

Enrollment, last year	None	77	16, classes begun through March	1,281	432, classes begun through March	230
Deserters, last year	80	90	30	199	233	30, to February this year
Enrollment, this year	225	300	158	953	925	70
Repeaters, this year	—	—	—	128	40	5
Average attendance, this year	—	No records kept	80%	74%	70%	74%
Average attendance, last year	65%	No records kept	80%	76%	75%	Not available

Source: A. John Vogt, "Report on Collection of Base Data for Study of Adult Basic Education, Ciudad Guayana," CSED, Harvard University.

to discourage the importation of skilled workers from Europe and the States, though by that time it made little difference anyway, as boom conditions in North America and northern Europe attracted workers who might once have come to Venezuela. There has been, and there still is, a propensity to import skilled labor on high priority construction jobs. In the middle sixties, with

TABLE 5.5
Gross Domestic Product by Major Sectors in Venezuela
(in Millions of Bolivares)

	1950	1955
Agriculture, livestock, and fishing	1,014	1,352
Mining	20	221
Petroleum	3,920	5,777
Manufactures	1,150	2,004
Construction	827	1,363
Water and electric power	69	159
Commerce	1,726	2,862
Transportation and communications	699	951
Rent and interest	1,161	1,752
Services	2,140	2,884
Total	12,726	19,325

Source: Memoria, 1959, Banco Central de Venezuela.

unemployment running higher than 15 percent in Guayana, construction companies were bringing equipment operators down from Maracaibo and the oil sites in El Tigre. Almost one hundred British timberers and several hundred Italian form-makers were brought in on an emergency basis for the all-Venezuelan-managed Guri Dam project.

INCE was modeled on a successful enterprise in Brazil, SENAI, which had been set up in 1942.[9] INCE was founded in Venezuela by a law dated 1959. In Chapter 1 of the *Ley Sobre El Instituto Nacional de Cooperación Educativa* (Law on the National Institute of Educational Cooperation), the objectives of INCE were stated as follows:

1. To promote the professional development of workers and to contribute to the development of specialized personnel.

TABLE 5.6
Gross Domestic Product in Venezuela, 1959, 1962, 1966

	Absolute			Relative			Annual Rate of Increase	
	1959	1962	1966	1959	1962	1966	1959–1962	1962–1966
1. Agriculture	1,625	2,029	2,760	6.2	7.1	7.1	7.7	8.0
2. Petroleum	5,482	6,253	7,315	20.9	22.0	18.9	4.5	4.0
3. Mining	447	383	561	1.8	1.4	1.4	− 5.0	10.0
4. Manufacturing	4,000	4,655	7,720	15.3	16.4	20.0	5.2	13.5
5. Construction I	1,881	1,450	2,523	7.2	5.1	6.5	− 8.3	14.9
6. Construction II	2,806	3,308	4,301	10.7	11.6	11.1	5.6	6.8
7. Electricity, gas, and water	313	440	853	1.2	1.5	2.2	12.0	18.0
8. Transport and communications	1,148	1,152	1,530	4.4	4.1	3.9	0.1	7.4
9. Commerce	4,214	4,332	5,337	16.1	15.2	13.7	0.9	5.4
10. Other private services	1,869	2,055	2,629	7.1	7.2	6.8	1.6	6.4
11. Government	2,374	2,381	3,228	9.1	8.4	8.4	0.1	7.9
I Agriculture	1,625	2,029	2,760	6.2	7.1	7.1	7.7	8.0
II Petroleum and mining (2 + 3)	5,929	6,636	7,876	22.7	23.4	20.3	3.8	4.4
III Industries (4 + 5 + 7)	6,194	6,545	11,096	23.7	23.0	28.7	1.9	14.1
IV Services (6 + 8 + 9 + 10 + 11)	12,411	13,228	17,025	47.4	46.5	43.9	2.1	6.5
Gross geographic product	26,159	28,438	38,757	100.0	100.0	100.0	2.8	8.0
Product per capital (Bs. 1960)	3,518	3,493	4,225				− 0.2	4.9

Construction I = highways, factory buildings, etc.
Construction II = housing, commercial buildings, etc.
Source: Plan de la Nación, Oficina Central de Coordinación y Planificacion, Caracas, 1966.
Tables 5.5 and 5.6 are a composite and the product for 1950 and 1955 is not compatible with the rest of the series. Even so, the general trend is clear.

Millions of bolivares 1960
$1 U.S. = Bs. 4.48

2. To contribute to the vocational, agricultural training of students coming out of rural schools in order to train farmers able to utilize the soil and natural resources of Venezuela.

3. To stimulate and develop the apprenticeship of young workers. This can be accomplished by creating special schools, organizing apprenticeship programs within factories and workshops with the cooperation of the management and in accord with the provisions fixed by law.

4. To cooperate in the struggle against illiteracy and contribute to the improvement of primary education insofar as it contributes to vocational development.

5. To prepare and develop the teaching material necessary for the improved training of workers.

Full-scale training operations began in 1961. Under the INCE law employers were required to provide training for one person between the ages of fourteen and eighteen for every thirty persons employed. Training could be on the premises of the industry itself or in INCE centers, such as the one in Guayana. INCE operations are financed by employers (taxed at 1 percent of the payroll), by employees who pay 0.5 percent of the annual share of company profits, and by the federal government which contributes 20 percent of the other contributions. The financing then is 80 percent from the payroll tax and 20 percent from the public fisc. In the Guayana INCE runs several different kinds of programs. Its major enterprise is the metal trades training center which sponsors courses in industrial formation, in-service improvement, and introductory and intensive apprenticeship programs.

INCE also administers two adult basic education programs, a literacy program and a cultural extension program, with the enrollments shown in Table 5.4. INCE, under the Directorate of Special Programs, runs prevocational training courses which attempt to provide youngsters in their teens some further basic education and entry-level skills in the construction trades. This was one of the first INCE programs begun in Guayana, and preceded the establishment of the metal trades training center which was planned jointly by CVG staff and INCE specialists in 1965. In 1966 there were about eight hundred enrolled in these prevocational programs, but the plan was to reduce these enrollments and increase activities in the metal trades training center.

The INCE literary programs are organized into four courses: language, reading, and writing (fifty hours); mathematics (twenty hours); social and natural sciences (five hours); drawing (five hours), giving a total of eighty hours.

Language covers grammar and composition; mathematics goes through the fundamental operations, the use of fractions, and stresses measurement; there is some rudimentary attention to geometry in drawing; science covers safety, health, matter and energy.

The INCE cultural extension program offers a complete primary school program in 480 class hours covering language, mathematics, natural sciences, social sciences, and drawing.

Table 5.4 summarizes the data on INCE and ODEA basic education programs in Guayana, as of March 1967. It is apparent that ODEA and INCE run very similar programs for very similar clients, and that the duplication and overlap between the two organizations is great. As originally conceived, INCE literacy and cultural extension programs catered to workers, often at their place of work, whereas ODEA programs were designed to serve the general population. As the programs actually function in any locality such as Guayana, there is not only duplication, there is even competition. Both INCE and ODEA employ program organizers called *promotores*. Perhaps it would be more accurate to translate promotores more literally and call them "promoters" instead of organizers. It is the promoter's job to advertise the courses, sometimes by hiring a sound truck and cruising the barrios, organize the courses at school or factory, set the schedule, enroll the students, recruit the teachers and pay them, provide the materials, and see that the classes run their entire course. In Guayana ODEA promoters sign up people who are workers and who should, under law, have been INCE charges, whereas INCE takes in as students persons who are neither employed nor economically active, and hence not workers under the usual definition.

INCE has greater material resources and slightly higher program quality. INCE programs could be an important way of providing Ciudad Guayana with shorter, less expensive training for the skilled workers its industries must have. There are plans to run programs jointly with industry and specific projects in the training of workers for the heavy machinery industry. To date the program is not as fruitful as it might be, but it is new and still recovering from disorganization and the rush to get started. INCE may well settle into an important center for producing skilled workers in informal education and training programs. In all of its programs it suffers from a shortage of instructors and shop supervisors. It also draws from a population with low general education, though when the primary schools improve in efficiency and quality this problem may be taken care of.

6
The Efficiency of
the Primary Schools

The future development of Ciudad Guayana and its industries will depend in large measure on the number and quality of citizens and workers who have middle school education and this might lead one to expect that research on education in Guayana would probe deeply into the problems facing middle schools. However, the state of education in the city, as in most of Venezuela and much of Latin America, is such that there are too few primary school graduates: primary schools are the major bottleneck in the flow of students through the educational and formational process and research should be directed at this level.

This chapter, and the four that follow it, deal exclusively with problems of primary education in Ciudad Guayana. Problems are analyzed from the point of view of the school as a "factory" producing human resources, which proceeds from a consideration of the school as a subsystem of the society, assigned the task of forming inputs to the society. An industrial conception of education is a useful analytical tool, but no argument is made that schools serve only the economic needs of a society, or that human beings can be treated as so many carloads of iron ore to be dumped into the schoolroom smelter. On the contrary, as will be shown, schools and educational institutions perforce must attend to much more than instruction and training in economically useful skills.

Several major problems facing primary education are considered. This chapter looks at the problem of providing sufficient numbers of schools to meet the demand for enrollment. Chapter 7 considers school failure from the point of view of the evaluation system employed by the school. Chapter 8 takes up an argument that what happens in school may not be the most important determinant of the school's success in educating children; the argument is developed further in Chapter 9 and summarized in Chapter 10. The official curriculum of the primary schools is not considered to be a major problem. It contains all the right course titles, but the problem in Guayana is not so much content of education as how to guarantee that children will be exposed to it. Instructional materials receive some attention but are considered a secondary problem. The quality of the instructional staff of Guayana schools is a central factor, but that quality must be judged in terms of what problems teachers must resolve and, as the findings will show, these problems have their locus outside of the classroom.

For the reader acquainted with education in Venezuela and other Latin American countries, the educational situation in Ciudad Guayana will seem familiar. The schools in Ciudad Guayana do almost as well as those of the country as a whole. As in other middle-size cities, they are more efficient than rural schools but much less so than the schools of Caracas which receive more attention and support. However, comparison with the national average is misleading, for Ciudad Guayana is not and cannot be allowed to be an average city of Venezuela. Continued development in Venezuela depends in very large measure on the industrial development of Ciudad Guayana, and that will be determined by the success of its schools. The schools of Ciudad Guayana should be, therefore, among the most "efficient" of the nation.

Measuring School Efficiency

The efficiency of a school system is determined by its ability to effectively "process" the raw material it receives. This depends on three requisites. First, schools must be able to attract the largest possible percentage of children eligible to enroll. Children should enroll as soon as they attain the minimum legal age so that the system can educate them to a desired level before they attain the minimum age for employment.

Once children are enrolled, the school must maximize their attendance. Daily attendance rates must be high so that opportunities for learning are greatest. The number of students abandoning school during the year must be kept to a minimum. All children should be enrolled the following year, whether they successfully passed the previous grade or not.

Finally, the efficiency of a school system is greatest when the system is able to bring all students to a sufficient level of knowledge to meet the requirements for promotion to the next highest level. This means several things. Instruction must be of a high enough quality for students to learn the necessary material. Conditions present in the school must facilitate the teaching and learning processes. The school must reduce to a minimum situational factors, both within the school and without, which impede teaching and learning.

Enrollments. The best estimates are that primary schools in Ciudad Guayana enrolled about 90 percent of the eligible students in September 1965. It is difficult to make an accurate estimate; the numbers of eligible children increase too rapidly to maintain a count. Enrollment figures include children above or below primary school age limits. Enrollment figures also exaggerate school holding power for some students enroll in September, attend only a few classes, and drop out.

About 70 percent of the children who enroll in primary schools in Ciudad Guayana enroll at age seven, the legal minimum age. Another 15 percent enroll at age eight; others enroll as late as ten or eleven. About 4 percent of the enrollments in first grade are children younger than the minimum age. Partly as a result of late enrollment, partly as a result of repeating grades, partly as a result of abandoning school for a year or more and then returning, the distribution by age in the six primary school grades in Ciudad Guayana shows large numbers of older students (Table 6.1). If the school system operated at a higher level of efficiency, there would not be so many overage children. Overage enrollment is serious because many children in primary school attain the minimum working age of fourteen before completing six grades of primary.

TABLE 6.1
Age Distribution of Children and Proportion of Repeaters in Primary Schools in Ciudad Guayana, 1963–1964

Grade	Correct Age	Total Enrollment	Older than Correct Age	% Overage	% Repeaters
First	7–8	3,076	792	25.7	20.0
Second	8–9	2,331	864	37.1	16.0
Third	9–10	1,952	831	42.6	16.0
Fourth	10–11	1,803	791	43.9	13.1
Fifth	11–12	1,162	495	42.6	10.0
Sixth	12–13	794	328	41.3	3.6
TOTAL	—	11,118	4,101	36.9	15.1

Source: Ministerio de Educación, Caracas.

The Efficiency of the Primary Schools   93

TABLE 6.2
Average Daily Attendance in Primary Classrooms in Ciudad Guayana in December
as a Percent of Enrollment in September 1963[a]

Classroom Attendance %	Grade						Total
	First	Second	Third	Fourth	Fifth	Sixth	
70 or less	26.9	9.8	7.3	2.7	—	—	10.0
70–80	19.2	27.5	14.6	21.7	20.7	13.1	19.1
80–90	32.8	35.3	31.7	37.8	41.3	34.7	35.7
90–95	17.3	19.6	36.6	27.0	27.7	17.4	24.3
95–100	3.8	7.8	9.8	10.8	10.3	34.8	10.9
Total %	100.0	100.0	100.0	100.0	100.0	100.0	100.0

[a] Average daily attendance is calculated by dividing the total number of pupils attending during a given period by the number of class days in that period.
Source: Ministerio de Educación, Caracas.

Given the poverty of many families in the city, some of these children are forced to try their luck in the labor market rather than continue in school to graduation. Large enrollments of older students also mean fewer places for young students entering school for the first time. This leads to more late enrollments.

Attendance. Table 6.2 shows that schools do not maintain high daily attendance rates. One of every three classrooms in Ciudad Guayana had less than 80 percent of their enrolled students attending daily in December 1963. Only 11 percent of the classrooms had optimal daily attendance rates.

In part the low daily attendance rates can be attributed to school dropouts. As shown in Table 6.3, about 6 percent of the students enrolled in September 1964 left school before June 1965. Some of these apparent "deserters" officially withdrew from school before June, that is, 5 percent of those enrolled in September 1964 had withdrawn officially by May 1965. (Official withdrawal permits the student to enroll immediately in any other school in the country. Without a withdrawal slip he must wait until the following September to enroll.) However, new students who enrolled after October 1964 added 4 percent to the total beginning enrollment. Therefore, about half of the apparent "desertion" is due to official withdrawals.

Another 5 percent of the students enrolled in Guayana schools in 1964–1965 disappeared between June and July, when final examinations are administered. Some of the children moved from the city during this period, but it is doubtful

TABLE 6.3
Examination Results in Ciudad Guayana in 1962–1963
and 1964–1965

	1962–1963		1964–1965	
Grade	N	%	N	%
First				
Enrolled September	2,453	100.0	2,970	100.0
Attending in June	2,249	91.6	2,695	90.7
Took examination	1,988	81.0	2,426	81.7
Passed examination	1,511	61.6	2,002	67.4
Second				
Enrolled September	1,812	100.0	2,317	100.0
Attending in June	1,765	97.4	2,248	97.0
Took examination	1,630	90.0	2,124	91.7
Passed examination	1,329	73.3	1,832	79.1
Third				
Enrolled September	1,770	100.0	2,047	100.0
Attending in June	1,661	93.8	1,905	93.1
Took examination	1,554	87.8	1,824	89.1
Passed examination	1,294	73.1	1,554	75.9
Fourth				
Enrolled September	1,337	100.0	1,764	100.0
Attending in June	1,248	93.3	1,660	94.1
Took examination	1,163	87.0	1,604	90.9
Passed examination	955	71.4	1,358	77.0
Fifth				
Enrolled September	949	100.0	1,472	100.0
Attending in June	921	97.0	1,363	92.6
Took examination	867	91.4	1,314	89.3
Passed examination	758	79.9	1,149	78.1
Sixth				
Enrolled September	637	100.0	966	100.0
Attending in June	610	95.8	900	93.2
Took examination	589	92.5	887	91.8
Passed examination	570	89.5	830	85.9
All Years				
Enrolled September	8,958	100.0	11,536	100.0
Attending in June	8,454	94.4	10,771	93.4
Took examination	7,791	87.0	10,179	88.2
Passed examination	6,417	71.6	8,725	75.6

Source: Ministerio de Educación, Caracas.

that all did. Teachers state that it is a common practice to advise students with low grades not to show up for the examination. No doubt some students come to the same conclusion on their own. About 12 percent of the original September enrollment did not make it to the examination stage in 1964–1965.

Achievement. If the job of a school is to educate, then the success of a school system must be measured in terms of its ability to communicate knowledge to students. The school sets its own standards of what knowledge should be communicated and has its own apparatus for measuring the amount received by students. Schools in Ciudad Guayana in 1965 failed one student of every ten who took the final examination in the primary grades. The most difficult examinations to pass are at the end of the first grade. About 17 percent of those taking the first grade examination at the end of the 1964–1965 year failed the examination and were kept back; over-all losses were greater in first grade than any other. Fourth grade is another difficult year (15 percent fail), but with the exception of the sixth grade, there is not a great deal of difference among the promotion rates for the other primary grades. The school rejects at least 10 percent of its products each year by virtue of low quality of education and inefficient testing devices.

These tables do not show the percentage of students who abandon school between years. It is difficult to determine the extent of between-year school desertion because there is no way of finding out if students no longer enrolled in the city's schools have enrolled elsewhere. There is no central file in Venezuela which maintains a permanent school record for each child (though there is a file of examination results). Later chapters present some results obtained directly from students which indicate the extent of between-year desertion, and some of its causes and consequences.

The Effects of Inefficiency. High rates of school abandonment, within and between years, and examination failure limit the number of graduates from school. Inefficiency also raises the total cost of producing a graduate, and limits the ability of the school to service more children.

Table 6.4 shows the effects of applying 1964–1965 rates of promotion and repeating grades to an imaginary cohort of 1,000 children. The table shows how many graduates there would be among every 1,000 students entering Guayana schools, if there is to be no change in efficiency. Some 208 students would graduate from the sixth grade after six years of education. Eventually, 435 students would graduate. However, 4,952 student-years of education would have to be given to produce this number of graduates. That is, it would take 11.4

TABLE 6.4
Number of Graduates in an Imaginary Cohort of 1,000,
Applying Continuance Rates for Academic Year 1964–1965

		0	1	2	3	4	5	6	7	8	9	10	Total	Continuance Rates
	1	1,000	190	36	7	1	0	0	0	0	0	0	1,234	1 → 1 0.19
															1 → 2 0.67
	2		670	221	55	13	3	0	0	0	0	0	962	
															2 → 2 0.14
															2 → 3 0.79
	3			529	249	78	21	5	1	0	0	0	883	
															3 → 3 0.14
Entering in Grade															3 → 4 0.76
	4				402	229	82	24	6	2	0	0	745	
															4 → 4 0.10
															4 → 5 0.77
	5					310	201	79	24	7	1	0	622	
															5 → 5 0.08
															5 → 6 0.78
	6						242	167	69	22	6	0	506	
															6 → 6 0.04
	6+							208	144	59	19	5	435	6 → 6+ 0.86

Total years given   = 4,952
Total graduates   = 435
Average years to produce a graduate = 11.4

years of education for each graduate of sixth grade. Were the schools operating at perfect efficiency the system would produce 1,000 graduates in six years. Of course, no system operates at perfect efficiency. There are always some students who must be held back, and others who leave because of poor health or mental inability. But in an efficient primary school system the great majority of students move through the six grades without failure and graduate after six years.

Costs per child enrolled in public schools in Ciudad Guayana have been estimated at about 400 Bs. ($88) a year, including teacher salaries, amortization of plant, maintenance, and equipment.[1] In the current system, the average cost per graduate is Bs. 4,560 ($1,003). If the system functioned with perfect efficiency, the cost would be Bs. 2,400 ($528). Because the Ministry of Education has limited funds with which to build and staff schools, the direct effect of inefficiency is to deny education to a number of children the schools could serve were they more efficient.

The Demand for Education

The general history of primary education in Latin America is no different from the experience of Ciudad Guayana. Dramatic improvements in health practices, increasing numbers of live births and reducing infant mortality rates, have effected pronounced increases in population growth. Even alert governments have been caught off guard by the masses of children demanding an education. Most governments have not been sufficiently prepared to meet the crises.

The situation in Venezuela before 1958 was one of nonchalance. Under the dictatorship of Pérez Jiménez, ended in that year, public education in Venezuela was almost totally ignored; private education increased dramatically to meet some of the unsatisfied need. The dictator lavishly spent public funds to create an image of Venezuela as a modern country, but this did not include investments to provide opportunities for development through education. Millions of bolivares were spent to build a superhighway from the port to the capital city, more millions were spent to erect a glamorous luxury hotel atop a mountain overlooking the city, accessible only by cablecar, and untold millions more were spent to build what has been termed the most luxurious officers' club in the world.[2] Meanwhile, a relative pittance was devoted to the development of the majority of the people in Venezuela, those not fortunate enough to own cars or to live in hotels or belong to the military oligarchy.

From 1948 to 1958, the number of public schools operating in Venezuela actually declined, from 6,369 to 5,606, although total enrollments in public schools increased from 395,804 to 608,428. In the same period private schools increased from 272 to 1,070, and numbers of students from 46,308 to 143,133 (see Table 6.5). In rural areas of Venezuela the problem was most serious; the dictator's social myopia allowed him to ignore the poverty and misery of the countryside.

TABLE 6.5
Public and Private Education in Venezuela during the Dictatorship
of Pérez Jiménez and during the Democratic Government

| | Academic Year | | | | |
	1948–1949	1952–1953	1957–1958	1960–1961	1963–1964[a]
Public Schools					
Buildings	6,369	6,685	5,606	11,043	10,000
Teachers	11,287	13,513	14,912	29,019	32,556
Students	395,804	485,215	608,428	1,080,714	1,188,742
Students/Teacher	35.1	35.9	40.8	37.2	36.5
Private Schools					
Buildings	272	556	1,070	914	974
Teachers	1,653	3,213	6,002	6,248	7,073
Students	46,308	85,071	143,133	163,234	181,923
Students/Teacher	28.0	26.5	23.8	26.1	25.7

[a] The decrease in number of public school buildings between 1960–1961 and 1963–1964 resulted from the closing of unitarias. The decline in *rate* of increase in school enrollments between these years reflects in part the absorption of late entrants to the system denied admission in previous years. By 1963–1964 most of these late entrants had been taken into the system. The decline also reflects a brief economic downturn in Venezuela during 1961 and part of 1962.
Source: Memoria y Cuenta, 1964 (Vol. II, "Annuario Estadistico"), Ministerio de Educación, Caracas.

The size of the task facing Venezuela after the overthrow of Pérez Jiménez is perhaps most clearly indicated by the massive effort which the national government has made in an attempt to alleviate the problem of school shortages. In the academic year 1957–1958, there were 5,606 public schools in Venezuela; in 1958–1959, one year after the overthrow, 6,577. In 1959–1960, the number increased to 8,746. By 1960–1961, the democratic government had provided as many new schools in three years as the dictator had in ten, and still there was no room for many children. At present, the Ministry of Education estimates that it has schools sufficient to enroll 85 percent of the nation's school-age children; it is now spending nearly three times as much on education as was spent during the last years of the dictatorship. It is not surprising, then, that many young and old adults in Venezuela have little education. There simply have been no schools for them to attend.

One could hope that in this day and age it would not be necessary to argue that the demand for education is real, that schools will be attended if they are built. But the fact is that the shortage of public schools is justified by some decision makers on the grounds that the poor little appreciate the value of education. They point to low enrollment rates, and high rates of desertion, as evidence to support their case. Later chapters in this book present findings which attack this point of view about the reasons for school dropouts, and this chapter makes a case for expecting maximum enrollments if schools are built in adequate numbers.

The argument could be applied to all of Venezuela, but it has special importance for Ciudad Guayana, where the educational system confronts a special challenge. The economic importance of the city for the nation is such that schools must *now* enroll as many students as possible, and train them and graduate them in the least possible time if the dream of industrialization is to take form.

Results of the June 1965 School Census provide some information about the demand for education by parents. The major purpose of the census was to determine the extent of nonattendance in primary schools in Ciudad Guayana. The census obtained information on reasons for not attending school, and provided a distribution of the school-age population of the city which could be used for locating needed new schools.

Table 6.6 shows how the children of the city were distributed in its five major areas, and where the nonattending children were most frequently found. Approximately 20 percent of the children between seven and fourteen years of age were not attending school in June 1965. The worst area, Dalla Costa, was also the one that most needed school buildings. The difference in attendance between Dalla Costa, the bottom of the socioeconomic heap in Ciudad Guay-

TABLE 6.6
Results of June 1965 School Census in Ciudad Guayana: Attendance

Zone	Children Attending	Children Not Attending	% Not Attending
San Félix	4,320	840	16.2
El Roble	2,407	611	20.2
Dalla Costa	855	554	39.3
Castillito	1,560	470	23.1
Puerto Ordaz	937	44	4.4
Ciudad Guayana	10,079	2,519	20.0

ana, and Puerto Ordaz, the top, is a dramatic demonstration of the inequities of the educational system in the city. In June 1965 Dalla Costa had one six-year school which operating two shifts a day could serve only 640 children, but there were 1,400 children of school age living in the neighborhood. Puerto Ordaz had two private schools, with a capacity of 1,100 children operating one shift a day, and only 1,000 children of school age. A third private school was under construction, to open in September 1966, but no new schools were being constructed in Dalla Costa.

TABLE 6.7
Results of June 1965 School Census in Ciudad Guayana:
Reasons for Nonattendance Given by Parents

Reason	Number	% of Total
No space	524	24.9
Insufficient economic resources	408	19.4
Recently moved[a]	362	17.2
Lack of interest	286	13.7
Health	165	7.8
School too far	100	4.8
No reason given	150	7.1
Various reasons	108	5.1
Total	2,103	100.0
Too young; attends kindergarten	416	Nonattendance of school-age children is 19.0 percent

[a] On moving, parents can obtain an official withdrawal slip which permits immediate enrollment in any other school in the country. Failure to obtain this slip indicates a lack of parental concern or ignorance of the procedure.

Table 6.7 presents reasons offered by parents and guardians of the children as to why they were not attending school in June, at the end of the school year. Twenty-five percent of the children were not enrolled in September because of closed enrollments in the schools. Teachers in public schools are usually instructed to close enrollments for their classes when the number of students reaches fifty.

Partly as a result of the school census, partly as a result of a desire to encourage both the Ministry of Education and the CVG to build new schools, the educational supervisor for the school district which includes Ciudad Guayana instructed public school principals to keep enrollments open in September 1965, with no upper limit. He also established more unitarias.

In September 1965, 91 per cent of the children of primary school age (seven through fourteen) in the city were enrolled in school, according to the results of a sample survey carried out in November 1965. Maximum enrollment can rise about as high as 96 percent of the school-age population; it would probably not go higher as there are always some chronically ill and handicapped children whose parents do not enroll them. The 91 percent enrollment figure of September 1965 suggested that the schools could attract almost all children to enroll, if sufficient schools and seats were available.

This confirmed expectations, although it ran counter to the belief of some officials that parents do not really care about the education of their children. The demand for education by the people had already led to the building, by parents, of two "schools," one described earlier as a chicken coop, with six rooms and 677 students, and a more recent coop with three rooms and 200 students enrolled. In October 1965, children in the latter school sat through their classes on cinder blocks and stones, as there were no chairs.[3]

The Crowded Schools of Guayana

An open door is not enough, children must find space within classrooms. The public schools of Ciudad Guayana experienced a steady increase in enrollments between 1961 and 1965, but without a concomitant increase in *adequate* facilities to receive and educate the children. Average class sizes increased dramatically, as Table 6.8 shows. School enrollments increased, but this was an increase in quantity with no increase in quality.

The problem in Ciudad Guayana was that public school students, 80 percent of the school population, were crowded together, fifty or more in classrooms designed to hold forty or less. In October 1965, the Human Development Section of the CVG published a memorandum which showed in the public primary schools of Ciudad Guayana three classes with less than forty students enrolled, thirty-two classes with between forty and forty-nine students enrolled, seventy-six classes with fifty to fifty-nine students, and thirty-two classes with sixty or more students enrolled. Pressure on some of the classes was somewhat relieved as students abandoned school during the year. But many classrooms were small, badly ventilated, and terribly noisy, even with only forty or fifty students. Except for the Felipe Hernández school, all of the public schools operated two shifts a day, whereas private schools had one shift a day.

TABLE 6.8
Enrollment in Public Primary Schools in Ciudad Guayana, 1962–1966,
Expressed in Terms of Average Class Size

	1962–1963		1963–1964		1964–1965		1965–1966	
	Enroll-ment	Average Class Size	Enroll-ment	Average Class Size	Enroll-ment	Average Class Size	Enroll-ment	Average Class Size
Antonio de Berrio	1,456	48.5	1,476	49.2	1,460	48.7	1,507	50.2
San Félix	1,208	54.9	1,139	51.3	1,210	55.0	1,306	59.4
José Angel Ruiz	948	43.1	1,076	48.9	990	45.0	1,424	54.5
Puerto Ayacucho	804	57.4	680	48.6	689	49.2	790	56.4
Tumeremo	696	38.7	949	52.7	983	54.6	1,101	61.0
Felipe Hernández	511	56.8	513	56.8	552	46.0	582	48.5
José Félix Ribas	289	41.1	381	54.4	388	55.4	534	53.4
Silvana de Irady	248	41.3	388	55.4	472	43.0	592	49.3
Mercedes Prospert	—	—	423	52.9	924	51.3	1,112	61.8
José L. Guzmán	—	—	—	—	497	49.7	500	50.0
Consuelo Navas	—	—	—	—	242	40.3	677	56.4
Total	6,160	47.5	7,025	50.5	8,407	49.5	10,125	56.4

All schools except Felipe Hernández have two shifts per day.
Source: Ministerio de Educación, Caracas.

A bright, motivated student can learn under almost any circumstances. He does not need a modern classroom with carpeting, indirect lighting, tinted windows, and floor-to-ceiling blackboards. Nevertheless, the teaching-learning process is facilitated when classroom temperature and noise levels are reduced, when teachers have available a full range of teaching materials, when teachers can afford more attention to individual students, and when children come to school well fed and healthy.[4]

The effects of overcrowding on the efficiency of a school system are difficult to measure. Unless one can apply a standardized examination measuring the achievement of students, the variation of grading procedures among the various schools obscures relationships between class sizes and promotion rates. No research of this kind in Latin America appears in the literature. However, a study in Argentina was able to demonstrate a significant inverse relationship ($r = 0.35$) between number of students per teacher and number of students going on to higher grades.[5] This relationship is also found in Ciudad Guayana, when one eliminates private schools from the comparison (promotion rates in private schools are higher than those of public schools, irrespective of class size).

A relationship between class size and promotion rate does not necessarily prove that the teaching-learning process per se is negatively affected in large classes. Teachers in public schools, confronted with many more students than can easily be handled, "push out" a number of students during the year in an attempt to reduce the magnitude of their task. This may be done by discouraging children from attending during the year (represented by within-year dropout rates), by discouraging children from attendance at the final examination, or by failing large percentages of students as standard procedure independent of the children's ability to master material at the next highest level. The examination procedures practiced in Ciudad Guayana and their relation to intellectual ability and other factors are reviewed in the next chapter.

The Need for a Program of School Construction

What is clear is that the school "system" of Ciudad Guayana was critically short of classrooms in 1965. No public primary school buildings had been built in the city since 1963, even though the school-age population had nearly doubled between 1963 and 1965. To reduce class sizes to an average of forty, to eliminate the dead-end unitaria schools, and to replace collapsing buildings, at least six twelve-room public schools should have been built by September 1965, and these new schools would have had to run two shifts per day.

Unfortunately, these urgent needs were not met with immediate action. The school census of June 1965 and the analysis made of school enrollment cards afforded an opportunity to demonstrate that 90 percent of the children in public schools lived in the immediate area, within the one-kilometer radius specified by the Ministry of Education. Planners from the Human Development Section of the CVG worked together in early 1965 to delineate those areas of the city which needed schools immediately, and to choose school sites which afforded easy paths of access to young students. Given the inability of the Ministry of Education to allocate resources to immediate primary school construction in the city, the CVG decided in May 1965 to build the needed six schools. Five of these schools were finally ready for occupancy in January 1967. As the plan for the development of the school system of the city projects a school-age population growth rate requiring at least four new primary schools per year every year, these delays in construction of public primary schools represent a serious frustration to the goal of providing *entrance* to school for the great mass of the city's children.

Construction of private school facilities has continued *ahead* of demand, as
is indicated in Table 6.9. Private schools operate only one shift per day, and
still have less than forty students per class. But all of the private schools charge
fees and are therefore not available to the large number of families with low

TABLE 6.9
Capacities and Enrollments of Primary Schools in Ciudad Guayana
in January 1966

Public	Enrollment	Capacity[a]	Area
Antonio de Berrio	1,507	1,200	
San Félix	1,306	880	
José Félix Ribas[d]	534	400	San Félix
José L. Guzmán[d]	500[b]	400	
Consuelo Navas	600[b]	200	
Silvana de Irady[d]	592	560	
José Angel Ruiz	1,424	960	
Mercedes Prospert	1,112	960	El Roble
Felipe Hernández	582[c]	480	
Puerto Ayacucho	790	640	Dalla Costa
Tumeremo	1,101	720	Castillito
Total	10,048	7,400	
Private			
Nuestra Sra. de Fatima	364	600[b]	San Félix
Emanuel	156	200	
I.M.C.O.V.	302	320	El Roble
La Salle	246	240	
Fe y Alegría	588	480	Castillito
Domingo Zorrilla	124	200	
Nazaret	288	400	Puerto Ordaz
Diego de Ordaz	727	720	
Total	2,795	3,160	

[a] For public schools calculated at 80 students per classroom, or 40 per shift.
For private schools calculated at 40 per classroom (all are on one shift per
day).
[b] Estimated.
[c] This is the only public school not on double shift. Enrollment capacities
are calculated at 40 per room.
[d] These schools are run by the state government. All others are supervised
by the federal government.

incomes. Further, construction costs for private facilities are two or three or four times greater than public schools of equivalent size, so that the economic discrimination favoring the middle and upper class is exaggerated by a higher investment per pupil ratio.

The Ministry has regarded Ciudad Guayana as just one of many regions in need of new schools; it has not assigned the city a special priority. Most personnel in the Ministry's planning department were unaware of the rapid growth of the city until the district supervisor hand-carried the results of the June 1965 School Census to his superiors. Even then, there was no full realization that the city would continue to grow at a rapid rate and no institutionalized means to be kept informed of the educational needs of the city.

The CVG was also unaware of the pressing need for new public schools. Out of touch with the Ministry, distracted by their own efforts in private education and the construction of highways, dams, and housing developments, CVG planners had failed to notice that the public education sector was not developing properly. When convinced of the need for construction of public primary schools, there was some hesitation to assume responsibility, as this would limit funds available to other projects of apparently equal importance. The CVG began public school construction with the understanding that this was an emergency measure and that theirs was a short-term commitment.

7
Some Characteristics of School Operation Affecting Efficiency

The construction of more public schools in Ciudad Guayana will contribute to a reduction in the wastage of talent which results from failure to educate all the children of the city. Smaller classes will help teachers in their constant struggle with unmanageable numbers; better built schools will replace dead-end unitarias and totally inadequate buildings now in use. The result will be an appreciable improvement in the ability of schools to carry their students through to graduation. More is needed, however.

Overcrowding is not the only problem which the schools of Ciudad Guayana face. Schools can also stand some improvement in instruction, instructional materials, and evaluation techniques. The problem of instruction is the subject of another research now being carried out. (The improvement of instructional materials in Ciudad Guayana has already begun; achievements to date are described in Chapter 14.) In the present analysis the argument is that attempts to improve the performance of teachers must attend to their extra-classroom activities.

This chapter examines patterns of success and failure among individual children in the Guayana primary schools. The presentation of aggregate statistics compiled by the Ministry of Education gave some idea of the wastage of children through failure in examinations or through leaving school during the year. But these statistics, however useful, do not fully reveal the extent to which large numbers of children flounder through school in what must seem to them an endless number of years of failing, dropping, repeating, failing. Part of this inefficiency of the schools can be attributed to evaluation practices.

Problems in Studying Performance in School

Ideally, one could study a child's experience in school by examining his permanent record file. However, only one public school in the city in 1965 kept a cumulative record on each child, and that practice began only a few years before. Most schools, public and private, keep only the enrollment cards filled out by the child's representative (if literate) at the time of enrollment. These cards provide information on birthplace, birth date, sex, school in which previously enrolled, previous grade and mark in that grade, and names of the child's representatives. Home addresses are not recorded as many parents do not know their own address. (Until 1966 most streets in Ciudad Guayana were unpaved and, not including Puerto Ordaz and San Félix, unnamed except by local residents. House numbers were usually those marked by the Public Health Service in its antimalaria campaign.) Some of the public schools have no filing cabinets, and cards stored in cardboard boxes mildew in a few months. Most schools keep the enrollment cards until the cards for the following year are filled out, and then destroy them. The Ministry of Education maintains end-of-year examination results in a central file in Caracas, but records for the early primary grades are usually destroyed after several years.

The problem of studying a child's record is further complicated by the frequency with which families change residences, and schools. Table 7.1 gives

TABLE 7.1
Migration between Schools of Students Entering Fourth Grade in Ciudad Guayana in 1964–1965

	Where Student Enrolled, 1963–1964					
Where Enrolled 1964–1965	Antonio de Berrio	San Félix	Mercedes Prospert	José Angel Ruiz	Puerto Ayacucho	Tumeremo
Antonio de Berrio	74.9	6.3	3.0	4.9	1.0	0.0
San Félix	7.1	73.8	1.3	0.0	1.9	0.0
Mercedes Prospert	1.6	1.9	86.7	14.8	15.2	2.1
José Angel Ruiz	0.3	1.9	0.0	65.6	1.0	0.0
Puerto Ayacucho	0.3	0.0	3.0	4.9	75.1	1.4
Tumeremo	0.0	0.0	0.0	1.6	1.0	79.6
Others in city	15.8	16.1	6.0	8.2	4.8	16.9
Total %	100.0	100.0	100.0	100.0	100.0	100.0
Total N	255	160	67	61	105	142

some idea of the movement from school to school between two school years. About 25 percent of the students entering fourth grade in the six largest public schools in September 1964 enrolled in a different school from the one in which they had enrolled in September 1963. There is more movement in the earlier grades, less in fifth and sixth grades. Students repeating grades move less than those not repeating, but this may be an artifact of the failure of the new schools to report the student as a repeater. Some of this movement results from changes of residence of families from one part of the city to another. However, parents may change schools because the child is failing in one school and they hope he will be more successful in another. Parents also believe that some schools are better than others.

For all these reasons it would be difficult if not impossible to measure the efficiency of schools in Ciudad Guayana by comparing enrollments in one grade in a given year with enrollments in the next highest grade the following year. Large numbers of new enrollees come into the city from other regions; families move within the city and leave the city for other areas. From a sample of 1,042 of the 12,000 families enumerated in the school census in June of 1965, only 633 of the families, about 63 percent, could be located in November 1965. According to interviewers, 19 percent of the 389 families not contacted had definitely moved out of the city. This represented about 7 percent of the original sample. Another 11 percent of the families had moved within the city. Interviewers reported that 65 percent of the families not found could not be located by the address listed or were not known at that address. Enough cases were double- and triple-checked to confirm the interviewers' reports. Great numbers of ranchos have disappeared, torn down by owners or demolished by construction companies' bulldozers. The areas of most difficulty were the areas of greatest flux. MacDonald is probably right in his assertion that Ciudad Guayana receives people who have come to stay,[1] but it is also true that many people still live a rootless life, endlessly swarming in the poorer barrios.

Studying year-to-year enrollment rates in Ciudad Guayana (as in the rest of Venezuela) can be misleading for other reasons. Ministry of Education reports do not provide information on the extent of enrollment after data collection in October of the school year. At least 4 percent of the total enrollment of schools in Ciudad Guayana occurs after enrollment data are collected. Nothing is known about the extent to which children once enrolled in school drop out between years and enroll at a later date. Furthermore, in some developing countries, especially those where enrollments are limited by lack of school facilities, parents may enroll their children in two or more schools to ensure admission into one. The effect is to exaggerate total enrollment counts. The problem has never been studied nationally in Venezuela. Research in Ciudad Guayana indicated that only 1 percent of the total enrollment in each of the first, fourth, and sixth grades in 1964–1965 could be explained on the basis of double enrollments. Double enrollments occur most frequently in first grade, when children are trying to enter school, and in fourth grade, when students transfer from unitarias.

Withdrawal from school is another source of error in official aggregate statistics. The Ministry of Education Statistical Office cannot subtract these from the enrollment figures of the school. Hence, students enrolling later in another school (if this occurs by mid-October) are counted twice in computing enrollment totals. Finally, year-to-year analyses of the schools of Venezuela in general, and Ciudad Guayana in particular, are subject to error because schools do not identify all the students who are repeating grades. Parents may enroll their repeating child in another school, without indicating that he failed the previous year. This is especially prevalent in the first grade, but may occur for higher grades too, because the parent need (in fact, though not according to regulations) only present the certificate of promotion from the previous grade to enroll the child; the school does not note the year in which the grade was passed. Even a child who has failed a grade and re-enrolls in the same school may not be listed by the school as a repeater. These sources of error make assessment of school efficiency based on analysis of national aggregate enrollment statistics extremely hazardous.

Nor can school efficiency be accurately estimated on the basis of the proportion of students passing each year. Some students who pass drop out of school permanently, others stay out one or two years and re-enter. Many students who fail leave school also. If the function of the school is to produce graduates in as short a time as possible, the efficiency of a system depends both on the pass rate of students, and the extent to which passing *and* failing students remain in the system. Inaccurate repeater rates make analysis difficult.

Another method to study the flow of children through schools would be to identify a cohort of children attaining their seventh birthday in a given year, and follow these students until they graduate or drop out permanently. Given the high mobility in general in Venezuela, a longitudinal cohort study would be extremely costly. It would require substantially more than six years to complete.

The research in Ciudad Guayana employed a compromise technique. Although not as satisfactory as the longitudinal cohort study method, it was within the realm of feasibility and offered more reliable information than could be obtained from the aggregate statistics compiled by the Ministry of Education. Parents of children of school age were asked to state for each year after age seven whether their child had enrolled in school, whether he had remained in school until the examination period, and whether he had passed the examination. Clearly the parents' memories would in some instances be spotty, but great stress was put on the importance of these data in training interviewers, and their reports and further checks suggest that this information was fairly accurate. Only 10 of the 640 respondents gave information that was obviously incorrect, and each case was corrected after reinterviewing the child's mother.

The study had several objectives, so that interviews were conducted with mothers of children from seven to fourteen years of age. The purpose of investigating academic histories would have been better served if interviews had been limited to older children. However, with complete age range coverage it was possible to examine patterns of student progress through schools over time to see what changes may have occurred. The data also permit comparisons of children who had been in Ciudad Guayana (and its schools) for at least five years with those who had lived in the city for less time.

The data presented are based on an expansion of the sample of 640 to the total school-age population of 11,000. The sampling procedure overweighted unsuccessful children in order to study fully reasons for their failure. This exaggeration is corrected by the expansion procedure used. The tables presented deal only with children who had spent at least six years of school age living in Ciudad Guayana. The numbers in the tables appear large, but it should be remembered that they are based on relatively small numbers of students, and therefore are likely to be fairly unreliable.

Rates of Passage

Table 7.2 shows what happened to students enrolling in schools in the city for the first time, beginning with the academic year 1956–1957. One of the two dramatic fluctuations in the number of students passing first grade occurred in 1960–1961, when Venezuela experienced a fairly serious economic depression and the Ministry of Education enrolled large numbers of students in unitarias and in schools with poorly prepared teachers. This was a national phenomenon, and is testimony to the wastefulness of programs which provide entrance to

TABLE 7.2
Performance in the First Year of School for Students Living in Ciudad Guayana More than Five Years, by Year of First Enrollment

	Performance		Year Entered School									Total Percent
			1956–1957	1957–1958	1958–1959	1959–1960	1960–1961	1961–1962	1962–1963	1963–1964	1964–1965	
First Year in School	Within-Year Drop	%	—	65.8	6.3	12.7	22.7	14.7	20.8	13.6	17.4	17.4
		N	—	48	19	68	274	120	188	152	210	1,079
	Failure	%	—	4.2	2.6	14.2	38.4	15.6	6.1	2.9	12.9	14.9
		N	—	3	8	76	464	127	55	33	155	921
	Pass	%	100.0	31.0	91.1	73.1	38.9	69.7	73.1	83.5	69.7	67.7
		N	7	22	276	392	469	569	660	936	840	4,171
	N Expanded Sample		7	73	303	536	1,207	816	903	1,121	1,205	6,171
	Percent		0.1	1.2	4.9	8.7	19.6	13.2	14.6	18.2	19.5	100.0
	N Original Sample		3	15	19	44	49	53	55	66	50	354

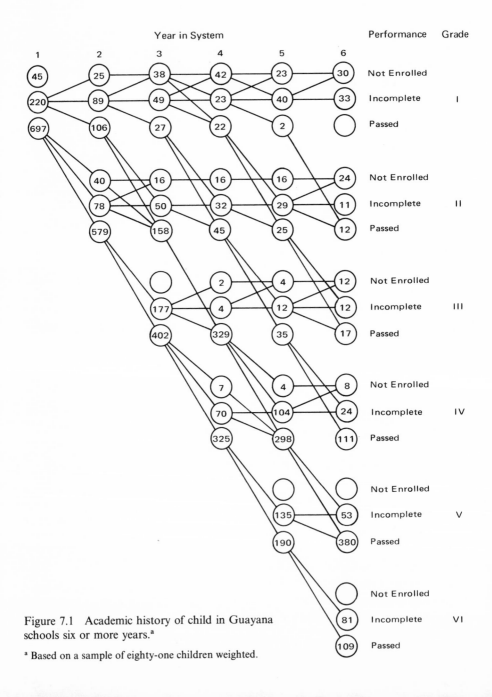

Figure 7.1   Academic history of child in Guayana
schools six or more years.[a]

[a] Based on a sample of eighty-one children weighted.

school for large numbers without making improvements in quality. The other significant decline in school effectiveness occurred in 1957–1958. Pérez Jiménez was overthrown in January 1958 and the country suffered a brief period of strife and turmoil. Other fluctuations might be explained on the basis of changes in promotion practices by the various schools or by sampling error.

Some eighty-one of the children included in the study had been in Ciudad Guayana for at least six years since attaining their seventh birthday. Figure 7.1 shows the results of weighting these children to represent the 900 children in the whole city who had been there for at least six years. This figure demonstrates the erratic progress, or lack of progress, of many children who entered schools in the city six or more years ago. The accuracy of the figures at the various levels in the chart are of less importance than the demonstration that a great variety of things must happen to children in school to produce such varied results. Because the figure is based only on children remaining in the city, it minimizes the educational discontinuities caused by migration. That is, it underestimates the variety of routes children take in their pursuit of education. On all measures children in the city for five years or less do less well than those in the city for six or more years. New migrants are more plagued with economic and marital instability in the city,[2] as well as with a series of disadvantages associated with life in rural areas.

The Examination System as a Source of Inefficiency

Figure 7.1 offers evidence to support a conclusion that the present examination system is an inefficient device for predicting which children will do well in school. First, the examination system makes many "false positive errors"; it lets children pass in early years who will fail later on. This is seen by following the progress of children who pass the examination at the end of first grade: only 16 percent (109) go straight through to sixth grade; 30 percent (208) do not reach the fifth grade in six years. If the examination were a more effective predictive device, more children would go through the upper grades without difficulty.

More serious is the fact that the examination system also makes "false negative errors." It holds back children who apparently are capable of successfully meeting requirements of the upper grades. Table 7.3 shows that children failing in a given year go on to do as well as or better than children who pass in that year. This is especially true in the upper grades. In the first grade the effect of failure is to discourage many children from continuing in the system. About

TABLE 7.3
School Achievement in Ciudad Guayana: Grade Level Attained Six Years after School Entry Age as a Function of Not Passing Various Grades

Grade Level at End of Six Years	Achievement in Grade							
	First		Second		Third		Fourth	
	Failed[a]	Passed	Failed	Passed	Failed	Passed	Failed	Passed
None	28.7	—	—	—	—	—	—	—
First	5.5	3.3	19.5	—	—	—	—	—
Second	13.7	0.9	0	1.0	3.4	—	—	—
Third	8.6	4.3	0	5.2	7.3	4.2	22.0	—
Fourth	26.7	30.2	20.3	32.1	89.3	7.0	36.4	0
Fifth	16.8	45.7	60.2	41.9	0.0	61.7	41.6	66.5
Sixth	—	15.6	—	19.8	—	27.1	—	33.5
Total %	100.0	100.0	100.0	100.0	100.0	100.0	100.0	100.0
Total N	220	697	118	579	177	402	77	325

[a] Includes those who dropped out for a year.

half the students who are listed as "flunking" first grade actually dropped out during the year. These students who leave during the year are less likely to enroll again the following year. If they do enroll, they are less likely to pass than are students who took the examination but failed it. In Table 7.4 most of the students who do not return after having "failed" a grade are those whose "failure" is attributable to not having attended to the end of the school year. This occurs most frequently in first and fourth grades. In fourth grade most dropouts are students who transferred from unitarias to six-year schools.

The burden of the school is increased when large numbers of students fail or leave during the school year, and enroll the following year or later. Students repeating grades take up seats that could be filled by new students. If most of those students failing did not go on to achieve in later years of schooling, they would represent a total waste for the school. If the school cannot educate them to some meaningful level (functional literacy attained at the fourth-grade level) but the students remain in the system (as do the majority), the effect is to reduce the ability of the school to produce graduates. Deadwood repeaters in the early grades take up space that could be granted to students who would eventually graduate. What should be the policy of the schools with respect to repeaters?

A conservative argument, seeking to minimize costs of education, would state that children fail in school because of their inability to master the material which the school believes necessary for achievement at higher grade levels. According to this argument, these children should be removed from school as soon as possible if the school does not provide special services for them (such as special classes and tutoring). The society should not invest in incompetent students if the economy demands the production of trained workers rather than services to less productive members of the society.

The findings indicate, however, that failure in school is not all explained by an irremediable lack of intellectual ability. Among the numbers of children who never reach any meaningful level in the educational system is a sizable group of considerable talent. Because Venezuela, and especially the Guayana, needs to have all educable children educated, the school system should attempt to

TABLE 7.4
School Achievement in Ciudad Guayana: Performance of Students Not Enrolling in Year Following Success or Failure

Record for Previous Year		Number Who Do Not Re-enroll	%	Never Return	Return to: Fail	Return to: Pass
	N					
1st Year	Failed 220	25	11.4	11	0	14
	Passed 697	40	5.7	9	0	31
2nd Year	Failed 167	20	12.0	13	7	0
	Passed 685	0	0	—	—	—
3rd Year	Failed 276	25	9.1	0	25	0
	Passed 587	9	1.5	2	0	7
4th Year	Failed 129	8	6.2	8	—	—
	Passed 721	4	0.5	4	—	—
5th Year	Failed 320	27	8.4	27	—	—
	Passed 550	0	0	—	—	—
All Years	Failed 1,112	105	9.4	59	32	14
	Passed 3,240	53	1.6	15	0	38
Total		4,352	158	3.6%	74	32	52

salvage as many children as possible. To support this argument it must be possible to show that lack of ability is not the principal reason for failure in school.

Examination Procedures. Examinations in primary schools in Ciudad Guayana are administered by a three-person panel including the child's teacher, another teacher from the same school or the principal, and a person connected with education from outside the school, usually a school principal. The examination has three parts, oral, written, and practical, but most emphasis is usually placed on the oral part of the examination for the grading is much easier. In grades four, five, and six, examination results must be certified by the district supervisor, and are recorded in the central file in Caracas for each child. In the early grades the school sends copies of examination results to the state supervisor.

Examinations require the recall of material memorized during the school year. The examination panel makes up questions from a set of basic topics, usually on the day of the examination. The oral examination is administered with all students present in the classroom.

A child's mark for the year is based half on the mark given him by his teacher, and half on his success in the examination. In Venezuela marks range from 0 to 20, with a minimum of 10 needed to be promoted. A child entering the examination with a class mark of 16 would have to score 3 or less on the final examination to fail the year.

Marks given in schools in Ciudad Guayana vary considerably from teacher to teacher, grade to grade, and between public and private schools. Private school marks average between 15 and 16, and many more private than public school children are exempted from the examination by virtue of receiving a class mark of 19 or 20. Public school marks average 13 to 14. This difference in average marks is *not* explained by differences in the social class levels of the students enrolled because marks are equally high in private schools which enroll poor children. Marks given are progressively higher as one advances in grade in the school; the failure rate in sixth grade is lower than in fourth chiefly because class marks are higher and not because the examination is less difficult. Differences in average marks between public and private schools, and between lower and upper primary grades, are testimony to the subjectivity of the evaluation process.

As far as is known, no study has ever been made of the reliability and validity of the current Venezuelan examination procedures. The procedure is supposed to guard against teacher favoritism while taking account of the students' over-all performance during the year. The Ministry of Education is considering the development of a national examination, such as that administered in Mexico, to permit studies of the effectiveness of Venezuela's schools.

Research in Ciudad Guayana attempted a preliminary analysis of the validity of examination and grading procedures by comparing marks obtained in school with a number of characteristics of the child, including scores made on tests supposedly measuring intelligence. Marks were obtained for 200 of the 640 students in the sample. School records in the city are so inadequate that information could not be found for more than half the students. Measures of correlation were calculated to assess the relationship between marks in school and social and economic variables. Three of the correlations (out of fifty-six) attained significance ($p < 0.05$). High marks are associated with mother's expectation that her child will go far in school ($r = 0.18$), with high occupational mobility of the father relative to the child's maternal grandfather ($r = 0.21$), and with mother's belief that education is important as a way of obtaining the means for a better life ($r = 0.15$). Although statistically significant, these correlations are small and given the large number of correlations calculated may very well be spurious.

Four tests were used to measure the intellectual ability of the 238 children who could be reached for examination. The psychologists administering the tests divided the children into three groups on the basis of presumed ability to read and write. The illiterate group, mostly young children seven and eight years of age, took the Detroit Non-Verbal test, and the Goodenough Draw-A-Man test. The Detroit test supposedly measures a child's memory, attention, motor control, numerical understanding, comprehension, and other intellectual abilities. Instructions are oral. The Goodenough requires the child to draw a human figure. Quality of the drawing and amount of detail determine the score. Children with some reading skill were given the Goodenough and the P. V. Simon, which supposedly measures the same intellectual capacities as the Detroit. The most advanced group was given the Simon and the Otis Short Form A, a power intelligence test requiring advanced reading ability.

Marks in school do not seem to be principally a function of the intellectual ability of the child. There were no significant correlations between the intelligence test scores and marks in school for a given year. However, intelligence test scores are related to measures of over-all success in school. For example, high scores on the Detroit Non-Verbal test were associated ($r = 0.30, p < 0.01$) with having more successful than failing years; high scores on the P. V. Simon were associated ($r = 0.24$, $p < 0.01$) with a higher grade level than expected given age. When children are grouped according to the income and education level of their parents there is a positive relationship between I.Q. scores and marks for the year for the group whose parents are high on both education and income. The relationship reverses in the low income-education group; *low* marks are more frequently obtained by those with *above* average I.Q. scores. This could result if teachers rewarded bright middle-class students with good marks; these are the children most likely to be well socialized and conforming. Bright lower-class students are more likely to be a source of difficulty for teachers. Not socialized into the middle-class value system of teachers, and easily bored by a school which offers little çhallenge, they are more likely than dull lower-class students to run afoul of the teacher and be punished with low marks.

If we assume a general (but small) relationship between intelligence and social class, and moderate unreliability in marks from year to year, the relatively low relationship found between intelligence test scores and over-all success in school makes sense. Dull lower-class students tend to drop out of school because of low parental motivation. Bright lower-class students may fail a year or two but return to school. Middle-class students generally move through the system without much failure, with duller students obtaining low, but passing, marks.

This is, of course, speculative. No brief can be made for the validity of the intelligence tests. The tests were adapted from another culture and they have never properly been validated in Venezuela (though they were used successfully in private schools in Caracas to predict grade point averages in high school). Conditions of test administration guaranteed some unreliability. The sample of children is too small to permit definitive statements about the adequacy of school marks. However, it does seem reasonable to conclude that, in the schools in Ciudad Guayana, there is no clear-cut relationship between the mark a child obtains in school and his ability to do well on tests purportedly measuring intelligence. The results suggest that grading and examination procedures in the schools must be studied carefully, for they may be contributing to the "inefficiency" of the schools.

To buttress this argument further it is worthwhile to look at what happens to children who fail examinations. Many teachers in Ciudad Guayana believe that children who fail examinations *should* fail because they are incapable of mastering material at higher levels in the school. If that were true, children who do fail in one grade and then try again should be unsuccessful in the following year.

But, as shown in Table 7.3, 17 percent of the children who fail first grade then go on to pass the next five years; 43 percent pass at least four of the next five years. However, only 60 percent of those passing first grade the *first* time pass four out of the next five years, a not much higher rate than that of those failing the first time in first grade. If the first grade mark is an accurate screening device, far fewer of those failing should be successful in later years. Instead, first grade failure appears to be a mechanism to arbitrarily delay some students. Similarly, failure in later grades, after having passed, seems only to have the effect of delaying students rather than screening out those who are incapable of achievement at a high level.

Nothing that has been said in this chapter should be taken as reflecting lack of dedication of the teachers of Ciudad Guayana. As a group, teachers in the city have earned their reputation as "those who are doing most for Venezuela."[3] The problem is that many teachers are undertrained and overwhelmed. Their secondary-level normal school formation ill-prepared them for coping with the hordes of children they face each day, under oppressive climatic and didactic conditions. In-service training now available does not fully remedy the basic inadequacy of their preparation. The middle-class-oriented normal school does not train teachers to understand or work with the impoverished.[4] Principals and the district supervisor are too burdened with other responsibilities to help teachers.

Examination and promotion policies in Guayana schools should be changed. It will be several years before stable communities are formed and the turbulence of life in the city diminished. Even then, children will enter schools with varying degrees of preparation, and with wide variability in intellectual development and cultural values. Schools and teachers should consider it their responsibility to educate the great majority of these children, and to bring them as quickly as possible to the sixth grade. To accomplish this, teachers will have to stop failing large numbers of children in the early grades and look outside of the school for causes of failure. The data reviewed to this point lead to the conclusion that failure in school in Ciudad Guayana probably results from more than just inattention or inability in the classroom. Sporadic school attendance of many children over the years suggests that what happens in the classroom may not be the principal factor in the inefficiency of schools.

It is the total environment in which children live in Ciudad Guayana which acts to promote or impede their education. The school, as it now operates, plays only one part, perhaps even a minor one, in that environment. This does not "excuse" the educational system from its responsibility to educate all children well. On the contrary, it suggests that the schools of the city are not now functioning so as to comply with their mandate. Schools seem to be run as centers of instruction, badly administered at that, but without attention to the broader, and more challenging, task of education of the people of the barrios.

8
The Family
and the Efficiency
of the School

If education systems in urbanizing Latin America were faced only with problems of lack of buildings, inadequate books and supplies, and poorly trained teachers, the educational planner would have a relatively easy task. These are tangible problems and the profession has experience in solving them. Schools can be built, books can be bought, teachers can be trained. The methods are known and the elaboration of a plan is not difficult. True, the financial resources are too often lacking: good plans are not carried out and the frustration is bitter. But planning at that level now presents only a secondary challenge. With increased resources and national commitment to fulfillment of educational objectives, the planner can and should look beyond the initial steps of planning to consider whether brick and mortar and teachers alone are all that go into the educational process. They are not, of course, and the planner is then faced with the task of allocation of time and resources to the solution of these other problems.

In Ciudad Guayana the evidence seems clear that the success of the school as an educational system is as much or more a function of factors external to the school than what goes on within its walls. The efficiency of the school depends as much or more on events and processes in parts of the social system other than the educational subsystem. This may not be an inherent rule, and it certainly is not desirable, but the condition prevails. As this and following chapters will show, events in the community have a pronounced effect on the efficiency of the school, and schools do little to counteract these negative influences. The suggestion is made that resources now spent on traditional aspects of the school might be better spent in activities not usually considered part of "schooling."

This chapter considers the influence of the family on the efficiency of the school. Later sections show how schools in Ciudad Guayana have failed to work with families, and the consequence of this lack of cooperation. In Ciudad Guayana, and in most of Latin America, the school has operated as though it had complete control over the educational futures of its pupils, but it has not attempted to make sure that this is so. The result is that the school accomplishes less than it could and wastes resources.

Characteristics of Families in Ciudad Guayana

The data reported in this chapter and the three that follow are based on interviews with a sample of 640 families in the city who have school-age children. The population from which the sample was drawn included 90 percent of the families with children of school age living in the city in November 1965. Only families from Puerto Ordaz were excluded: the conditions of living and educational opportunities in that section of the city are sharply different; few families in Puerto Ordaz have children who do not attend school, salaries are high, and unemployment is minimal. The sampling procedure yielded a disproportionately large number of families with children who do not attend school. This was done deliberately to provide a large number of cases for analysis. At the same time, characteristics of the total population of families are represented fairly by weighting the sample appropriately.

Information about conditions of life in the city has been presented in earlier chapters. Some of that is repeated here, for purposes of emphasis, to call attention to the fact that Guayana families with children are generally more disadvantaged than unmarried persons and families without children.[1] That is, conditions are even worse than suggested in Chapters 3 and 4. Table 8.1 summarizes data on characteristics of families with children of school age. Several features of the data merit special attention.

TABLE 8.1
Family Characteristics of Children of School Age in Ciudad Guayana in 1965

A. Region of birth of mother:		Birthplace of students in:		
		sixth grade	fourth grade	first grade
Ciudad Guayana	6.9%	12.4%	18.0%	32.6%
Bolívar, urban	12.1	12.3	12.1	10.8

TABLE 8 (continued)

Bolívar, rural	8.1	9.1	11.1	9.2
Other states, urban	35.4	43.6	36.8	29.7
Other states, rural	34.2	20.9	20.6	16.8
Foreign countries	3.3	1.3	1.4	0.9

B. Number of cities in which mother has lived:

One	2.6%	Four	20.5%
Two	20.2	Five or more	24.4
Three	32.3		

C. Facilities of house:

Flush toilet	21.3%	Refrigerator	50.0%
Latrine	61.9	Washing machine	21.6
Nothing	16.8	Radio	66.8
		Electricity	77.0

D. House type:

Rancho	28.5%	Cinder block or brick	43.4%
Bahareque	28.1		

E. Persons in household:

Two–five	13.6%	Eight–nine	31.5%
Six–seven	26.5	Ten or more	28.4

F. Persons per room (counting all rooms in house):

One or less	8.1%	Three	25.0%
Two	45.4	Four or more	21.5

G. Family stability:

Natural mother and father	53.2%	Mother only, no spouse	21.2%
Natural mother or father, living with new spouse	16.5	Other relationship or none	9.1

H. Education of male head of house:

Female head of house:

No education	30.6%	37.1%
One–three years	22.8	28.2
Four–five years	19.8	21.6
Graduate of primary school	21.8	8.6
Some secondary	5.0	4.5

I. Occupation of male head of house:

Professional, administrative	5.4%	Skilled labor	22.5%
Office worker	3.4	Unskilled labor	38.4
Sales	9.8	Services	9.1
Transportation	11.4		

J. Monthly income of family in dollars:

Less than $44	9.9%	$121–154	15.2%
$44–$88	18.2	$155–$188	20.0
$89–$120	15.8	More than $188	20.9

Families in Guayana came to a city in the making, as yet incapable of providing adequate housing or services for many of its inhabitants. Many have had to seek temporary solutions until facilities are made available. A family arrives and stakes out a piece of the virgin plain which surrounds the city, in an area without roads, water, or electricity. Because land on the Puerto Ordaz side of the river is controlled by the CVG or the Orinoco Mining Company, almost all of the "squatting" families have built their homes in the empty areas between Dalla Costa and El Roble, and on the far side of San Félix, away from the pole of growth of the "planned" city. As a result, many families are without basic services. In November 1965, 17 percent of the children of school age in Ciudad Guayana lived in homes with no sanitary facilities, another 62 percent had latrines only. Twenty-three percent of these homes were without electricity and less than 50 percent had piped-in water. Families without running water usually bought from the city's truck, fifty gallons for one bolívar ($0.22). The city was drawing its water from a well located next to an open sewer; health officials claimed the water was contaminated. Fortunately, the CVG-built water-treatment plant will supply water to all the city when pipes are laid. Twenty-nine percent of the houses in which school-age children lived were made from sheets of aluminum, or of pressboard, cardboard, or beaverboard. These are euphemistically called ranchos. Houses of *bahareque* (mud and sticks), typical rural construction in Venezuela, housed another 28 percent of the children. These houses are more adequate than the rancho; rooms are larger, the house is cooler in the day and warmer in the evening. But mud walls provide breeding places for many insects, including the vector of Chagas disease (a debilitating disease with no known cure), and grass roofs afford welcome habitats for rats and vermin.

Families in Ciudad Guayana in 1965 were large, crowded, and many had only one parent. Typical sleeping arrangements for young children are four to a double bed; hammocks are often slung in what during the day serves as living room and kitchen. Most families were nuclear, that is, including children and mother and father, but 21 percent of the families had no male head of the house (see Table 8.1G). In 9 percent of the families there was at least one child who did not have a direct blood relationship to either housewife or her spouse.

The cost of living in Ciudad Guayana is higher than in Caracas or other parts of Venezuela, and as high as in the United States. Because of low incomes (Table 8.1J) and the persistence of rural customs, many families follow a diet unlike that of the typical inhabitant of Caracas or the United States; they are accustomed to a fare low in proteins, high in starch and bulk.[2] Efforts to educate these families in the use of a more nutritious diet, of meat and eggs and milk and bread, must overcome traditional eating habits. And families must have incomes sufficient to provide themselves with these foods in quantity.

A typical family in the city might be that of Félix González, who lives in an abandoned housing development in El Roble. Félix and his wife Julia came to Ciudad Guayana more than five years ago from San Juan de los Morros in the State of Guárico. Félix had worked in the eastern oil fields in Anzoátegui. He came to Ciudad Guayana when the mill opened; he had heard of the employment opportunities. Félix's father was an illiterate farmer and Félix considers himself lucky to have finished the fifth grade before beginning work. Although his wife never went to school and does not read or write, "she has been a good woman." The couple came to the city with their four older children, and have had three more children here. Their oldest reached the third grade; he is now looking for work. Félix Jr. and Rafael will be better educated, their father believes. He is upset about Ali, who is thirteen and has only finished the first grade. Ali does not want to return to school. The Gonzálezes live in a two-room "house" that Félix built with aluminum sheets. The children are outside during the day, so the cramped quarters are not too bad. The house has electricity and the water truck comes by several times a week. Félix dug a latrine behind the house. He works in construction, and is happy now to be working again, after having been out of work for awhile. Félix earns about Bs. 120 a week ($110 a month). This is not enough, but he expects things will get better.

Like Félix González, most of the people in Ciudad Guayana are not well off, most do not yet share in the great riches that the city promises for the future. They hope that they will, and that their children will lead better lives, and they understand that education is the key to the future for their children. But to a certain extent the child is father to the man, and today's conditions of poverty sharply limit opportunities for the future.

The Influence of the Family on Educational Attainment

Family Income. All schools involve some costs to parents. Even though the public schools of Ciudad Guayana are free, families have to spend some portion of their meager incomes to equip children for school. This is a strong belief of parents: children need shoes and clothing, textbooks, and other school supplies. In addition to these direct costs, families forego income which could be provided by children working, or by children tending the home while the mother works.

Given the low income levels of many of the families in Ciudad Guayana, the costs of schooling represent a serious burden, and for many families the load is too great.

Even if a family is above the minimum level of income necessary for meeting costs of schooling, the family's economic position affects the educational progress of the child. Higher incomes can mean better diets, more thorough medical attention, books other than those needed in school, and a wider range of "luxury" items which serve to enrich the child's intellectual development. In Chile children from low-income families leave primary school at an earlier age than do children from higher income families; those poor children who do stay are less likely than their wealthier schoolmates to graduate.[3] Primary school desertion rates are higher in those Argentine provinces with lower per capita incomes, and promotion rates are higher in the more wealthy provinces.[4] Lower-class children are grossly underrepresented in primary schools in Brazil, and the disproportion increases with grade.[5] Research in the United States and England, where abject poverty is not as serious a problem as in part of Latin America, shows the same relationship.[6]

In Ciudad Guayana, too, family income (represented in Tables 8.2 to 8.4 as per-family-member income, to control for family size) relates to attendance at school, to the age-grade standing of the child, and to his academic history. Children from families with higher incomes are more likely to be enrolled and

TABLE 8.2[a]
Per-Person Monthly Family Income and School Attendance

			Income Level in Bolivares					
			Bs. 25	50	75	125+	N	%
	Yes	%	67.8	76.5	78.5	84.3		
		N	78	127	142	140	487	77.5
Does S	No	%	32.2	23.5	21.5	15.7		
Attend Now?		N	37	39	39	26	141	22.5
	Total		115	166	181	166	628	
	Percent		18.3	26.4	28.8	26.4		100.0

Chi-square Statistic = 10.826 with 3 degrees of freedom, $p < 0.02$.

[a] The tables that follow are based on results from the sample of families of 640 school-age children, stratified for age, place of residence, and school attendance (see Appendix A). Total number of respondents is sometimes less than 640 when information could not be obtained from the housewife participating in the interview. S refers to the school-age child drawn into the sample.

TABLE 8.3
Per-Person Monthly Family Income and Success in School

| | | | Income Level in Bolivares | | | | | |
			Bs. 25	50	75–100	125+	N	%
	Correct	%	13.9	22.3	24.3	32.5		
		N	16	37	44	54	151	24.0
	One year behind	%	19.1	24.7	24.9	24.1		
		N	22	41	45	40	148	23.6
Age-Grade	Two-three behind	%	40.9	27.7	30.4	25.9		
Standing of S[a]		N	47	46	55	43	191	30.4
	Four + behind	%	26.1	25.3	20.4	17.5		
		N	30	42	37	29	138	22.0
	Total		115	166	181	166	628	
	Percent		18.3	26.4	28.8	26.4		100.0

Chi-square Statistic = 20.388 with 9 degrees of freedom, $p < 0.02$.

[a] Based on whether the student has attained a grade level to be expected given his age.

TABLE 8.4
Per-Person Monthly Family Income and School Achievement Pattern

| | | | Income Level in Bolivares | | | | | |
			Bs. 25	50	75	125+	N	%
	Nonenroller	%	32.7	20.5	25.9	21.4		
		N	37	32	43	33	145	24.6
	Nonattender	%	31.9	23.1	18.7	14.9		
		N	36	36	31	23	126	21.4
School	Nonachiever	%	21.2	34.6	27.1	24.0		
Achievement		N	24	54	45	37	160	27.2
Pattern	Achiever	%	14.2	21.8	28.3	39.6		
		N	16	34	47	61	158	26.8
	Total		113	156	166	154	589	
	Percent		19.2	26.5	28.2	26.1		100.0

Chi-square Statistic = 37.372 with 9 degrees of freedom, $p < 0.01$.

to do well in school. The relationship would probably be stronger in a more established city; economic instability still threatens many families in Ciudad Guayana. Some families have made good in the city, others who previously had good incomes are now unemployed.

We can perhaps see the relationship between family income and education of children more clearly by using a measure of the length of time that the family has had a "high" income. The number of possessions and facilities (electricity, refrigerator, washing machine, radio) a family has is one index of the extent to which the family has enjoyed "good times." Those who have enjoyed a stable income for some time would have acquired more things. The number of these possessions is more closely related to educational attainment than is income (see Table 8.5). The kind of housing that the family has been able to afford, another kind of index of income over a period of time, is even more closely related to educational attainment (see Table 8.6).

Other Variables. Until recent years Venezuela was a rural nation, as most Latin American countries still are. In the struggle for individual progress it is the rural dweller who suffers most, for schools and other services seldom drift into the backwater of the village. Ciudad Guayana children born in small cities and towns are more frequently behind in school than are those from larger

TABLE 8.5
Possessions in the House and Success in School

			All four	Three of four	Two of four	One of four	None	N	$\%$
				Number of Possessions					
	Correct	$\%$	32.9	31.8	27.9	19.2	13.7		
		N	27	48	38	24	20	157	24.5
	Year behind	$\%$	29.3	19.9	25.0	22.4	23.3		
		N	24	30	34	28	34	150	23.4
Age-Grade	Two–three behind	$\%$	28.0	32.5	25.0	32.8	31.5		
Standing of S		N	23	49	34	41	46	193	30.2
	Four + behind	$\%$	9.8	15.9	22.1	25.6	31.5		
		N	8	24	30	32	46	140	21.9
	Total		82	151	136	125	146	640	
	Percent		12.8	23.6	21.2	19.5	22.8		100.0

Chi-square Statistic = 33.808 with 12 degrees of freedom, $p < 0.01$.

TABLE 8.6
Type of Housing Construction and Success in School

			Zinc	Bahareque	House Type Block	N	%
	Correct	%	20.1	17.4	35.5		
		N	51	30	76	157	24.5
	Year behind	%	22.0	25.6	23.4		
		N	56	44	50	150	23.4
Age-Grade	Two–three behind	%	28.3	32.6	30.4		
Standing of S		N	72	56	65	193	30.2
	Four + behind	%	29.5	24.4	10.7		
		N	75	42	23	140	21.9
	Total		254	172	214	640	
	Percent		39.7	26.9	33.4		100.0

Chi-square Statistic = 36.676 with 6 degrees of freedom, $p < 0.001$.

cities. The relationship between the average size of all cities in which the child's mother has lived and his age-grade standing is even stronger.

And the depressing effect of rural life weighs heavily not only because of the lack of opportunity, but also because of a culture that little values education. The conuquero sees little obvious need for education to carry out his role in life. So it is that families which continue a rural style of living after arrival in the city also may maintain attitudes and habits unfavorable to education. Families now living in Ciudad Guayana who live in a house of bahareque, who do not bother with latrines, and who raise animals for food are more likely to have children behind in school than persons with a more "urban" style of life (see Table 8.7).

Families in eastern Venezuela are characterized by a relatively low degree of permanency. Most unions are not legally sanctioned, and a sizable minority end in mutual separation or, as is more common, abandonment by the father. The impact on children in the family could be expected to be negative. Not only are there psychological effects, but children are often removed from school until the family crisis is resolved. As Table 8.8 shows, children with a father living at home more frequently are at the correct grade level for their age than are children without a father at home. This finding is similar to results of research in the United States where dropouts more frequently come from unstable

TABLE 8.7
Rural-Urban Living Style and Success in School

			Rural	Rural Slum	Living Style Urban Slum	Urban	N	%
	Correct	%	18.3	17.2	26.0	37.3		
		N	20	36	44	57	157	24.5
	One year behind	%	21.1	24.4	22.5	24.8		
		N	23	51	38	38	150	23.4
Age-Grade	Two–three behind	%	31.2	32.1	27.2	30.1		
Standing of S		N	34	67	46	46	193	30.2
	Four + behind	%	29.4	26.3	24.3	7.8		
		N	32	55	41	12	140	21.9
	Total		109	209	169	153	640	
	Percent		17.0	32.7	26.4	23.9		100.0

Chi-square Statistic = 36.688 with 9 degrees of freedom, $p < 0.01$.

TABLE 8.8
Adult Male's Relation to Child and Success in School

			Father	Relationship Not father	No spouse	N	%
	Correct	%	35.2	12.7	19.0		
		N	105	26	26	157	24.6
	One year behind	%	21.8	25.5	24.1		
		N	65	52	33	150	23.5
Age-Grade	Two–three behind	%	27.9	31.9	32.1		
Standing of S		N	83	65	44	192	30.0
	Four + behind	%	15.1	29.9	24.8		
		N	45	61	34	140	21.9
	Total		298	204	137	639	
	Percent		46.6	31.9	21.4		100.0

Chi-square Statistic = 41.554 with 6 degrees of freedom, $p < 0.001$.

families than do children who remain in school.[7] The findings in Guayana suggest that children in families with no adult male are somewhat *less* disadvantaged academically than children in families where the adult male is not their father. Furthermore, other findings indicate that children with unemployed fathers are behind in school more frequently than children in families with no adult male. These results suggest not only that marital and economic instability have negative effects on the ability of children to be educated, but that "father" is not always a positive influence favoring efforts of the school.

The ability of the school in Guayana to "process" its students effectively might also be a function of the size of the families from which they come. Families are large in Guayana, and research in other countries has shown relationships between family size and academic achievement: children of large families tend to be less successful.[8] Several kinds of reasons are offered to explain the relationship. It is suggested that size of family reflects the planning ability of the family, and therefore the intellectual climate in which the child is raised. Large families are often crowded, and crowding can have a serious effect on mental and physical health. It is also argued that intellectual development of children is strongly determined by the amount of contact the young child has with adults, that children in large families cannot, on the average, receive as much stimulation from adults as those in small families, and that first-born children are more likely than later-born brothers and sisters to enjoy academic success because of their closer and more prolonged contact with parents.[9]

These arguments, based on research in a different culture, do not hold in Ciudad Guayana. Children from large families are just as likely to be successful in school as are those from small families. In Guayana, the middle class has families as large as those of the lower class and, perhaps even more important, it is large families which are more often stable, that is, include an adult male who is father of at least some of the children.

Crowding is a serious problem in about half the homes in Guayana where, as was shown in Table 8.1E, three or more people occupy each room in the house. The findings in Table 8.9 appear to suggest that this piling together of bodies does have its effects; children from crowded families are less likely to be at the correct age-grade level than are those from families with only one person per room. However, if the same table is constructed for only middle-income families, or only low-income families, the relationship disappears. Apparently crowding per se has little effect, at least when compared to the powerful impact of other conditions.

TABLE 8.9
Crowding: Persons per Room in the House and Success in School

| | | | \multicolumn{4}{c}{Persons Per Room} | | |
			One per room	Two	Three	Four or more	N	%
	Correct	%	32.9	21.6	22.7	20.5		
		N	53	38	34	30	155	24.5
	Year behind	%	24.8	22.7	25.3	21.2		
		N	40	40	38	31	149	23.5
Age-Grade	Two–three behind	%	27.3	33.0	31.3	27.4		
Standing of S		N	44	58	47	40	189	29.9
	Four + behind	%	14.9	22.7	20.7	30.8		
		N	24	40	31	45	140	22.1
	Total		161	176	150	146	633	
	Percent		25.4	27.8	23.7	23.1		100.0

Chi-square Statistic = 17.881 with 9 degrees of freedom, $p < 0.05$.

TABLE 8.10
Birth Order and School Achievement Pattern

| | | | \multicolumn{3}{c}{Birth Order} | | |
			First-born	Middle-born	Last-born	N	%
	Nonenroller	%	27.7	21.4	32.1		
		N	43	64	17	124	24.5
	Nonattender	%	27.1	20.4	7.5		
		N	42	61	4	107	21.1
School	Nonachiever	%	22.6	31.8	17.0		
Achievement		N	35	95	9	139	27.4
Pattern	Achiever	%	22.6	26.4	43.4		
		N	35	79	23	137	27.0
	Total		155	299	53	507	
	Percent		30.6	59.0	10.4		100.0

Chi-square Statistic = 22.331 with 6 degrees of freedom, $p < 0.01$.

Nor in Guayana can we find evidence that first- or early-born children do better in school. As Table 8.10 indicates, last-born children are most likely to do well in school. (They are also most likely to be not yet enrolled, but this is because many of these late-born children are eight-year-olds who soon will be in school.) Older children in Guayana are more likely to have been born in rural areas where schools did not exist, and to have reached school age when the family's economic position did not permit enrollment. Younger children are more likely to be city-born, with the advantages of schools next door and higher family incomes. The effect of income is seen again to be the most powerful determinant; the relationship between birth order and academic achievement disappears if the children are divided up according to level of family income.

A student's sex is also often related to success in school. In the developed countries boys often leave school earlier than girls, and are less successful, academically, while in school.[10] This is not the case in Ciudad Guayana. Boys do as well as girls in primary school and are more likely to continue into secondary school. The major reasons are most likely cultural; education of women traditionally was not considered very important in the countries of Latin America and some of this persists today.

The value of this review of factors which do *not* appear to have a marked influence on the success or failure of children in school in Guayana is to indicate that individual characteristics, often demonstrated to be important in the more developed countries, are relatively less salient in this setting. Of course a child's personality and intelligence will affect his ability to achieve in school, and teachers can take that into account within the classroom. But in developing regions of the world other factors also operate against successful completion of the school, and the radius of activity of these factors extends beyond the walls of the school.

Motives and Education in Ciudad Guayana

High income, family stability, good health, good housing, and other amenities provide conditions under which parents can educate their children. That has been shown clearly, and it is no surprise. But more is needed for the child to be sent to school, for him to continue in school and do well. The family must motivate the child so that he is willing to suffer endless hours of boredom and fatigue in pursuit of a highly intangible goal. The child must be taught to conform to the discipline and regimen imposed by the school. Through their own behavior parents must establish for their children a hierarchy of values in which the pursuit of an education can take precedence over all other interests. When this happens, when the child is so taught and formed, then he overcomes fatigue, irritation with tyrannical and deadly dull teachers, and hunger pangs. He achieves despite the school or his family's economic status. This is possible, of course, only when sickness or hunger or fear are not so powerful as to incapacitate him.

No doubt the relationship between social class of family and educational attainment of children represents more than differences in income levels between the working and middle classes. Middle-class parents are better educated and create for their children an environment in which intellectual achievement is valued. The positive association between education of parents and academic achievement of children in the United States and England has been demonstrated in a number of studies.[11] In Ciudad Guayana the average education of adult family members is more closely related to the child's educational attainment than is the family's income. When families are compared within levels of income the relationship between parental educational attainment and that of the child is still fairly strong. But comparing within levels of parental education, the relationship between income and age-grade standing of the child is all but eliminated. This suggests that family income appears related to the education level of the child chiefly because of its association with parental education. This is an important finding with implications for adult education and we shall return to it later.

Education of the child's mother is more closely associated with his attainment than is the education level of his father. This is consistent with research findings that the mother plays a dominant role at all ages in the education of children in the United States.[12] The argument has been offered that when the mother is better educated than the father[13] or from a higher status level,[14] the child is more often the target of pressure to achieve. For example,

... many parents who push children toward social mobility are members of mixed-class marriages.... A lower-middle class woman who marries a man from the upper part of the working class usually begins to try and recoup her original social class status either by reforming and elevating her husband's behavior to meet lower-middle class standards or by seeking to train and propel her children toward the status she once had.[15]

In Ciudad Guayana children advanced in age-grade standing are only slightly more likely to have a mother with education superior to the father than are children retarded in age-grade standing (Table 8.11). There is also a slight

TABLE 8.11
Spouse–Wife Education and Success in School

			Spouse more	Who Has More Education Equal	Wife more	N	%
	Correct	%	21.0	27.3	31.9		
		N	45	41	45	131	25.9
	One year behind	%	22.4	25.3	22.7		
		N	48	38	32	118	23.4
Age-Grade	Two–three behind	%	34.6	24.7	27.0		
Standing of S		N	74	37	38	149	29.5
	Four+ behind	%	22.0	22.7	18.4		
		N	47	34	26	107	21.2
	Total		214	150	141	505	
	Percent		42.4	29.7	27.9		100.0

Chi-square Statistic = 8.487 with 6 degrees of freedom, $p < 0.25$.

tendency for children to attend school more frequently or to be advanced in age-grade standing when their father has a lower status occupation than their mother's father, but this relationship also fails to attain statistical significance. Furthermore, the extent to which mothers want education for the children is as strong among women with less education than their husbands as those with more. Although women who "marry down" tend to have better educated children, there is no evidence to support the hypothesis that this results from the woman trying to "realize herself" through her child.

Level of parental education may be an important influence on the educational attainment of the child by virtue of the intellectual model which parents furnish for the child. If this is true, there should be a relationship between the parents' intellectual activities and the child's educational attainment. In Ciudad Guayana there is a strong relationship between the presence of reading matter in the home and the age-grade standing of the child, a relationship which holds up even within levels of parental education and income. Similarly, variables measuring the extent to which parents attend to the mass media (radio, news-papers) or belong to associations (union, clubs, church) are strongly related to age-grade standing. And mothers who actually do read are more likely to have

TABLE 8.12
Mother's Intellectual Activity and School Achievement Pattern

| | | | Has Housewife Read Book Lately? (includes literates only) | | | |
			Yes	No	N	%
	Nonenroller	%	18.3	23.1		
		N	37	42	79	20.6
	Nonattender	%	14.9	27.5		
		N	30	50	80	20.8
School	Nonachiever	%	29.7	25.3		
Achievement Pattern		N	60	46	106	27.6
	Achiever	%	37.1	24.2		
		N	75	44	119	31.0
	Total		202	182	384	
	Percent		52.6	47.4		100.0

Chi-square Statistic = 14.238 with 3 degrees of freedom, $p < 0.01$.

achieving children than those able to read who do not exercise their literacy (Table 8.12).

More important than the passive example offered by parents are the direct motivational inputs which they feed their children. Working-class students in the United States are more likely to drop out of high school if their mothers do not believe they should get further education.[16] Working-class students who "strive to get ahead" are more likely to report parental advice to enter a profession[17] and to be successful in school.[18] The following description of "common-man" parents is frequently associated with children motivated to achieve in school.

[They] started to apply pressure from the beginning of the school career. They encouraged high marks, they paid attention to what was happening at school, they suggested various occupations that would be good for their sons. Their boys reached high school with a markedly different outlook from those who were not pushed.[19]

The relationship between the student's motivation to succeed in school and his performance is straightforward. Highly motivated students are less likely to discontinue their studies, more likely to obtain high grades. Most of the sources of motivation of these children are external to the school.

Guayana mothers readily talked about their ambitions for their children. All of the women interviewed said they think education is important. More than 31 percent of the mothers wanted their child to finish secondary school, and 19 percent hoped that the child would attend the university. In most cases these goals are unrealistic in the sense that few of the children will actually attend secondary school, much less finish, and even fewer will ever be able to reach the university. But unrealistic ambitions have their impact, and there is a strong association between the kind of educational goals mothers have and the child's success in school to date. Children who have been enrolled in school and have passed a grade or two are expected to go further than those with a history of nonenrollment or dropping out during the year, or failing. At least mothers are realistic enough to plan for the future on the basis of past success. And they also know the economic returns of education, as shown by the strong relationship ($r = 0.60$) between how far they hope their child will go in school and the income they believe he would receive if he did get that far.

The realism of Guayana mothers emerges clearly with another set of questions. When housewives were asked, "What do you hope to obtain for yourself in the future?" 69 percent of them named education of their children as a goal. And 93 percent of the women staked out education as a goal they wanted for their children. But the world is cruel and these women know it; only 47 percent

TABLE 8.13
Interviewee's Goals for Herself and School Attendance

			Wants to educate child and thinks it possible	Wants to educate child but not possible	Goals Does not mention education	N	%
	Yes	%	83.6	75.2	69.7		
		N	249	106	140	495	77.3
Does S Attend Now?	No	%	16.4	24.8	30.3		
		N	49	35	61	145	22.7
	Total		298	141	201	640	
	Percent		46.6	22.0	31.4		100.0

Chi-square Statistic = 13.730 with 2 degrees of freedom, $p < 0.01$.

TABLE 8.14
Interviewee's Goals for Child and School Attendance

			Specific educa-tional achieve-ment likely attain	Specific achieve-ment not likely	Study or learn likely	Study or learn not likely	Does not mention educa-tion	N	%
	Yes	%	84.1	82.7	76.6	62.7	57.8		77.3
		N	190	91	141	47	26	495	
Does S	No	%	15.9	17.3	23.4	37.3	42.2		22.7
Attend Now?		N	36	19	43	28	19	145	
	Total		226	110	184	75	45	640	
	Percent		35.3	17.2	28.8	11.7	7.0		100.0

Chi-square Statistic = 26.760 with 4 degrees of freedom, $p < 0.01$.

TABLE 8.15
Interviewee's Goals for Herself and Success in School

			Wants to educate child and thinks it possible	Wants to educate child but not possible	Does not mention education	N	%
	Correct	%	27.9	20.6	22.4		24.5
			83	29	45	157	
	One year behind	%	22.8	22.7	24.9		23.4
		N	68	32	50	150	
Age-Grade	Two–three behind	%	29.9	35.5	26.9		30.2
Standing of S		N	89	50	54	193	
	Four + behind	%	19.5	21.3	25.9		21.9
		N	58	30	52	140	
	Total		298	141	201	640	
	Percent		46.6	22.0	31.4		100.0

Chi-square Statistic = 7.207 with 6 degrees of freedom, $p < 0.30$.

of the women felt that they would be able to achieve their personal goal of educating their children. Only 35 percent felt that the child would get as far in school as they hoped he would.

The broad disparity between ambition and realization is shown more poign-antly by comparing the relationship of motivation to present attendance and past success. Questions about goals for the future distinguish fairly well between attenders and nonattenders, but the relationship between over-all success and motivation is insignificant (compare Tables 8.13 and 8.14 with 8.15 and 8.16). *Motivation leads to enrollment, but other factors determine attendance and success once enrolled.* Within income-education groups the slight association between educational motivation and academic realization is almost completely accounted for by what happens in the group above average on both education and income. In the fortunate-educated group of families only, there is a strong relationship between desiring education and getting it. In the groups less fortunate, and/or less educated, education is just as much desired but the hope

TABLE 8.16
Interviewee's Goals for Child and Success in School

			Specific educa-tional achieve-ment likely attain	Specific achieve-ment not likely	Study or learn likely	Study or learn not likely	Does not mention educa-tion	N	$\%$
					Goals				
	Correct	%	27.4	27.3	25.5	14.7	15.6		
		N	62	30	47	11	7	157	24.5
	One year behind	%	24.3	25.5	23.9	18.7	20.0		
			55	28	44	14	9	150	23.4
Age-Grade	Two–three behind	%	27.9	31.8	30.4	33.3	31.1		
Standing of S		N	63	35	56	25	14	193	30.2
	Four+ behind	%	20.4	15.5	20.1	33.3	33.3		
		N	46	17	37	25	15	140	21.9
	Total		226	110	184	75	45	640	
	Percent		35.3	17.2	28.8	11.7	7.0		100.0

Chi-square Statistic = 17.421 with 12 degrees of freedom, $p < 0.20$.

TABLE 8.17
Reasons Why Education Considered Important by Housewives, and Attendance

Reason	Attend Now		Total	
	Yes	No	N	%
To be cultured	87%	13%	53	5
Intellectual development	81	19	141	13
General ignorance (he who isn't educated isn't worth anything)	78	22	394	36
Get work	78	22	277	25
General success	74	26	241	21
			1,106[a]	100.0

[a] More than one response was permitted.

of getting it is less, and wanting it is often unrelated to obtaining it. For these people, carefully made plans and cherished dreams collapse when faced with cruel reality. A child's future, at least for many low-income families in Ciudad Guayana, is subject to a whimsical fate.

Some parents continue to hope in their children. Their children are their only hope; they realize that their own lack of education dooms them to a marginal existence because they are unable to obtain secure and well-paying employment. This importance of education of children as a means of escape from poverty is reflected in the belief of 92 percent of the mothers that their children will help the family.[20] And the children can be educated; in the new society the city offers promise. Education is the key for a more prosperous future. It means more income, work, and a more meaningful life (Table 8.17).

The Educating Family

One can imagine a family which presents the child with all the conditions, necessary and sufficient, for attendance and achievement in school. Such a family has been labeled the "educating family"[21] and studied in various forms.[22] It is the family, not just the parents, and the situation in which it finds itself, which is important for the education of the child. In Ciudad Guayana the average education of all adults in the family (parents, older children, relatives, other persons) is more closely related to the educational attainment of the child than is education of the child's mother or father, or both combined (see Table 8.18). All adults in the family serve as examples for the child, educated aunts and uncles exert pressures for achievement, and the better educated adult members of the family are the more likely that the family will possess the economic wherewithal for education of the children.

Some of the characteristics of educating families in Ciudad Guayana have already been discussed. For example, the family may not be in a position to afford the child the opportunity to be educated. The income level of the family, the family's stability, and the availability of schools are indicators of opportunity. Families located in rural areas where schools are unavailable are less likely to have been able to educate their children than are families which have more often lived in urban areas.

A second condition for education of the children is that families commit themselves to goals for their younger members which can be realized through education. The evidence is that most families in Ciudad Guayana do have goals which they believe can be reached through education of the children. When the family has the economic means to attain these goals, families planning for the future do a better job of educating their children.

The effect of the family on the child is often attained, as we have argued, through active means. A principal vehicle for carrying the child through the system is parental participation in the child's school experiences. Housewives

TABLE 8.18
Average Education of Adults in Family and School Achievement Pattern

			None	One–three years	Four–five years	Six or more years	N	$\%$
					Amount of Education			
	Nonenroller	$\%$	38.2	28.9	17.1	14.7		
		N	21	90	28	10	149	24.9
	Nonattender	$\%$	23.6	25.4	17.7	10.3		
		N	13	79	29	7	128	21.4
School	Nonachiever	$\%$	16.4	25.7	36.0	19.1		
Achievement		N	9	80	59	13	161	26.9
Pattern	Achiever	$\%$	21.8	19.9	29.3	55.9		
		N	12	62	48	38	160	26.8
	Total		55	311	164	68	598	
	Percent		9.2	52.0	27.4	11.4		100.0

Chi-square Statistic = 57.061 with 9 degrees of freedom, $p < 0.001$.

were asked whether they helped their children with their schoolwork. Almost half of the women with children attending school stated that they do not. Some mothers who do not help are illiterate, so that participation is naturally limited. But among literate housewives, those involved in their children's schooling to the extent of helping with homework are more likely to have a child who is successful in school (Table 8.19). This is true no matter what the income and education level of the family.

It might also be expected that parents who get along well with their children would be able to generate more pressure on them to attend and succeed in school. For example, in five countries (United States, England, West Germany, Italy, and Mexico), the possibility of reaching secondary school is inversely related to dominance by parents, controlling social class.[23] Another research reports that high-achieving boys described their parents as approving, trusting, affectionate.[24] Research on this question is summarized as follows:

When this quality of family living is more closely analyzed it becomes clear that affective relationships between the child and his parents, the concern which the parents show for the child's welfare, the consistency or otherwise of discipline, and, in consequence, the atmosphere of security in the home, are all of great importance for determining school success or failure.[25]

TABLE 8.19
Maternal Involvement in Education and School Achievement Pattern

| | | | Does Respondent Help Child with Schoolwork? | | | |
			Does not help	Helps	N	%
	Nonenroller	%	22.2	16.4		
		N	61	46	107	19.3
	Nonattender	%	24.7	21.1		
		N	68	59	127	22.9
School	Nonachiever	%	31.6	26.4		
Achievement Pattern		N	87	74	161	29.0
	Achiever	%	21.5	36.1		
		N	59	101	160	28.8
	Total		275	280	555	
	Percent		49.5	50.5		100.0

Chi-square Statistic = 14.771 with 3 degrees of freedom, $p < 0.01$.

TABLE 8.20
Maternal Attitude toward Child Rearing and School Achievement Pattern

| | | | How to Treat a Nonachieving Child | | | | |
			Reward	Oblige	Punish	N	%
	Nonenroller	%	19.6	26.7	27.2		
		N	37	40	59	136	24.5
	Nonattender	%	16.9	26.7	23.0		
		N	32	40	50	122	21.9
School	Nonachiever	%	27.0	22.0	28.1		
Achievement		N	51	33	61	145	26.1
Pattern	Achiever	%	36.5	24.7	21.7		
		N	69	37	47	153	27.5
	Total		189	150	217	556	
	Percent		34.0	27.0	39.0		100.0

Chi-square Statistic = 16.671 with 6 degrees of freedom, $p < 0.02$.

It seemed unlikely that Guayana housewives would be able to give an unbiased estimate of their relationships with their children. But their preference for rewards or punishments in disciplining children should reveal their attitudes toward relationships with children. Table 8.20 shows a clear and close relationship between preferring reward as a disciplining technique and a positive academic history for the child. Although it is true that middle-class families are more likely to use rewards, and lower-class families to use punishments, the relationship between attitudes toward discipline and school achievement holds up across classes. As discussed earlier, fathers are sometimes more important as a negative rather than a positive influence on the children's schoolwork. Within various levels of income, involvement of the father is positively related, in all socioeconomic groups except that which contains the largest proportion of unemployed men, to the child's academic record. In the "unemployed" group, the relationship is negative.

Of course, a number of these characteristics of the educating family must be interrelated and codeterminant. Taking the *set* of factors which is most closely associated with the child's age-grade standing, some of the relationships reported drop out. The following are the findings with respect to factors that work together in their relationship with school achievement. Children advanced in age-grade standing are more likely to come from families where the mother has high educational aspirations for the child and from families with few adults (that is, nuclear and young families). The families of the achieving child have enjoyed a period of marital stability, and the adults in the family tend to have attained higher than average educations, and to have lived in large cities. These families also tend to have higher incomes and to have had these incomes for a longer period, as indicated by the quality of their housing and number of possessions. These are the families in which the mother indicates that rewards are preferred to punishment as a means of discipline. And they are more frequently families in which the mother is better educated than the father. This set of variables accounts for 27 percent of the variability among children in terms of age-grade standing. (For a detailed multivariate analysis, see Chapter 10 and Appendix C.)

The family of Jesús Luis Hurtado has many of the characteristics associated with the educating family in Ciudad Guayana. Jesús Luis is now fourteen. He entered school at age seven and went through the sixth grade without failure. He did not enroll in high school immediately because his mother could not find a place for him, but she did enroll him the following year. Jesús Luis's mother, Marcelina Jiménez (she is not married to her husband, but has lived with him for the last twenty years) was born in El Pilar, a small town in the state of Sucre, where her father was a constable. Her husband is also from El Pilar. Marcelina Jiménez finished the fourth grade in school, her husband the third. He has always been a small businessman in the furniture line. The business brings home about $250 a month. There are six persons in the house: two older brothers of Jesús Luis, both of whom are in high school now, and a younger sister, also in high school. They live in Dalla Costa, the poorest section of Ciudad Guayana, but Mr. Hurtado has built a block house with four rooms. There is a latrine in back (no running water in Dalla Costa), he has wired the house, and there is a refrigerator and radio. The family is waiting for the CVG to build houses because they think their present one is inadequate.

But Marcelina Jiménez' first goal for herself is to educate all of her children. Her husband is now sixty (she is thirty-five) and she hopes that her sons will support her when she is widowed.

She says that she often talks to her sons about the need "to be someone in life," and that only by going to school can one become a man of importance. In Dalla Costa it is hard to convince her sons of this: there are many families who let their children run loose, and the character of the neighborhood is expressed well by a street called Lawless Avenue. She warns Jesús Luis of the bad influence others can have. Marcelina Jiménez helps her sons with their homework, as best she can, but now that the children are all better educated than she, she is mostly limited to making sure that they do study. She gives her children little presents when they bring home good marks, hoping that this will make them more interested in studying. Both she and her husband keep after the children—they consider that they are doing well as they almost always bring home good marks.

Less than half the families in Ciudad Guayana have been as successful as this one. The Hurtado-Jiménez family is fortunate not only in enjoying economic and marital stability, or in having bright children, but because it has suffered few of the vagaries of life which plague so many families, including those economically well established.

Were the family variables discussed here the only antecedents of academic success, it might have been possible to generate a much larger multiple correlation with age-grade standing. But success in school is also a function of a series of events which occur to (instead of within) families, preventing families with ambitions from realizing them, penalizing those who have made every effort to educate their children. The nature of these events is best understood by studying in more detail the reasons why children do not regularly attend school or finish the school year.

9
Factors Affecting the Family's Ability to Educate Children

The necessity and importance of education for children are constant themes in conversations with Guayana parents; the future of the child is seen to rest solely on how far he goes in school. For many parents their future, too, rests on the child's shoulders as he goes through the educational process. Their chances for advancement are now lost, they believe, but the child can gain a better life; the school's diploma promises larger incomes and greater job security, and with education one earns dignity and respect from the community. Parents have missed their chance in life, but the child is just beginning and his success can be shared with them.

Are these whimsical dreams, based on short-lived motives? The finding that parents' motivation is associated with enrollment in school, but not with continued success, might be interpreted in that way. The relationship might suggest that Guayana parents can only see to the immediate tomorrow and do not have deep-rooted values which would lead them to make the day-after-day sacrifices necessary to keep a child in school once enrolled.

This chapter examines that possibility. It looks at reasons given by parents for failure to enroll children in a given year and at reasons offered for not finishing a year successfully once enrolled. Several case histories are presented which typify the erratic school histories of Guayana's children. The argument is made that what we might consider a normal school history of enrollment, passing the year, enrollment again, through the sixth grade, is in eastern Venezuela and perhaps other regions of Latin America an *abnormal* occurrence which can take place only if families escape the normal crises that confront them. The bitter roots of school failure lie largely in conditions that pervade the lives of the poor majority. The chapter also briefly considers the relationship of the school to the amelioration of crises that plague families. In this analysis the issue is taken up once again of the need for schools to consider ways to increase their efficiency.

Reasons for Failure to Progress in School

Rapid changes in the educational situation of Ciudad Guayana have offered a unique opportunity to study motives for education. Historically, the lack of school buildings has been the principal reason for failure to enroll in school. Adults now in the city often lived in areas where schools did not exist and the validity of this reason has tended to obscure the importance of other kinds of factors. A decision by the primary school district supervisor in Ciudad Guayana to enroll as many children as applied in September 1965, irrespective of resulting class sizes, effected a dramatic increase in the number of spaces available to parents seeking to enroll children, much as if several new schools had been opened. Despite this, a number of children still remained out of school. The school census carried out in late June 1965 had asked parents why their children were not enrolled or attending school; more detailed questions on the same theme were asked of mothers of a sample of the same children in November 1965.[1] Table 9.1 compares the reasons offered for nonattendance in June and November.

The category most frequently used by interviewers in November to record reasons for nonattendance was "lack of interest" on the part of the parents or the child. This exaggerated the frequency of lack of motivation of parents for interviewers tended to place in this classification those who did not offer a clear reason for the failure of their child to attend school. An attempt was made through other questions in the interview to discover if parents felt that education was a waste of time or that schools were poorly run. For those cases where lack of interest as recorded by the interviewer was attributed to the parent, about half the group offering this reason, there were no responses which could be interpreted to suggest that parents see the schools of Guayana as so deficient that a child's time there is wasted. It is most likely that many of these children were not attending for other reasons, which the parents preferred not to tell the interviewer. The suggestion is also clear that parents did not see the school as a prime cause of academic failure.

A different situation exists for the cases in which parents stated that their *children* were not interested in attending school. Here it was clear that both

TABLE 9.1
Reasons for Nonattendance at School in June and November
1965

Reason	June 1965 Census	November 1965 Sample Survey
Space	24.9%	8.6%
Economic reasons	19.4	26.0
Moving	17.2	2.4
Lack of interest	13.7	26.5
Health	7.8	14.6
Distance	4.8	2.7
Various	5.1	7.2
No reason offered	7.1	5.8
Documents	—	7.2
$N = 171^a$		

[a] The survey included 320 children who had not been attending school in June 1965. Of these children, 139 were not in school in November; 8 of the 320 children in the survey group who were attending in June were not enrolled in November. The respondents sometimes gave more than one reason for not enrolling the child.

parents and child considered school a waste of time. In every case, the child was at least twelve years of age, and had not reached fifth grade. School must be seen as a waste of time by older children who spend several years in each grade, although not necessarily because these children can find more productive ways to employ their time. Less than 10 percent of the children were not attending school because they were working. This low figure may not accurately represent the situation in other cities. Unemployment levels are high in Ciudad Guayana and independent of the minimum employment age of fourteen, seldom enforced in Venezuela. There are few ways in which a young boy or girl can be employed when many grown men look unsuccessfully for work.

"Economic resources" as an explanation of nonattendance in school may often be taken at face value. Many families feel themselves too poor to afford even the minimal costs presented by public education. Although some highly motivated families struggle to overcome economic disabilities, to make sacrifices necessary to buy clothes, shoes, and books for their children, many families are so poor that the sacrifices necessary to overcome their poverty require heroic effort, a rare commodity in any class.

On top of this, conditions of life in Ciudad Guayana are unstable to the point that the tragedy of sudden poverty or sickness may simply immobilize the family on all fronts. Families which one year enjoy a good income may, when the breadwinner loses his job, find themselves in dire economic straits. Children are pulled out of school because they play a vital role in the family's survival. In families which lose their male head, older children may be employed within the home while the mother works, a factor mentioned several times by the group offering "economic resources" as a reason for nonattendance. Even in families with both parents present, children may be kept home to look after younger siblings when the mother is sick or pregnant. In half the cases in which "poor health" was given as a reason for nonattendance, the child remained at home because his or her mother was sick. These illnesses may be of relatively short duration but, although the schools officially permit a child to enroll any time before January, children are discouraged from enrolling late. Furthermore, when the child or mother is sick for awhile absence from school makes it difficult for the child to return successfully to classes.[2]

Some parents asserted that they could not enroll their child in school until they had either a birth certificate (in the case of children entering first grade) or proof that the child had successfully completed the previous grade. In all instances parents complained that they must return to another place (of birth or last residence) to get these "documents" required by the school for enrollment. The use of the "excuse" might seem to imply a lack of motivation for few residents in Ciudad Guayana have migrated from long distances and they have had sufficient time to make the trip home before the opening of school. On the other hand, given the education level of rural migrants, it smacks of bureaucratic unrealism for the school system to put the burden of handling papers on the shoulders of illiterates and semiliterates. To compound the error, the bureaucracy recognizes privilege in its demands: at least 4 percent of those enrolling in the first grade for the first time have not yet reached their seventh birthday (the stated minimum age), and most of these children come from higher income families.

"Distance from school" should not be taken as a valid reason in Ciudad Guayana for nonenrollment: there is a school (if the unitarias are included as schools) within one kilometer of the homes of all children in the city. Perhaps there are a few parents in the less urbanized sections of the city who delay enrolling their young children because they have to cross busy highways or overgrown ravines in order to reach the school.

TABLE 9.2
Reasons for Nonprogression in School and Academic History

	School Year Lost because of						
Parent's reason	Nonenrollment		Nonattendance		Nonachievement		Total
	N	$\%$	N	$\%$	N	$\%$	N
Space	45	49.4	27	29.7	19	20.9	91
Documents	14	46.7	8	26.7	8	26.7	30
Resources	24	42.1	18	31.6	15	26.3	57
Work	11	36.7	9	30.0	10	33.3	30
Moving	25	25.0	36	36.0	39	39.0	100
Sickness	39	31.5	32	25.8	53	42.7	124
Motivation	43	31.4	35	25.5	59	43.1	137
Dead-end school	8	29.6	5	18.5	14	51.9	27
							596[a]

[a] Of the 640 children studied in the survey, 112 had never failed in school, 44 were seven years of age and enrolling for the first time. That leaves 484 children who had lost at least one year of school, because of not enrolling, not finishing the year, or failing the year. The respondents were asked to give a reason for each lost year, so the total N is greater than the number of students being considered.

"Moving" is a less frequent reason for nonattendance in November because school had only been in session for two months.

The reasons offered by parents in Guayana for nonenrollment, nonattendance, and failure in school indicate clearly that the chief causes of the inefficiency of schools in Ciudad Guayana cannot be attributed to defects in the academic curriculum or the instructional techniques employed by teachers in the classroom. Table 9.2 complements the data presented in Table 9.1. It presents all of the reasons why some of the 640 children included in the November sample lost school years. There is a slight relationship between the type of failure experienced by the child and the parent's reason for why the year was lost. A lack of school facilities, document requirements, and, to some extent, lack of economic resources are barriers which families must surmount to enroll their children in school. Moving and sickness, on the other hand, tend to work against the child completing the year successfully. But in all cases it is clear that what takes place within the classroom could have only little effect in increasing the efficiency of schools. Better books and more exciting classes, important as they are for the intellectual development of the child, would do little to diminish the negative consequences of sudden unemployment, to prevent the family from moving when faced with crisis, to change the health conditions in the home, to get parents the documents they need to enroll their children. Teachers can have little effect on the academic histories of their children, these findings suggest, if they restrict their role to that of intellectual formation of the child through instruction in traditional areas.

Withal, academic programs cannot be unresponsive to the peculiar conditions which poverty and deprivation bring. Curricula designed for middle-class children with high verbal skills cannot be thrust, without modifications and carefully designed bridging materials, onto children with limited vocabularies, limited experience of the wider world, and the consequent problems of concept formation which these limitations bring. C. B. Cazden has recently reviewed the vast literature on subculture language differences and the problems these differences cause in teaching culturally deprived groups.[3] A vast number of studies have established beyond doubt that these do exist, and the deficiencies in vocabulary and grammar of children from culturally deprived homes have been extensively catalogued. There is also evidence, less clear, that these language deficiencies (there is argument as to whether to call it "a difference" or "a deficiency") affect the process of concept formation and retard learning. This is not surprising because achievement in school is measured by tests in standard language. There is much less clear evidence on how these deficiencies are overcome in school programs. However, there is agreement that recognition of the language problem by teachers and sympathetic attention to its solution are gains in themselves.

Test performances of children from the shanty barrios did indicate that many —but by no means all—had verbal and conceptual problems which could be related directly to the deprivation of their backgrounds. The curriculum of the primary schools of Guayana is, as has been said, extremely rigid. First-grade children are expected to sink or swim and the majority of barrio children are allowed to sink. There is no attempt to modify and grade institutional materials to fit the groups or individuals who cannot measure up in the first year.[4]

Case Histories of Failure

The impact of the extra-school events which impede academic progress is seen even more clearly by examining the year-by-year histories of children. Here are three examples of children whose academic achievements will be limited because of a slow start in school.

Arquimedes Hernández was not enrolled in the first grade at age seven because his parents lived in an area where there were no schools. He enrolled

the following year but did not pass because, according to his mother, he had no
help with his schoolwork. At age nine he enrolled again, passed the first grade,
and has now passed second and third. He is thirteen and in the fourth grade.
The Hernández-Merida union (Arquimedes' mother identified his father as her
concubino) has been plagued with difficulties. Since their arrival in Ciudad
Guayana, for example, Mrs. Hernández was sick for several months with
amoebic dysentery. She did not seek medical treatment. In addition, her husband has been without steady work for one year (he makes what little income
the family receives by selling vegetables), and the family lost their first home in
the city in the floods of 1964. Mrs. Hernández hopes that her son Arquimedes
will continue in school, "to learn so that he can help us."

Victor Sifontes lives with his aunt, and her "husband," in Dalla Costa, the
most impoverished area of the city and that with the least adequate school
facilities. Victor lost his first year of school because his family arrived in
Guayana in January (without having officially withdrawn Victor from his
previous school). He enrolled again at age eight but failed the year, even though
he passed the final examination. The following year he contracted measles just
before the examination, and so had to repeat the first grade again. The next
year his father ran away and took Victor with him. Victor came back to his
mother when she became ill. Victor is now twelve. He is not now enrolled in
school because he has lost interest.

Benjamin Caraballo has a similar history. He enrolled in school at age seven,
but his family moved. The following year he was sick. The next year Benjamin's
father left home and took Benjamin with him; he was not enrolled in school
that year. At age ten he enrolled in first grade for the third time, passed the year,
and the following year passed second grade. But he then failed third grade two
years in a row. Benjamin's mother now manages her ten children by herself.
They live together in a one-room rancho without electricity, refrigerator, or
radio. Mrs. Caraballo claims an income of only $44 a month, which she earns
making *arepas* (corn pancakes) and by taking in laundry. She may also function
as a "grocery" prostitute, that is, taking in men from time to time without
intending to form a stable union. Her income could not possibly support her
children and she has had several children since her husband left. Mrs. Caraballo's father was a farmer. Although illiterate herself, she clearly understands
the importance of education. She states that her own poverty is a direct result of
her ignorance. She wants to educate her children and has done the best she can,
but between her illnesses and theirs, and her inability to manage the children

now that they are older, she feels helpless. She wishes the government would launch a campaign to oblige children to go to school.

Here are three histories of children who started off well in school, but are now behind.

Yraida Gómez passed first and second grades without difficulty, but failed third. She failed third again, and then passed. She is now enrolled in the fourth grade. Yraida's failures of the third grade occurred during the period when her mother (abandoned some years before) took on another man and bore two of his children. That man is now gone; Mrs. Gómez is left with nine living children, and an income of about $50 a month which she earns by sweeping out the hospital. She is thirty years old. Yraida is likely to continue her education, despite the relatively adverse conditions of her family life. Mrs. Gómez reached the fifth grade and is highly motivated to ensure that at least one of her children finish high school. She tries hard to interest her children in school. So far none of her children has been sick.

Antonio Blanca also passed his first two years in school without difficulty. However, his parents had to send him to live with relatives in Puerto La Cruz while they worked out some difficulties and, unfortunately, the move out and back took place each time in the middle of the year. Antonio is now enrolled in the third grade in Ciudad Guayana.

Nildes Guevara had completed third grade after three years in school. But at age ten she became ill and was not enrolled in the fourth grade. The following year Nildes was kept at home to watch the younger children while her mother worked selling *hallacas* on the street. Her mother's husband has been out of work for the past year. He lives with the family but does not help with the children. Nildes is the oldest of seven.

Although they resulted in wasting years of children's school lives, none of the circumstances described here was of such gravity that it could not have been prevented. Families could have delayed their moves until the children had finished the school year, or could have withdrawn their children officially and re-enrolled them in a new town. Children could have passed completed years if their parents had paid a bit more attention to their schoolwork. Working mothers could have made arrangements for neighbors to watch the younger children instead of withdrawing the older children from school. Even illnesses could have been shortened in duration; the government provides some medical attention through the social security hospital and a rural medical outpatient service.

The "self-made man" reading these histories might wish to argue that the families do not really care for education. He might argue that lower-class parents mouth educational aspirations but are not committed enough to take the steps necessary to guarantee it. They live in a culture of poverty and never think to delay gratification of immediate needs in order to achieve long-range goals.

But this argument runs counter to two facts which have already been mentioned. First, even middle-income, and educated, and motivated families experience, to some extent, problems of moving during the middle of a school year, of living in rural areas, of prolonged and serious illness, of abandonment by a feckless husband. Faced with several of these problems, middle-income families too may fail to educate their children. And low-income families which have been so fortunate as to have been spared illness, or the need to move, or family disunity, or other causes of school failure and desertion, *do* manage to educate their children.

Second, the economic situation of many of these families is so tenuous that even responsible parents are forced to assign first priority to moving to a better job. Some of them are tempted to feel that they must delay pursuit of long-range goals, such as education, in the interest of survival. Many of the families who have come to Ciudad Guayana, and those that will continue to migrate there, have known poverty for many generations. The promise of an escape through steady and remunerative employment is a lure to abandon cherished dreams for their children in order to secure bread today: the promise of a job means a move and the child will be educated in the next town. Other families have been exposed to middle-class values long enough to be tempted by the prospect of the prosperous tomorrow which Venezuelans believe can be obtained by those who sacrifice enough. They bounce about searching for the better future for their children and themselves.

This striving and struggling occurs in Venezuela without the host of public and private assistance agencies which are omnipresent in the developed countries. There is no aid to dependent children, no unemployment compensation, no social security retirement. In Ciudad Guayana, with 85,000 people, there is no YMCA, no Boys' Club, no Police Athletic League, no Big Brothers, no Catholic Youth Organization, no Neighborhood Association, no League of Women Voters. What organized "charity" there is, is handled by a private agency which cannot begin to reach the numbers of people whose diet is below subsistence levels. Each family must "make it" on its own in Ciudad Guayana.

Many families, overwhelmed with hungry children, constant illness, miserable quarters, and a hostile climate, just cannot make it. Education for their children *is* their chief ambition, but they must eat today if their children are to survive to go to school tomorrow.

In the wasteland of family failure stand the schools. In most areas of Ciudad Guayana the school building is the *only* institutional facility, the only agency which provides any service to the community. Outside of downtown San Félix, Puerto Ordaz, and areas where the CVG has scattered its offices, the only building which is not a home, bar, or store is the school. Do people then turn to the school when they meet difficulties which threaten the education of their children? They have nowhere else to turn. Does the school help parents overcome their problems so that it can more effectively carry out its role of educating all children without discrimination? Or is it merely a building where children must go for a certain number of years to receive a passport to a better life denied to their parents?

Extra-School Effects of the Educational System on Families

Logic dictates that the more a person is involved in the activities of an organization the more likely it is that he will subscribe to the norms of behavior which the organization promotes. This logic has been supported by a number of studies on organizations, including those which serve clients.[5] In this case the argument is that the more Guayana parents are involved with the school, the more they will see education as important, help their children in school, and have successful children. Data presented earlier showed a strong association between educational aspirations and enrollment in school. And mothers who claimed to help their children with their schoolwork were more likely to have children successful in school than those who were less involved in the learning process.

Involvement in the educational system can also be indirectly measured in terms of parental contact with the schools. Parents of children who finish high school in the developed countries are more active in school affairs than those whose children desert before graduation.[6] But in Guayana there are few school activities that involve parents. Not all of the public schools have even the ubiquitous parent-teacher association, although the Ministry of Education urges its formation. Nor do many schools regularly have events that the parents are expected to attend. Teachers seldom visit homes of their students, and the teacher is not a well-known person in the community, although as a symbol he is highly respected.

As a result, even though highly visible, the school is an unknown entity.
Some 15 percent of the parents of children of school age attending school in
Ciudad Guayana were unable to name *any* of the schools which their children
had attended. In fairness to the parents, it should be noted that unitaria schools
do not have names but rather numbers, which are more difficult to remember.
Also, some of the schools in Ciudad Guayana were only recently begun.
However, even eliminating these cases it was possible to find a sizable number of
mothers who could not name their child's school. Acquaintance with the
school building is usually guaranteed through the requirement that some adult
(the child's "representative") must enroll the child at the beginning of school
and assume responsibility for him. But the mothers of 10 percent of the children
attending school in the city have *never* been to their child's school, and another
55 percent visit the school only once a year, at enrollment time. As Table 9.3
shows, mothers of only 15 percent of the children have attended a parent-
teacher association meeting; another 17 percent of the children have mothers
who, with no invitation from the school, visited it.

Perhaps more meaningful than acquaintance with the school building is the
knowledge parents might have of the school as a social institution. According to
the respondents (see Table 9.4), more than 50 percent of the children in Ciudad
Guayana live in families where the mother has never met her child's teachers.
Contact with the teacher has apparently been limited to going to school once to
enroll the child or attendance at a parent-teacher meeting. Those very few
parents who have received a visit in their home by their teacher were so blessed,
in most instances, only because their child was failing in school. Teachers do
not frequently visit the homes of children who do well in school.

TABLE 9.3
Contact with School by Mothers in Ciudad Guayana

Reason for contact	N	%
Never visited school	1,024	10.0
Enrollment only	5,682	55.5
Parent-Teacher Association meeting	1,545	15.1
Called by teacher	242	2.4
Went on own account	1,746	17.0
Total	10,239	100.0

TABLE 9.4
Contact with Teachers by Mothers in Ciudad Guayana

Reason for contact	N	%
Never met teacher	5,279	51.5
Enrollment	1,648	16.1
Parent-Teacher Association meeting	1,545	15.1
Called by teacher	242	2.4
Teacher visited house	238	2.4
Went on own account	1,285	12.5
Total	10,237	100.0

The lack of contact between teachers and parents is unfortunate for a visit by the teacher could have a strong impact on the family. Mothers who had been visited by a teacher responded to the question, "How do you know that teachers are interested in the children?" by saying that the visit of the teacher proved his interest. On the other hand, persons who had never met a teacher explained the teachers' interest on the basis of their position, for example, "because they are teachers." The visits to homes by interviewers in the study, asking people about

TABLE 9.5
Knowledge of School and Achievement Pattern

			Does Respondent Know School Name?			
			Yes	No	N	%
	Nonenroller		14.7	32.5		
		N	63	37	100	18.4
	Nonattender	%	21.2	28.1		
		N	91	32	123	22.6
Academic	Nonachiever	%	29.5	29.8		
Achievement Pattern		N	127	34	161	29.6
	Achiever	%	34.7	9.6		
		N	149	11	160	29.4
	Total		430	114	544	
	Percent		79.0	21.0		100.0

Chi-square Statistic = 36.596 with 3 degrees of freedom, $p < 0.001$.

TABLE 9.6
Reason for Visiting School and Achievement Pattern

| | | | Why Respondent Visited School | | | |
			Never visited	Enrollment	Teacher contact	N	%
	Nonenroller	%	22.7	19.1	14.0		
		N	17	56	24	97	18.0
	Nonattender	%	29.3	25.6	14.5		
		N	22	75	25	122	22.6
Academic	Nonachiever	%	26.7	27.6	34.9		
Achievement Pattern		N	20	81	60	161	29.8
	Achiever	%	21.3	27.6	36.6		
		N	16	81	63	160	29.6
	Total		75	293	172	540	
	Percent		13.9	54.3	31.9		100.0

Chi-square Statistic = 17.470 with 6 degrees of freedom, $p < 0.01$.

TABLE 9.7
Contact with Teacher and Achievement Pattern

| | | | How Respondent Knew Teacher | | | |
			Did not know	Teacher initiated	Self-initiated	N	%
	Nonenroller	%	20.7	19.7	8.8		
		N	63	24	10	97	18.0
	Nonattender	%	24.9	27.0	11.5		
		N	76	33	13	122	22.6
Academic	Nonachiever	%	29.8	25.4	34.5		
Achievement Pattern		N	91	31	39	161	29.8
	Achiever	%	24.6	27.9	45.1		
		N	75	34	51	160	29.6
	Total		305	122	113	540	
	Percent		56.5	22.6	20.9		100.0

Chi-square Statistic = 28.145 with 6 degrees of freedom, $p < 0.01$.

their hopes and dreams for the future and the education of their children, resulted in a number of families seeking enrollment for their children.[7] Furthermore, knowledge of the school's name and contact with the child's teacher by his mother is associated with enrollment in school and academic success. This is shown in Tables 9.5, 9.6, and 9.7. Children are more likely to be doing well in school if their mother knows the school's name, if their mother has met a teacher, and especially if their mother took it on herself to meet the teacher.

Of course, these tables could be interpreted to mean only that more highly motivated parents are more likely both to visit the teacher and to see to the education of their children. The associations cannot be explained on the basis of the income and education level of the family for they are equally strong in both low and high groups. This is not the case for groups of mothers high and low on motivation for education. Within the group of highly motivated mothers, children are more likely to be doing well in school if their mother has met a teacher than if she has not. For those with moderately ambitious plans for their children the relationships become somewhat confused; there is no pattern of success associated with contact with a teacher. Children with mothers without motivation (that is, those who failed to mention education as a goal for their children) are again more likely to be successful in school if their mother has met a teacher. These findings suggest that the contact of mother and teacher affects the child's school success independently of how motivated the mother is.

The extent to which parents are involved in or committed to the school system can also be tapped by asking about friendship with teachers. Parents who count a teacher among their acquaintances might feel less "social distance" from the school, and would be more likely to emphasize education positively to the child. There was a strong relationship between academic standing and friendship with a teacher (see Table 9.8).[8] There is, however, also a relationship between social class (that is, family income and education) and friendship with a teacher; 65 percent of the above average education and income families claim a friendship with a teacher as compared to 47 percent of the whole sample. When family income and education are controlled, the relationship between friendship with a teacher and school success disappears for the higher income and education group, *but not for the low income and education group*. For these persons, friendship with a teacher, who has both higher economic and social status than low-income parents, is associated with educational attainment for the child.

None of these arguments should be taken as positive proof of a causal relationship between contact with the school system and educational achieve-

TABLE 9.8
Friendship with Teacher and Achievement Pattern

| | | | Is Respondent Friend of Teacher? | | | |
			Yes	No	N	%
	Nonenroller	%	18.7	30.3		
		N	52	97	149	24.9
	Nonattender	%	20.9	21.9		
		N	58	70	128	21.4
Academic	Nonachiever	%	28.1	25.9		
Achievement Pattern		N	78	83	161	26.9
	Achiever	%	32.4	21.9		
		N	90	70	160	26.8
	Total		278	320	598	
	Percent		46.5	53.5		100.0

Chi-square Statistic $= 14.493$ with 3 degrees of freedom, $p < 0.01$.

ment. It seems only logical to expect that more motivated parents will seek out the contact and that they will also educate their children. But the findings do indicate strongly that increased contact of teachers with parents should result in increased achievement of children, that is, increased school efficiency.

Perhaps more important is the role the school could play in supporting families in their attempts to educate their children. Given the still anomic state of life in Ciudad Guayana, the absence of private or governmental organizations that aid families in distress, the school stands alone as an institution which can help parents to carry out their responsibilities and fulfill their dreams. If the school system is considered as conceived here, as having the role of educating children, then it follows that the schools must attempt in every possible way to create conditions under which children become educated. In Ciudad Guayana this means three things. First, the school must be omnipresent. There must be buildings to receive all those who wish to apply, sufficient in quantity and size to form groups of students of manageable number. Second, teachers and school administrators must be capable of imparting instruction. Finally, probably of greatest importance, teachers and school administrators must be trained to promote family and community conditions which foster enrollment, attendance, and achievement of the children. The school must consider its task to include attempts to ameliorate the disruptive and destructive effects of the conditions which families experience. Failure of the school to assume this responsibility in Ciudad Guayana (and in many of the cities and towns of Latin America) can only mean that the school will continue to be a highly inefficient organization, serving well only a privileged minority.

Recognition of the differing needs of families in the community which it serves will permit the school to reach into each home with programs designed to maximize school attendance and achievement. Chapters 10 through 13 sketch out the frame of one possible set of programs. The idea is that the school needs to take up the challenge of human resource development in the total community, rather than limit itself to "education" of a few fortunates. The school in Ciudad Guayana must, because there is no one else to do it, serve to stimulate within the community those attitudes and skills necessary for the people of the community to begin to resolve their own problems. The school must create a "critical mass" of informed, active, and competent citizens who will demand and/or create services and organizations necessary for families to plan and realize their futures. Until this is done, the school will continue to be inefficient and discriminatory.

10
A Multivariate Characterization of Schooling and the Barrio Family

Introductory Note

Multivariate analysis preceded the nonparametric testing of the antecedents and consequences of school success and failure in Ciudad Guayana. The more general analysis indicated possible relationships for testing in later variable-by-variable comparisons. Additionally, it yielded useful insights into the relationships among main variables and the influence of zero, first, and higher order relationships.

It is best to be quite explicit about what the multivariate analysis did and did not do. It provided far richer insights into relationships among variables than the simple analysis did. But the insights came at some cost. In most cases the analysis furnished indications, not confirmation of hypotheses by tests. On the other hand, the more straightforward variable-by-variable test obviously provided no tests of interaction with other variables that did not enter into the comparison. Any choice has costs and benefits. The rich can choose to do analysis both ways, but not both at once. The very smart may even devise a way to get both rigor and richness simultaneously.

In this chapter, the indications furnished by the multivariate analysis are woven into narrative form to make reading more tolerable for all, and to spare those who do not have the patience to piece out the how and why of the analysis scheme. For those interested in peeking behind the prose facade, Appendix C presents indications based on key tables and, in some cases, statistical tests. For the more persistent still, there are many volumes of computer print-out; and for the absolutely unflagging, there are the data cards; but it is impossible to guarantee access to the original respondents. Interviewing was heavy among the shifting populations of the poor barrios where tenure is brief in a boomtown such as Ciudad Guayana.

Correlates of School Success

Seven variables indicated school enrollment, attendance, and achievement measured by regular grade promotion. In the analysis these can be viewed as dependent or criterion variables.

Forty variables showed the status of the mother and the family and may be viewed as antecedent or independent variables. The more modest term "correlate" is perhaps better. The forty correlates may be sorted into six major groupings of variables.

1. *Economics A:* Income, consumption, living standard reflected by amenities.
2. *Economics B:* Occupation and job status.
3. *Social-Cultural:* Education, cultural patterns, and life style.
4. *Urban-Stability:* Urban-residential stability versus rural-migrant.
5. *Family:* Family stability, marital status.
6. *Psychological-Motivational:* Goals and ambitions of mother; views on child rearing.

There is overlapping inasmuch as some variables can be assigned to more than one group. Family education, for example, could go into Category 3 or 5. There is also communality, in that large numbers of families tend to be high on all variable groups and all variables, whereas others are uniformly low.

The multivariate analysis sorted out two extreme groups at once. There were those who were high on all correlate variables and high on the criterion measures of school enrollment, attendance, and achievement. As expected, the analysis tended to throw into sharp relief the deprived or poverty culture family, and to indicate the enormity of the task of the school in doing something about the very poor family because of the self-perpetuating nature of poverty— it was precisely those who needed education most who got the least of it.

The highly successful families and the highly unsuccessful families were not the most interesting. It is the deviant cases, the poor but successful and the affluent but unsuccessful, that merit closer study.

Economics A: Income and Consumption. Not surprisingly students from economically favored families, as measured by family income, showed successful school histories. By and large, children of parents with higher earnings enrolled early, attended faithfully, and were promoted regularly. But this was not always the case. Some children came from fairly high-income families and showed poor school performance; some children came from low-income households and showed highly successful school histories. There were some marked deviations in the relationship between income or earnings and school performance which suggested the boomtown nature of Ciudad Guayana.

Some parents, recent migrants from rural poverty, were earning substantial incomes, but this had not yet had a chance to affect the school performance of the children. This was shown most clearly by the fact that possession of material goods and household amenities (refrigerators, washing machines) was much more closely related to school success than income. The possession of amenities marked families that had sufficient earnings over a period of time to affect their consumption patterns. Lack of possessions and amenities also characterized households where high earnings were dissipated in less wholesome forms of consumption. In households with possessions, school success was much higher than in families where earnings were merely high. When earnings and possession of amenities went with high cultural and social attainment (for example, newspaper readership or club membership), school performance was almost always high among children in the family. In summary, then, although income was an important correlate of school success, it was not in and of itself sufficient to guarantee school performance.

In view of the failure of income alone to relate unambiguously to school success, one wonders how effective negative income tax proposals or family subsidies will be in bringing families rapidly out of the culture of poverty to self-sustaining improvement. Money alone will not do it. Only after the money brings amenities and comforts and these bring leisure and cultural exposure will there be a very marked change. It would be interesting to study the time required to effect these changes. Is it a generation? Less? More? Some of the individual cases of rural migrants who climb in one generation suggest that it does not require more than one generation for many individuals who are not operating under other kinds of disadvantages, physical, psychological, social, or racial.

Economics B: Production and Occupation. If the first group could be called the consumption variables, the second might be called production variables, inasmuch as they measure the performance or status of the spouse in the work force. The situation is somewhat analogous to the consumption side where the possession of household amenities, mirroring stability and earnings over a period, is highly related to school success. The production variables show that occupational stability is more significantly related to school performance than current occupational status. Occupational status may have only recently been attained, but steady employment over a period of years means that children have enrolled early and attended faithfully. Job stability appears to be more highly related to school success than high earnings. High earnings come and go for some of the barrio families. When "The Big Money" comes, it sometimes gets used up on senseless consumption. When the money goes, it creates chaos in the family. Nothing is perhaps worse than bouts of affluence alternating with unemployment. This devastates school performance, as other data in the study show. Often, it is the family crisis—father loses job and migrates or deserts— which puts an end to schooling early for the children.

Whatever is done to aid the barrio dwellers must be steady and consistent, or it is likely to create more harm than good. This certainly has clear implications for social assistance policies in the barrios. Anti-poverty campaigns featuring large labor-intensive work projects are good if they are sustained over a suffi- cient period of time—for some this will be indefinite—but they may do more harm than good if they are one-shot temporary measures. The one-shot tem- porary measure raises expectations and ambitions, only to dash them when the project ends. The end of the project brings unemployment and family crisis such as desertion, and schooling dies.

Occupational mobility (moving to increasingly higher status jobs) showed very different relationships from other measures such as earnings, job status, and job stability. Mobility had, however, too erratic a relationship to reveal clear patterns, other than the fact that it was different. On the negative side low status occupation went with school failure, but not as clearly as high status went with school success.

Social-Cultural Correlates. Social-cultural correlates went much more closely with school achievement than did economic status. It is scarcely surprising that family education went with school success. The educational level of the mother, but not the father, the average education of the family, which is natural inas- much as it included the children's educational attainment, the average education of adult members of the family, the mother having more education than her spouse, all correlated highly with school enrollment, attendance, and achieve- ment of the children. Education tends to run in families and there is nothing surprising in this except that again it indicates the enormous task that schools have educating the noneducated family and the relatively easier task schools

have in bringing education to children of families where family education level
is already high. Again, education is a stable possession.

It is more interesting, perhaps, that certain indirect measures of cultural
attainment also correlated very highly with school success. Cultural contacts of
the family, reflected by reading newspapers, listening to radios—television was
not then common in the Guayana—all went with school achievement. Urban
life style and high contact with the world through communications media and
club membership went with educational attainment. There were also indications
that church membership went with school success and that the general cultural
level of the home was importantly related to school performance. Again there is
nothing startling about this. There is no evidence that listening to the radio,
reading newspapers, belonging to clubs, discussing affairs with friends, and
attending church had a direct effect on the children's education. These
characteristics simply were high in families where the children succeeded in
school.

Urban-Residential Stability. Parents and children from rural backgrounds
showed marked disadvantages in their school careers. Children from rural
backgrounds enrolled late in school and this related to lack of success, but the
strong relationship was between rural background and late age at initial enrollment rather than rural background and attendance and achievement. Many
children from rural areas, once they gained access to the schools, showed
steady progress through the grades. Indications were that the deprivations
of life on isolated conucos were not lasting, and that the schools could
overcome these deficiencies if the families could stay together and escape
crises.

The other side of this was the urban opportunity factor. Families, otherwise
quite poor, that had long been resident in urban areas had marked advantages
in schooling. Their children enrolled early, attended regularly, and passed. If the
mother was born and lived in a large city, if the family had generally resided in
large cities, and if the children had lived in cities, this showed in school enrollment and achievement. The families who come to urban areas to gain educational advantages for the children seem to have reason on their side. Whatever
other disadvantages they suffer, the children do get into school in numbers that
would be impossible in rural areas. Partly, the rural disadvantage is a function
of time and history in Venezuela. Currently and in the future, children will have
greater opportunity at schooling, even in the rural areas. Under Pérez Jiménez
opportunity was minimal.

Urban residence also tended to go with a more cultured life style and exposure to mass media and social club membership. Subjects born in cities other than Guayana did better than those born locally, and so did their children. The reason is obvious. Mothers born in and around Guayana were born into an isolated, semi-rural region which was what the area around San Félix was until 1955. Now that Guayana is a larger city, its native-born are favored compared with migrants from other areas.

In Guayana the schools may have an important task of "urbanizing" rural migrant families, in addition to merely providing formal education to the children. In the section on adult education, which highlights the necessity of developing school programs to meet the needs of the entire barrio family, there are details as to what "education for urban intelligence" may mean for the barrio families.

Migration also affected school enrollment and achievement. Rural migrants had more difficulties than migrants from urban areas but the mere instability of migrant life, reflected in frequency of moves, also affected schooling adversely. There were probably a variety of reasons for this. First, the moving itself had an unsettling effect on families and on the children. Second, the frequent moves often indicated family crises and the escape from joblessness or desertion. Last, school transfer required the parents to secure a grade completion paper which they often did not do. Without the transfer paper children lost progress in school and probably interest as well. A moderate amount of moving had little effect on school success in Guayana, inasmuch as almost all families were fairly recent migrants and the most stable residents date back to the rural depressed past of San Félix. When there were a great many moves, however, schooling was indeed affected. In those cases where there was a good deal of migration, but always within urban areas, there was much less effect on education of children. These could be families of fathers with fairly high skills, who are moving in order to profit from better job opportunities.

Family Stability and Marital Status. A variety of measures of family status were highly related to school enrollment, attendance, and achievement. The marital status of the mother had a definite relation, although it may not always have been the possession of a piece of paper or a church-blessed union so much as the stability of union with the same partner, whatever the legal or religious niceties. Unions outdating the children were more highly correlated with school success than more casual arrangements, though not vastly so. School success went with the children's belonging to both parents rather than to the mother alone. Mothers almost always kept the children, in the event of a split, so this would reflect whether or not the child belonged to the present male partner. When the child did belong, the child did better in school.

Family stability was more important for school enrollment and achievement than income. The stable, educated family had children who almost always succeeded in school. Average education of the family, naturally, was a strong correlate of school success. This is hardly surprising. It takes a bit more ingenuity to explain why the average number of adults in the family also correlated highly with school performance. Specifically, families in which there were a low number of adult members had children who succeeded in school. This seems to mark a young, nuclear family, in which the father is living with the mother and the children. Low average number of adults, then, is taken as a measure of nuclear families and stability.

In general the family that had all the advantages had children who did well in school. The effect of halo was widespread. In households where earnings were high, possessions and amenities high, education and culture high, and family stability high, children succeeded in school.

There is one other group of correlates which will be discussed next that also went with school success. However, before leaving the family one anomaly should be noted. Or perhaps it is not such an anomaly. Average family education, average adult education, and education of the mother all went with school success. When the mother had more education than the spouse, this also related to school success. But the relationship of schooling with the male spouse's education and behavior was opposite. Low education of the spouse went with school success. And low participation of the spouse in the rearing of the child also went with school success. When the man participated—or was it interfered?—in the rearing of the children, school success was lower. The relationships of low spouse participation in child rearing and education of the spouse with school success are difficult to explain. Obviously, a mother's status and behavior are more important to the children than her husband's, but why an uneducated and indifferent father should enhance his child's education is difficult to explain. Perhaps in some situations a mother, despite her own level of educational attainment, dominates her husband and forces the children to enroll and study. This is wild conjecture and the analysis did not provide any means to corroborate it.

Psychological: Goals and Motivations of the Barrio Mother. Most interesting of all was the indication that more than income, more than material possessions, more than culture, and more than family stability, the mother's expressed goal that her children should be educated related to school enrollment. The legendary indifference of the Latin American poor toward education did not appear among this group of barrio mothers. The presumption—or rationalization—that poor barrio dwellers were uninterested in education and unwilling to make necessary sacrifices had no confirmation. In this study mothers stated that they wanted education for their children, and they took measures, some relatively heroic given the costs and their income, to see that their children got education. In the poor barrios the mother could be a powerful instrumentality for improving schools if some way were found to harness her energy and dedication. The motivation is there.

The mother's desire for education for the child is more significant than the mother's desire for education for herself. The mother's general goals are unrelated to the children's school performance. The specific motivation for education is more realistic than long-term and general goals, which may merely reflect wishes with little realism. The long-range goal variable may be picking up unrealistic dreams and aspirations from mothers who are not cognizant of the necessity of taking steps early, especially in school, so that the child will have the basis for attaining the ambitious goals envisaged for later life. Some mothers do not perceive the means-end relationship between education and future economic and social attainment for their children. It is a task for the school to establish this awareness. But at least there is realistic motivation specifically addressed to schooling on which the schools may build.

Although there is a high relationship between the mother's motivation for education and the education attained by the children, the relationship between mother's motivation for education and her own educational attainment is not high. This is scarcely surprising given the lack of educational opportunity for rural women in past years. But at least motivation for education exists, and the adult education authorities must do everything possible to build on this. The mothers are far more interested in education for their children than for themselves. Usually this reflects past discouragement, present irrelevance of adult education programs, and lack of knowledge of the programs and their relevance to the work world on the part of mothers with limited education and urban and world experience.

The authorities in adult education must face the problem of informing and recruiting mothers—who are the sole support of many large families—so that they are equipped to do something more useful than perform menial services, do itinerant peddling, or become grocery prostitutes. Again and again the study showed that the mothers were highly motivated to make sacrifices for their children's education, but much less so to make any moves to educate themselves. Perhaps most of them feel that the chance is gone, and that if they attempt to get education and training they are diminishing the possibility of education for their children. Actually, the contrary is true, but the adult education authorities must inform the mothers of this. Feminine training courses help mothers to produce more and consume more wisely, and this will result in more resources available for the children's education rather than less.

The motivation variable is particularly high in families which seem otherwise disadvantaged in earnings and material possessions yet fairly high in educational success. It is the mother's motivation which makes the difference. If the mother has high goals for herself, particularly for education but for general accomplishment also, then the children enroll and succeed in school. These are families in which the mother has general pride and spirit with which she imbues the children. If the mother expresses wishes about improvement of her living standard in the event that the household moves, this does not go with high school achievement. These are the very poor mothers who wish for everything under the sun, but have little initiative or power in moving toward their dreams. Above all, the women of Guayana were realistic where their children were concerned. The highest single correlate of children's success in school was the educational attainment level the mother had for the children. However else mothers in the barrios dream, when they think of children's education they make sacrifices to attain their dreams.

The second most important finding in the analysis of psychological correlates with school success was the mother's preference for using reward rather than punishment in the rearing of the children. The mother who says she rewards rather than punishes her children usually has children who enroll early and succeed. There are a number of explanations for this. Perhaps reward takes more time and patience than punishment. A whack on the head requires less forethought and effort than the preparation of a birthday piñata or the planning of an excursion or the making of a dress. The mother who rewards might also be inclined to spend more time and effort seeing to it that her children attend and succeed in school. There is also sound theory from psychology to back the finding, in that reward is more effective in stimulating learning than punishment in forfending against nonlearning. Whatever the explanation, the multivariate analysis indicated beyond cavil of doubt that the preference for reward in child rearing was a correlate of school success.

An Educational Program for the Barrios

Based on the findings of the multivariate analysis, what can educational programs do to enhance the development of poor people in the barrios of Guayana? First, the school must mobilize the motive force of the barrio mothers. In the beginning, mothers will be more strongly motivated to provide education to their own children rather than to sacrifice for education generally on a community-wide basis. But broader and less individualized motivations can be generated. After motivations are broadened, authorities must stimulate interest among mothers to get education and training for themselves in the ODEA and adult education INCE programs. If a total community program offering education for the entire family could be created, it would accomplish many things at once. The sequence of barrio programs should be, first, reward through entertainment, second, attraction through practical relevance to life requirements, and last, intellectual and spiritual stimulus and reward. Unless the programs run through all cycles and provide entertainment, practicality, and intellectual and spiritual sustenance, they will be less than complete, less than penetrating, and less than lasting.

It seems obvious that whatever program is devised, it cannot be in the form of a quick or crash solution. Poverty is not broken in quick or massive campaigns. The effects of poverty are cumulative and persistent and only lengthy periods of stability in employment and earnings will affect the problem. Still, the study did give signs that money is not everything and that many useful things can be done despite limited resources. Similar studies merely reveal that the overwhelming shortage of money affects everything so that all other problems and possibilities are insignificant by comparison. But programs aimed at capitalizing on the motivation of barrio women need not be expensive. Programs which contribute to communication and to raising the general cultural level and world awareness of barrio dwellers are not expensive on a unit cost basis. Programs which provide orientation to urban living and which assist and orient the migrants in their early days are not expensive. The quicker the new migrant can be reached, the better.

It is not easy to promote programs which develop morality and family stability, but it can be done, given skilled and dedicated workers and some degree of economic stability. It cannot be done by preachment and moralizing, but it can be done by demonstrating the rewards of healthful consumption and avoidance of abuse. Such programs take time. Human development can be aided by programs which make the general surroundings less harsh. Cleanup campaigns are not vastly expensive. The study indicated, however, that education and training must go beyond meeting the mere work force requirements of the people. The spirit of the barrio people must be animated and the value structures influenced or the result will merely be higher earnings that permit greater indulgence and waste. Venezuela and Guayana show some signs of tending toward the latter.

The most important characteristic of any program for children, adults, or for general barrio development is continuity and stability in the allocation of resources, rather than the absolute amount. Programs must be run on the most even keel possible for it is this very evenness and continuity that are missing from the lives of the poor who live on the margins of crisis and disaster. Far better to promise less and deliver less, but to deliver it steadily and with a predictable rhythm over a long period. The level of resources should be even and kept this way over a long time, and the intervention of outside agents of change should also be consistent and lasting. The long-term resident agent works more effectively not just because he learns the situation better, but because the people in the situation come to know him better and to rely on him and believe that he will stay.

Avoidance of the large initial splash is one of the most difficult things to accomplish in Latin America. Avoidance of the grandiose promise, for education or for any other social benefit, is difficult in Guayana and Venezuela generally. The most difficult achievement in education and development is sustained effort.

There are some encouraging signs. The clustering of good and bad correlates indicates that although the initial breakthrough may be extremely difficult, once it has been accomplished, interaction will work the other way and the spread can be much faster. The wellsprings of motivation are there. The new educational programs need only tap them. Average education of children and the percentage of children attending also had a high relationship. If one child goes to school and succeeds, the probability is that all will go and do fairly well.

For those charged with providing school opportunity in Ciudad Guayana, the social and economic implications are clear. Effective programs can be run for adults at low cost, but school programs will require a large investment. Poverty, discomfort, and lack of educational opportunity tend to cluster in certain families and there are large pockets of thoroughly disadvantaged families in Ciudad Guayana. Poor and without the means to ensure education for their children, the likelihood is that poverty, ignorance, and disease are going to be transmitted down through the generations. It is not enough that a wisp of educational opportunity is available to these people. Only a very aggressive educational operation is going to bring the children into the schools and keep them there. The study demonstrates that the barrio families will take advantage of education when they have a halfway decent chance of getting it. But an indifferent and low-cost and low-quality program is not going to reach the hard-core cases. Required is an approach that covers the entire family and is supplemented by social welfare action; and this will be expensive if all that needs to be done is done well. It is no exaggeration to say that the present low unit cost education provided to children of the very poor in the Guayana public schools represents almost a total waste of resources. As a minimal estimate, the per unit cost must be tripled. It is also clear that Guayana is a compensatory education problem area. The "normal" educational opportunity—normal meaning low quality—will not serve the barrio populations of Guayana any more than it has served the ghetto and slum populations of the central cities of the world.

The barrio mothers are the key to educational development in Guayana. They have high motivation to educate their children. There are two possible approaches. The motivation can be capitalized on directly and mothers can be involved in assisting educational programs for their children. Or the motivation can be exploited more indirectly. Mothers can be enrolled in adult education and training courses which will raise their earnings and improve home management and ultimately enhance the educational possibilities of the children. This may, in the long pull, be the best way, but adult education authorities must convince the mothers of this.

Part Two
From Study to School Program: The Utilization of Research Findings

The research reported in the previous chapters has intrinsic interest, but the main objective of the authors was to use it as the basis for developing actual school programs in Ciudad Guayana. Throughout the research report there have been recommendations for translating the research results into educational planning and the development of school programs. In this part of the book the matter is taken up more explicitly and a prescription for an education and training program for Ciudad Guayana is written. There are two main points of emphasis in the plan: formal education which is confined to day school programs at the preprimary, primary, and middle school levels; and informal education which includes programs of education and community development for adults.

11

The Design of an Efficient School System for Ciudad Guayana

It will do no real good to modify only some parts of the educational programs of Ciudad Guayana. The system must be redesigned. The need is not to pick out a few programs piecemeal from all the possible remedies needed in the schools of Ciudad Guayana, for piecemeal remediation will, beyond a certain point, yield very little. As fast as one part of the system is fixed, another will break down and require attention. To write out a list of such projects is the same as preparing detailed instructions for bailing a very leaky boat. The enrollments and graduates projected in the previous chapters can come only if major changes are made in the educational system of Ciudad Guayana. The word *system* is important.

The study revealed clearly that there was no school system in Guayana and that this had a pronounced effect on the efficiency of the schools as reflected in the attendance and promotion of the children of barrio families. For example, children who had dropped out temporarily during a family crisis, brought on through illness or financial difficulties, often did not secure the necessary papers to assure re-entry when their home situations improved. For barrio children, as the study showed, the likelihood of at least one major family crisis during the course of their primary school years was very high.

The schools of Ciudad Guayana, as presently organized and staffed, have no school guidance or pupil welfare services whatsoever. Much less do they have any social service worker who can maintain family contact and assist the poorer families and their children in the face of emergencies that are almost chronic. The schools do not even have an effective administrative service which would handle the paper work to guarantee orderly withdrawal and protect the child's right of re-entry at the proper grade. The burden is thrown on the parents and the children, despite the educational level of the parents and the marked social distance between barrio family and school which the study reveals. The result, predictably, is chaos; wastage measured by retardation and dropout is high and efficiency low.

No very rich input for social services and guidance is outlined in the organizational plan which follows. The plan recommended would provide for organizing some centralized services such as pupil accounting and records and rudimentary guidance services. The central staff would also have a business manager. This would permit centralized purchasing and cut present wastefulness in the business management of the schools of Ciudad Guayana. The study showed that individual schools often purchased their own supplies retail from local stores. They were assigned a meager allotment and out of this they made do.

If the wastage within school levels is high, the wastage between them is even more appalling. There is currently no articulation between primary and middle schools in Ciudad Guayana. One can imagine the situation which faces the barrio mother when and if her child has been persistent and lucky enough to win through to a complete primary education. The child, age twelve to fourteen, aided by a parent with less than a primary education, must now choose a special purpose middle school, and in Guayana the choices are artisanal, technical-industrial, commercial, and general preparatory. This is an unaided choice which will affect the child for life.

There is not one iota of help available to parent or child in the schools of Ciudad Guayana as they are now organized. There is no one in the primary school assigned to encourage the child to go forward, and the staff of middle schools only discourage the child by complaining about his poor primary preparation without even knowing what goes on in the primary schools. But the situation is even worse than this. Inasmuch as there is no effective system even within the primary level, the preparations of the children differ greatly from school to school. Yet there is no cognizance of this in the middle schools. Each middle school sets its own rigid standards, teaches all courses at exactly the same level, and offers no remediation. It is, to use the Spanish phrase, degüello—no quarter is given.

The schools must be linked within and between levels. Primary teachers must know what will be expected of their students at middle school level, and middle school teachers must know what their children are supposed to learn in the primary level. This is particularly necessary to ensure adequate supervision and in-service training of teachers. The teachers in Ciudad Guayana are certified but at a minimal level of competence. Currently, in-service training programs operate out of the Instituto de Mejoramiento Profesional of the Ministry of Education in Caracas. Under such a system attention can only be sporadic; there are only occasional short courses by experts who fly into the zone. There is no possibility of follow-up and day-to-day supervision.

The same difficulties are observable in curriculum development. There is no continuity in science, mathematics, language arts, or social studies among the present isolated schools. The system proposed attempts to begin a solution of this problem by breaking down the barriers between levels and developing and coordinating curriculum and in-service training from grade one through middle level.

The survey revealed that the barrios are culturally barren. There are few books in the homes, and newspapers and magazines are equally scarce. This is hardly surprising in view of the literacy level of the parents. This being so, a heavy burden falls on the schools which provide about the only contact with the printed word the child will have. Under the proposed system there will be a school library and librarian in each primary school.

The library should serve not only the children but also the teachers who are woefully short of instructional materials. It must also someday serve the surrounding barrio through programs of cultural extension. The libraries must serve the children not only with supplementary reading materials but also in some cases by providing textbooks that parents cannot afford to buy. The study showed that many mothers had insufficient income to buy the cheapest school books for their children. Some mothers had incomes of less than $400 a year and the provision of textbooks for all their children would have cost $60. Under such circumstances it is impossible to expect them to buy books for the children.

A pilot program has already been started to remedy this hardship. In September of 1965 the CVG, in cooperation with the Ministry of Education and the Banco del Libro (a private organization which assists in establishing school and public libraries and in selecting and procuring textbooks), established a school library and free textbook program in seven of the public primary schools of the city. The program provides textbooks for all children in the seven schools, sets up a school reference library of 1,500 volumes, and trains teachers in library management. This program must be expanded to reach more of the poor families of the barrios, and perhaps should be broadened to include community

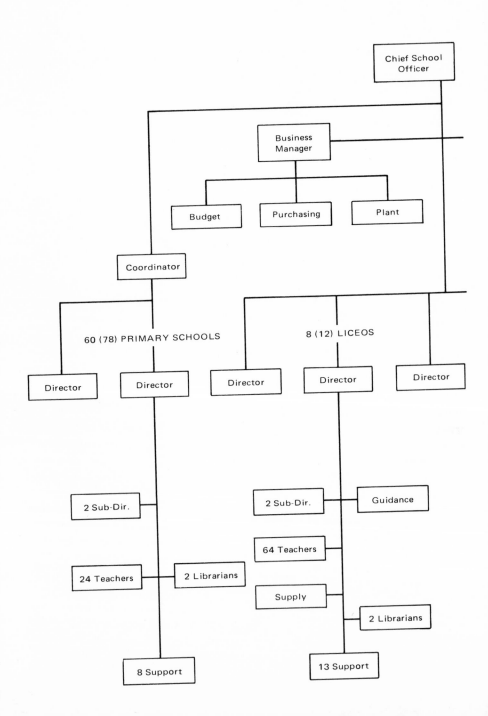

Figure 11.1 A model school system for Ciudad Guayana, 1975 (1980): Administrative staffing pattern.

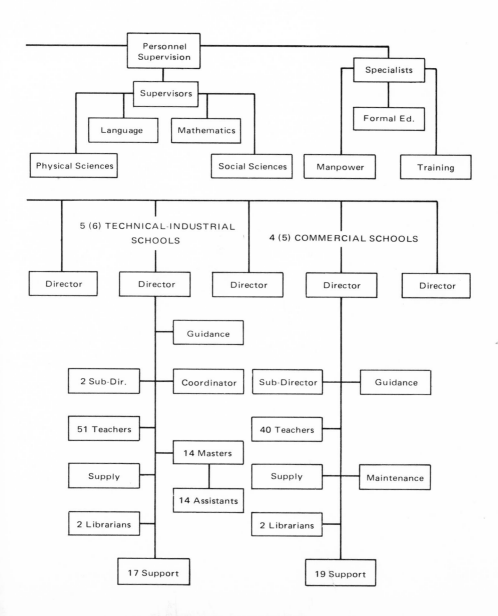

reading programs for the adults. One of the major weaknesses of conventional literacy campaigns and programs is the lack of graded reading materials to follow up the initial development of reading skills. This is reflected by the large relapse and loss rates observed some years after the first instruction. The notion is that the community school library program could provide the setting for graded, follow-up reading for adults.

In this chapter, system specifications and costs are written out in considerable detail. They imply programs and actions that should be taken as rapidly as possible, if anything approximating the system is to be in operation in Ciudad Guayana by 1980. The system is outlined in Figure 11.1 and the proposed organizational patterns for the various types of schools described in Tables 11.2 through 11.8. To reach the output targets proposed in Chapter 5 would require investment and expenditures which are summarized by educational levels and types in Table 11.1.

TABLE 11.1
Summary Table of Aggregate Operating Costs[a] for Guayana
Schools in 1975 and 1980 (Constant Prices)

1975	Total Cost	Students	Unit Cost
Primary Schools	29,280,000	55,770	525
Liceos	9,460,000	7,420	1,275
Technical-Industrial	12,464,000	8,200	1,520
Commercial	4,505,000	3,900	1,155
Total	55,709,000	75,290	740

1980			
Primary Schools	39,638,000	75,500	525
Comprehensive High Schools	45,451,000	30,200	1,505
Total	85,089,000	105,700	805

[a] Operating costs include proportionate costs for central administration of the system according to the model. All figures are bolivares. BS. 4.5 = U.S. $1.00.

A Central Administration for the City's Schools

The positions in central administration charted in Figure 11.1 and costed in Table 11.2 do not exist in the Ciudad Guayana schools as they are currently

TABLE 11.2

Staff Requirements and Costs of a Model School System for Ciudad Guayana, 1975–1980

Central Administration

Number	Title	Salary in 1966 Bs.
1	Chief school officer	31,300
1	Assistant business manager	28,200
1	Assistant personnel and supervision	28,200
1	Primary school supervisor	28,200
1	Fiscal officer (budget and central)	22,500
1	Purchase-supply officer	22,500
1	Physical plant officer	22,500
4	Supervisors (physical sciences, social sciences, language, arts, mathematics)	86,000
3	Guidance-testing specialists	64,500
	Manpower-vocational guidance	
	Formal education-educational guidance	
	Training systems	
3	Private secretaries	27,900
3	Secretary-accountants	31,800
6	Secretaries-clerk typists	45,000
2	Messenger-clerks	13,500
2	Janitors-maintenance men	13,500
	Total Staff Salaries	Bs. 465,600
	Benefits 46,600	
	Supplies 34,000	
	Misc. services 18,600	
	Total central administration cost per year	Bs. 564,800

managed, but there is nothing preventing such an organization except resistance to change. The salaries are based on Venezuelan experience. The system, as outlined, does not exist anywhere in Venezuela. The job titles are reasonably obvious and require no special comment, except to emphasize these points:

1. The chief school officer will have under his immediate control the seventeen directors of secondary schools. The coordinator of primary schools will also report to the chief officer. This will give him a larger number of people reporting directly to him than is usually recommended, but the alternative of naming an assistant in charge of primary and an assistant in charge of secondary schools may well bring the system back to the same divided and unarticulated state in

which it currently exists. The problem requires study and possible modification. The major objective in setting up the central office is to unify the system. It should be noted that the present administrative structure adds only Bs. 6 a year to the per-pupil costs of the system, an incredibly low cost when the possible benefits are accounted.

As is currently provided by law, the private schools will be under the jurisdiction, at least for curriculum, of the public school officer. An exact programing of public and private school share of the enrollment load of the future is not possible at this time. The assumption is that the number of private schools will increase very slightly, if at all, up to 1975. Private schools will handle a larger share of the enrollment load than presently, but this can be effected with the existing capacity. The study showed that almost none of the barrio children was attending the formally organized private schools. For many of the barrio families even the expense of sending the children to regular public schools was formidable and parents could not afford the shoes, clothing, books, and educational materials required. In some cases the parents sent the children to neighborhood dame schools, buying an "education" of unknown and dubious quality. These schools, as well as the unitaria schools, should be suppressed during the plan years.

2. The supervisory staff, under the assistant chief school officer, is divided by major curriculum areas and not by levels or kinds of schools. Their major task would be curriculum development. Again the objective is system unity and articulation among levels. More supervisors would have to be added to handle the other special fields. This is a most moderate staffing proposal. The objective is to have coordinators in the curriculum areas who work at all levels. This approach has been tried in other countries and has provoked problems, but they seem to have been often less serious than problems caused by the absence of such a system.

3. The guidance specialists are not conventional counselors and this group might better be called the Human Resource Development Planning Section. There is a specialist in vocational guidance and manpower planning and development who would keep the school system informed of major developments in industry and the labor market. There is a specialist in educational guidance who would advise on opportunities for further education within and outside of the region. The same specialist would administer scholarship and student welfare funds. Each secondary school would have its own guidance personnel. The educational guidance specialist in the central staff would also assist and

advise primary school directors. The third staff member would be charged with the planning and implementation of school-industry related training programs. He would keep in close touch with INCE and with the larger industries and their apprenticeship programs. Such an assignment is not common in any existing school system anywhere, but there is a need for it and nothing has demonstrated that it will not work.

No costing for office space or building has been included.

Preprimary Sections

Table 11.3 sets out the cost of running one preprimary section with each shift of the basic primary school. Provision of preprimary education is fundamental for the barrio children of Ciudad Guayana, and ideally a much larger program would be recommended. There are, of course, no guarantees that if preprimary programs were developed they would be any less rigid and arid than the present first grade programs are. Still, if the insistence on "standards" could be relaxed a bit in preprimary level by emphasizing that it is a vestibular experience and a readiness stage rather than a criterion situation in which youngsters must perform or perish, the preprimary experience could be most fruitful. The likelihood is that it would be possible to introduce such notions to Latin American preprimary teachers. Experience in other countries suggests that preprimary programs are free of the rigid standards that are clamped down once

TABLE 11.3
Costs of Model Primary School

	Students	Total Annual Operating Cost	Unit Costs[a]
Basic Primary School	960	Bs. 498,700	Bs. 519.4
Preprimary Added	1,040	540,000	519.2
Capital Investment			
Basic Primary			
Construction, Installation		Bs. 575,000	
Land		300,000	
Preprimary Added			
Construction, Installation		639,000	
Land		330,000	

[a] Per pupil enrolled.

primary school begins. But teachers would have to be specially trained for the
level and many of the current primary school teachers are unsuited for it. They
would merely move their standards down one more grade and start the children
reading a year early. This is one reason for recommending a modest beginning,
with two sections in each primary school. The second reason is the availability
of funds.

Later a proposal will be made for making the school more responsive to the
total economic and social needs of the surrounding barrios. One important
service could be that of providing day care and some instruction for children in
the preprimary years. Kindergarten and nursery schools, even if devoid of
instructional content, could be important contributors to the socialization of
children from restricted homes, and child health and nutrition programs, so
pitifully inadequate in Ciudad Guayana, could be run more effectively at school
centers. Classes in child care could also be run at such centers more effectively
and less expensively than by random visits to homes scattered through the chaos
of the unurbanized barrios. Much of the later absenteeism, a result of illness and
malnutrition, could be cut if preventative programs could be launched earlier.

Primary Level Schools

The School and Community Social Work. The plan for day primary schools
includes no provision for social workers attached to the schools. This should be
part of the total school-community program which would be run in the informal
or adult education program to be described in the next chapter.

Despite the appalling problems of barrio families it is unclear how much the
schools can do to help in the broader aspects of social and moral regeneration.
In the next chapter it is proposed that social workers be attached to the schools
to assist in planning education and training programs to meet the wider economic and social needs of the barrios and to contribute maximally to community
development. The social workers would plan programs to involve the total
barrio family, and in this sense something would be contributed toward assisting
children in the regular day primary programs. They would also be able to
contribute to improving pupil welfare services which are now nonexistent, but it
seems naive to hope that any major program of social work can be centered in
the day primary schools during the next few years.

It is unclear whether the school could teach anything that would be directly
addressed to promoting family stability. The birth rate in Ciudad Guayana is
one of the highest in the world and this undoubtedly contributes to the general

misery. Whether or not the schools could become involved in population control is debatable. Perhaps the school could contribute by informing people of the seriousness of the situation and referring families to sources of aid. The schools could also incorporate information in their curricula about the general problem and presumably make some contribution to changing the attitudes of indifference which now prevail. But the area is too sensitive for an abrupt beginning. There would first have to be research into possibilities and limitations.

Primary School Operating Cost. A model primary school operation is detailed and costed in Table 11.4. This minimal staff is necessary to operate the Ciudad Guayana primary schools at a level of efficiency sufficient to reach the enrollment and graduates projected in the previous chapters. The total annual

TABLE 11.4
Model Primary School Organization for Ciudad Guayana

Primary School (960 students, double shift, 1975)			
1	Director	Bs.	18,000
2	Subdirectors		32,000
24	Classroom teachers		270,000
4	Special teachers		30,000
2	Librarians		22,500
2	Secretaries		15,000
2	Cleaning and maintenance men		13,500
	Total Staff Salaries	Bs.	401,000
	Benefits		40,300
	Medical services		10,800
	Repairs and maintenance		8,600
	Services (water, light, gas)		7,000
	Expendable supplies		6,300
	Furniture, equipment		15,500
	Library equipment		3,800
	Library books, Texts		5,400
	Total Primary Operating Cost	Bs.	498,700
	Unit Cost		519.4
	To Add Preprimary Capacity (double-shift, 80 students)		
	2 Preprimary teachers		22,500
	2 Teaching assistants		15,000
	Total	Bs.	37,500
	Benefits		3,800
	Total Preprimary Operating Costs		41,300

operating cost of a model primary unit is Bs. 498,700, at 1965 prices. The staff
is not overly elaborate and, in fact, corresponds to Ministry of Education
standards. The supporting costs also correspond to recommended costs,
although they are not the actual costs of schools that are currently operating in
Ciudad Guayana. The schools are actually operating at lower costs because the
necessary and recommended inputs are simply not assigned.

Even if the general system staff recommendations are not followed, the model
primary school costs in Table 11.4 should be useful for planners, and the
pattern should be adopted by 1975.

Middle-Level Schools: Operating Costs

Liceos. The staffing pattern, operating costs, and cost per pupil enrolled in
academic secondary schools (liceos) are shown in Table 11.5. The per-student
current cost is substantially higher than existing costs but efficiency will be

TABLE 11.5
Model Liceo Staffing Pattern, Operating Costs, Costs per Pupil Enrolled, and Capital Cost

Liceo (1,600 students, double shift, 1975)

1	Director	Bs. 25,000
2	Subdirectors	45,000
1	Career guidance officer	22,500
64	Classroom teachers	1,363,200
8	Special teachers	160,000
2	Librarians	27,600
1	Secretary-accountant	10,600
2	Clerical secretaries	15,000
1	Supply and equipment officer (repair and maintenance)	17,700
1	Watchman	6,800
	Total Staff Salaries	Bs. 1,693,400
	Benefits	169,300
	Medical services	18,000
	Repairs and maintenance	22,200
	Services	15,200
	Supplies (incl. furniture, equipment, replacement)	64,000
	Library (equip. and texts)	42,400
	Total Operating Cost	Bs. 2,024,500
	Unit Cost	Bs. 1,265.3
	Capital Investment	
	Construction, Installation	Bs. 2,000,000
	Land	1,046,000

TABLE 11.6
Model Technical-Industrial School Staffing Pattern, Operating Costs per Pupil Enrolled, and
Capital Cost

Technical-Industrial School (1,600 students, double shift, 1975)		
1	Director	Bs. 25,000
2	Subdirectors	45,000
1	Vocational program coordinator	22,500
1	Guidance-placement officer	22,500
51	Classroom teachers	1,086,300
8	Special teachers	160,000
14	Shop masters	280,000
14	Assistant shop masters	172,200
2	Librarians	27,600
1	Secretary-accountant	10,600
2	Clerical secretaries	15,000
1	Supply and equipment officer	17,700
2	Repair and maintenance men	15,600
2	Janitors	13,500
1	Watchman	6,800
	Total Staff Salaries	Bs. 1,920,300
	Benefits	192,000
	Medical services	20,000
	Repair and maintenance	35,500
	Services	17,300
	Expendable supplies	177,000
	Furniture, equipment replacement	13,700
	Library	42,400
	Unit Cost	Bs. 1,511.4
	Total Operating Cost	Bs. 2,418,200
	Capital Investment	
	Construction, Installation	Bs. 3,550,000
	Land	1,775,000

substantially improved and a later chart will demonstrate that per-graduate
costs, a better measure of output, will not be higher. The present system, rather
than a comprehensive pattern, is assumed.

Technical-Industrial Schools. The staffing pattern, operating costs, and costs
per pupil enrolled in technical-industrial schools are shown in Table 11.6. The

same observations may be made about technical-industrial education as were made about liceo education. The costs are higher but the benefits greater with such a system.

Commercial Schools. The staffing pattern, operating costs, and costs per pupil enrolled in commercial schools are shown in Table 11.7, and the same observations apply.

Comprehensive Secondary Schools. Table 11.8 shows the staffing pattern, operating costs, and costs per student enrolled for a model comprehensive secondary school. This is planned for the year 1980 when presumably the

TABLE 11.7
Model Commercial School Staffing Pattern, Operating Costs, Costs per Pupil Enrolled, and Capital Cost

Commercial School (1,400 students, double shift, 1975)		
1	Director	Bs. 25,000
1	Subdirector	22,500
1	Guidance-placement officer	20,500
40	Classroom teachers	852,000
15	Special teachers	279,000
2	Librarians	27,600
1	Secretary-accountant	10,600
2	Clerical secretaries	15,000
1	Supply and equipment officer	17,700
1	Equipment maintenance man	17,700
1	Watchman	6,800
	Total Staff Salaries	Bs. 1,294,400
	Benefits	129,400
	Medical services	18,000
	Repair and maintenance	22,200
	Services	17,000
	Supplies, equipment replacement	86,000
	Library	37,100
	Total Operating Cost	Bs. 1,604,100
	Unit Cost	1,145.8
	Capital Investment	
	Construction, Installation	Bs. 2,000,000
	Land	1,000,000

TABLE 11.8

Model Comprehensive High School Staffing Pattern, Operating Costs and Costs per Pupil Enrolled

Comprehensive High School (2,300 students, single shift, 1980)

1	Director	
2	Subdirectors	Bs. 31,300
3	Program coordinators (academic, industrial, commercial)	45,000
1	Guidance director	67,500
1	Placement officer (vocational education)	22,500
78	Classroom teachers	20,500
10	Commercial teachers	1,661,400
16	Special teachers	212,500
7	Shop masters	320,000
7	Assistant shop masters	140,000
3	Resource librarians	86,800
2	Secretary-accountants	41,400
3	Clerical secretaries	21,200
1	Supply and equipment officer	22,500
3	Repair-maintenance men	17,700
2	Watchmen, security guards	20,700
		13,600
	Total Staff Salaries	Bs. 2,744,600
	Benefits	274,400
	Repairs and maintenance	25,000
	Services	51,100
	Supplies (incl. furniture and equipment)	220,300
	Total Operating Cost	Bs. 3,315,400
	Unit Cost	Bs. 1,441.5

secondary school pattern in Venezuela will be modified toward the comprehensive. Venezuelan educators have discussed the possibility of a comprehensive pattern at the secondary level. Plans for pilot schools have been drawn. It is impossible to predict whether or not the pattern can be established by 1980, but a glimpse of the model is worthwhile. The feature to note is that the unit is for single session. Presumably, by that date resources should permit this pattern. Despite the single session, unit costs are not appreciably higher. This is a feature of the scale of the operation. The unit, as is common with most efficiently run comprehensive schools, is large. Certain improvements in educational technology have also been assumed. There seems ample justification for assuming that large classes will feature instruction through television, although no specific allocation was put in for a closed circuit installation. Programed instruction through machines should also be a feature by that year, and the technology should lower teacher ratios and costs for instruction. Because changes in technology are presumed, it is difficult and perhaps useless to estimate the capital cost for building, installations, and equipment.

The presumed advantages of the comprehensive school should be noted here. There should be greater efficiency because of the unitary management and the larger size. There should also be greater flexibility in student programing. Students should be able to transfer from one program to another within a school more easily than they now transfer from one school, a liceo for example, to another, for example, a technical-industrial school. Vocational commitments will not have to be made as early and they can be made with more basis in experience than is currently the case. It is doubtful if the present *ciclo basico* serves any purpose when it is divided into special schools. Furthermore, in a comprehensive school, program emphasis can be changed in accord with shifts in the economic and work force demand. The comprehensive school also attacks the harmful problem of social and economic divisiveness and snobbism that is bred by the present separate schools. If a work force is to cooperate in productive enterprise in Guayana, there is some advantage in not segregating those destined to be professionals from future skilled workers and tradesmen. These are only a few of the commonly cited benefits of the comprehensive school, but they should be reckoned with.

School Construction and Capital Investment in Ciudad Guayana

Table 11.9 shows the demand for primary school construction in Ciudad Guayana from the fall of 1966 through 1975. There is also an estimate of schools required by 1980 and the aggregate number of all new schools required during the period. Capacity scheduled is that which must be available in September of each year. The table was prepared on the basis of projected enrollments. An attempt has been made to schedule probable private school construction during the period, but it should be noted that this is not based on any declaration by private school authorities that they will build any given number of schools. The table shows private school construction which is firmly planned by the private schools. All the rest is attributed to public schools, either from the Ministry of Education, the state of Bolívar, or possibly from CVG on emergency bases.

TABLE 11.9
Demand for Primary School Construction in Ciudad Guayana, 1966–1975 and 1980

	1966– 1967	1967– 1968	1968– 1969	1969– 1970	1970– 1971	1971– 1972	1972– 1973	1973– 1974	1974– 1975	1975– 1976
Capacity Existing	12,280[a]	20,240	23,720	27,560	32,360	36,200	41,000	45,800	50,600	56,360
Enrollment	16,235	19,365	23,033	27,069	31,705	36,231	40,775	45,417	50,248	55,770
Capacity minus Enrollment	−3,955	+875	+687	+491	+655	−31	+225	+383	+352	+590
Needed Classrooms[b]	50	37	35	42	52	49	58	56	56	63
Projected Private Classrooms[c]	7	0	15	0	0	—	—	—	—	—
Projected Public Schools[d]	—	8	3	4	5	4	5	5	5	6

	1980
Capacity Existing	75,560
Enrollment	75,500
Capacity minus Enrollment	+60
Needed Classrooms[b]	240
Projected Private Classrooms[c]	—
Projected Public Schools[d]	20

Schools needed 1967–1975   45
1967–1980   65

[a] Capacity needed to accommodate public school students 40 per classroom, two shifts per day, private schools one shift per day.
[b] Capacity of 80 students on double shift.
[c] Capacity of 40 students.
[d] Public schools may vary in size. For analytical purpose they are assumed here to have 12 classrooms each, and to accommodate 960 students on double shift.

TABLE 11.10
Demand for Middle School Construction in Ciudad Guayana, 1966–1975 and 1980

		1965–1966	1966–1967	1967–1968	1968–1969	1969–1970	1970–1971	1971–1972	1972–1973	1973–1974
Liceos	Expected Enrollment	1,292	1,701	2,074	2,848	2,910	3,424	4,098	4,930	5,695
	Public School Classrooms[a]	8	20	20	20	40	40	40	60	60
	Private School Classrooms	18	18	18	35	33	33	33	33	33
	Total Capacity	1,360	2,320	2,320	2,920	4,520	4,520	4,520	6,120	6,120
	Capacity minus Enrollment	+68	+619	+246	+72	+1,610	+1,096	+422	+1,190	+425
	Projected Public Classrooms	0	20	0	15	0	0	0	20	0
	Private Classrooms	0	0	0	0	0	0	0	0	0
	Public School Construction[b]	0	1	0	0	1	0	0	1	0
Technical	Expected Enrollment	549	792	1,271	1,583	2,195	2,868	3,557	4,218	4,996
	Capacity	1,600	1,600	1,600	1,600	3,200	3,200	4,800	4,800	6,400
	Capacity minus Enrollment	+1,050	+808	+329	+7	+1,005	+332	+1,243	+582	+1,404
	Construction Needed[c]	0	0	0	1	0	0	1	0	1
Commercial	Expected Enrollment	578	600	600	953	1,624	2,054	2,417	2,781	3,147
	Capacity	600[d]	600	600	2,000	2,000	2,000	3,400	3,400	3,400
	Capacity minus Enrollment	+22	0	0	+847	+376	−54	+988	+619	+253
	Construction Needed	0	0	0	1	0	0	1	0	0
Artisanal	Expected Enrollment	42	63	122	212	338	514	735	1,011	1,349
	Capacity	300	300	300	300	300	900	900	900	1,500
	Capacity minus Enrollment	+128	+237	+178	+88	−38	+368	+165	−111	+151
	Construction Needed[e]	0	0	0	0	0	1	0	0	1

[a] 40/room/shift, 2 shifts/day. Existing capacity of 8 classrooms, will become primary school in September 1966 when new liceo is opened.
[b] 10 classrooms each double shift.
[c] Double shift capacity 1,600.
[d] Existing facility is adequate.
[e] To be built by private sector.

TABLE 11.10 (continued)

		1974–1975	1975–1976	1980	Total to 1975	to 1980
Liceos	Expected Enrollment	6,683	7,418	13,600		
	Public School Classrooms[a]	80	80	145		
	Public School Classrooms	33	33	50		
	Public Capacity	6,400	6,400	11,600		
	Private Capacity	1,550	1,550	2,000		
	Total Capacity	7,950	7,950	13,600		
	Capacity minus Enrollment	+1,037	+302	0		
	Projected Public Classrooms	20	0	65		
	Private Classrooms	0	0	17		
	Public School Construction[b]	1	0	4	3	7
Technical	Expected Enrollment	5,928	6,646	9,000		
	Capacity	6,400	8,000	9,600		
	Capacity minus Enrollment	+472	+1,354			
	Construction Needed[c]	0	1	1	4	5
Commercial	Expected Enrollment	3,517	3,904	6,000		
	Capacity	4,800	4,800	6,200		
	Capacity minus Enrollment	+1,283	+896	+200		
	Construction Needed[d]	1	0	1	3	4
Artisanal	Expected Enrollment	1,759	1,800	1,600		
	Capacity	2,100	2,100	2,100		
	Capacity minus Enrollment	+341	+300	+500		
	Construction Needed[e]	1	0	0	3	0

[a] 40/room/shift, 2 shifts/day. Existing capacity of 8 classrooms, will become primary school in September 1966 when new liceo is opened.
[b] 10 classrooms, each double shift.
[c] Double shift capacity 1,600.
[d] Existing facility is adequate.
[e] To be built by private sector.

TABLE 11.11
School Construction and Investment for September of School Year, 1967–1980 in Ciudad Guayana: By Years and Total

	1967–1968	1968–1969	1969–1970	1970–1971	1971–1972	1972–1973	1973–1974	1974–1975	1975–1976
Primary Schools Needed									
Public, 12 rooms, double shift	8	3	4	5	4	5	5	5	6
Private, 12 rooms, single shift	0	1	—	—	—	—	—	—	—
Investment required[a]	4,600	1,725	2,300	2,875	2,300	2,875	2,875	2,875	3,450
With preprimary									
Academic High Schools									
Public, 10 rooms, 4 laboratories, double shift	0	0	1	0	0	1	0	1	0
Private, single shift	0	2	—	—	—	—	—	—	—
Investment required	0	0	2,220	0	0	2,200	0	2,200	0
Technical-Artisanal Schools									
Public, capacity 1,600 on double shift	0	0	1	0	1	0	1	0	1
Private, capacity 300	0	0	0	2	0	0	2	2	0
Investment required	0	0	3,550	0	3,550	0	3,550	0	3,550
Commercial Schools									
Public, capacity 1,600 on double shift	0	1	0	0	1	0	0	1	0
Investment required	0	2,000	0	0	2,000	0	0	2,000	0
Total construction cost[b] with preprimary	4,600	3,725	8,070	2,875	7,850	5,095	6,425	7,095	7,000

[a] Each school costs Bs. 575,000 at 1965 prices. Investments are expressed in thousands of 1965 bolivares. Costs do not include land value or capital recovery.
[b] Thousands of 1965 bolivares.

Table 11.10 shows the demand for secondary school construction in Ciudad Guayana from 1966 to 1975 and for the year 1980. The programs listed included artisanal, even though this is not recommended as part of the model system for 1975. The evidence suggests that the pre-industrial programs of the artisanal school are insufficient to guarantee entry-level skills for the work force and that demand for this program will fall markedly before 1975. Nevertheless, such a school type does exist in Ciudad Guayana and there is the possibility that this type may expand. It is more likely that the artisanal will evolve into a school with liceo and technical programs and thus be the first approximation of a comprehensive high school in Ciudad Guayana.

Table 11.11 aggregates construction investment for all types of schools from 1966 to 1975 and for 1980. It indicates that the staggering total of Bs. 52,735,000 will be needed for investment in school construction by 1975, and Bs. 78.7 million by 1980. This does not include any investment in the construction or equipment of more artisanal schools. When the needed investment is added to the costs of operation presented in Table 11.1, the price of human resource development in Ciudad Guayana assumes proportions consonant with investment in exploitation of physical resources.

Costs Per Student Enrolled and Costs Per Graduate: A Note of Cheer

Figures 11.2 to 11.6 are included to offer a note of cheer to alter the depressing effect of the estimate of required investment in the preceding section. The figures attempt to relate cost to quality and quality to productivity and productivity back to cost again. The true measure of what the schools are doing in Guayana is not the number of students enrolled but the number brought to some meaningful level of education or training. It is not possible to measure exactly or directly the achievement that is attributable to the schools, but the schools have their own standards which are reflected in promotion and graduation rates. These are school standards. Students have their own standards which are often reflected by retardation and dropout. Neither set of standards is completely adequate but it reflects quality in some indirect manner. Schools with high rates of retardation, failure, and dropout and low thruput are bad schools. Schools which graduate high proportions of their students enrolled are, by and large, good schools. The proportion of students-who-graduate to students-who-enroll is one measure of school productivity and quality.

Figure 11.2 shows that although the cost per student enrolled in the primary schools of Ciudad Guayana goes up rather sharply in the years 1966 to 1975,

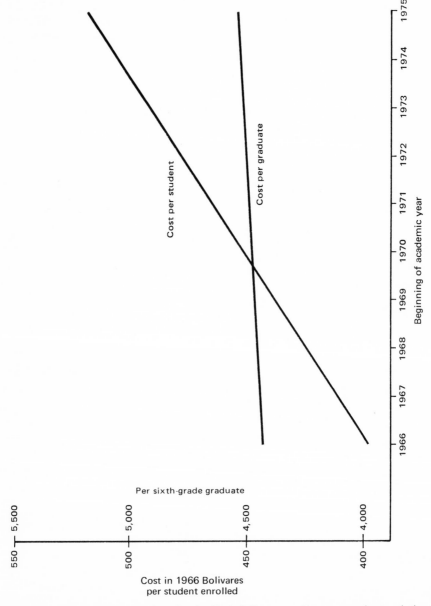

Figure 11.2   Costs of primary education in Ciudad Guayana: Cost per graduate relative to an increased investment in quality of education.

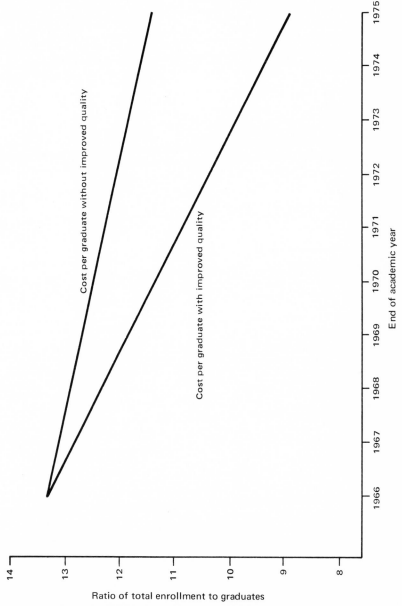

Figure 11.3   Productivity of primary schools in Ciudad Guayana with and without increased investment in quality of education.

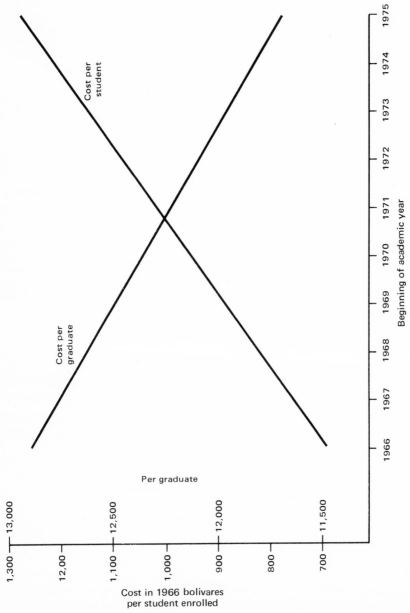

Figure 11.4   Costs of secondary education in Ciudad Guayana: Cost per liceo graduate relative to an increased investment in quality of education.

the cost per graduate does not go up appreciably. The reason is that the increased costs bring increased efficiency as measured by proportions of students who graduate to students enrolled. Figure 11.3 shows this productivity more directly. It shows that the ratio of enrollments to graduates—a high ratio reflects high retardation, dropout, and failure—will fall rapidly given the efficient system called for in this plan. The ratio falls far more gradually without the investment. The increased investment will bring increased productivity in the Guayana schools. The concept of productivity can be applied to schools just as easily as it can be applied to any enterprise where there are costs and outputs.

Figure 11.4 shows that the cost per graduate of the academic high schools (liceos) actually goes down with the improved quality and promotion rates implied in the plan. The cost per student, of course, rises from 1966 to 1975. The difference in the cost ratios reflects the tremendous wastage and inefficiency of the present secondary school system in Ciudad Guayana. Currently, costs are low, about Bs. 700 per student, but output and efficiency are outrageously low as well. It is probable that inputs to Ciudad Guayana secondary schools are too low to reach the minimal point necessary to guarantee any worthwhile output. The resources are largely wasted.

Figure 11.5 shows a more complex picture for technical-industrial education in Ciudad Guayana. The cost per graduate of the three-year program falls markedly as the system is improved. This is because there is very high retardation and dropout in the early years. The cost per graduate at the fifth year rises very slightly over the years as compared to the cost per student. The cost per graduate of the highest level program (the proposed six-year program began in 1967–1968) goes up as the cost per student goes up. This trend has no history to support it because the program does not exist. Technical education will be an expensive program, at least in the early years of the plan.

Figure 11.6 shows that the cost per graduate for both the four- and five-year commercial program go down, whereas the cost per student enrolled goes up. Again the cost per graduate of the higher level program goes down more slowly than the lower level one because dropout and retardation are much less severe in the higher grades. The system has already screened out the dropouts and failing students in the lower grades. The cost per graduate will, of course, not continue to go down as the trend on the graph indicates. It will stabilize near some ideal level. This will be the level where the number of years to graduate a student is the same as the legal or stated number of years in the program. If the program is a six-year program, the cost per graduate in the ideal system is six

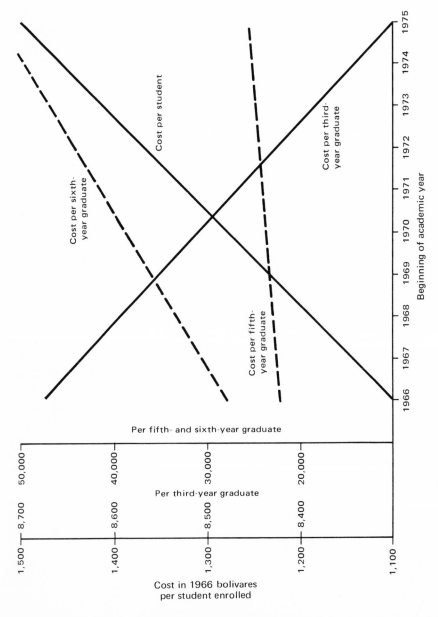

Figure 11.5   Costs of technical education in Ciudad Guayana.

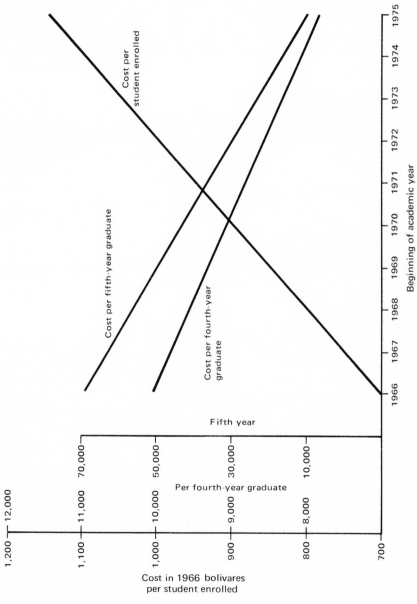

Figure 11.6   Costs of commercial education in Ciudad Guayana.

multiplied by the cost per year for a student enrolled. This will not be quite reached in Guayana, even by 1980, and a certain amount of improvement will depend on factors not within school control, that is, student selection and home background, economic demand in the work force, and economic condition of families.

12
A Program for
Informal Education
and Training

Even under the most optimistic assumptions about improvement in the formal school system of Ciudad Guayana, the primary and secondary schools cannot completely satisfy the demand for educated and trained people before 1980. Much of the deficit must be supplied by migrants who have been flooding into the city since the middle 1950's and who will supply the bulk of the population projected for 1975 and 1980. If these migrants came already educated and trained there would be no problem, but they come not only with little education and training, but also with little experience of urban and industrial living. Both to meet the deficits in formal education and training and to serve the mass of migrants from rural areas and deprived educational backgrounds, a substantial effort must be made in informal training.

Proposed Programs in Basic Informal Education

To plan an informal education program, a literacy campaign for example, by the numbers and without respect to the particular characteristics of the people and their particular needs is to prolong the same weary and unsuccessful history that literacy campaigns have had the world over. First, there must be intimate knowledge of the people, their life styles, and their needs. Then there must be programs tailored specifically to the people and their needs. This was the purpose of the study of the characteristics and attitudes of the mothers of school-age children in the poorer barrios of Ciudad Guayana. Some of the results should form the basis for programing informal education and training in Ciudad Guayana. The requirements of the economy and the work force will also give direction and shape to such programs, and these are the two bases on which the following programs are built.

Earlier chapters examined the influence of the family on school attendance and achievement in Ciudad Guayana. The schools do not have control over all factors which influence enrollment, attendance, and achievement, and all the ills of a community cannot be remedied by improvement of instruction within the schools. As noted, the study showed that many of the causes for failure and dropout were beyond the direct influence of the school and were embedded in the economic and social deprivation which afflict the families of the shanty barrios. The school can move against these ills only indirectly and over the long run. It cannot function solely as a social welfare agency even if it were assumed that social welfare agencies could do very much about solving the chronic problems of poverty and misery in the barrios.

A detailed description of the families from which barrio children came was presented in earlier chapters as well. The salient features should be kept in mind as a frame for the design of programs for adults of the barrios. Adult courses must be even more specially tailored to the needs of the underprivileged than those in the day schools inasmuch as barrio parents have been buried in poverty and cultural deprivation much longer than have their children. Education and training programs must be designed to free them from this morass.

Barrio men must be trained to acquire work discipline, and this must be an essential feature of any training program. Given the social system, all benefits in Guayana flow from regular employment and union membership. One would expect that this fact would suggest to the man that he must equip himself for work (through education and training). This does not happen however. More often the father becomes discouraged and immobilized in his barrio. He may never hear of training opportunities, even if they are available. This suggests that any program which is to work must actively seek out its clients. It must follow them into the barrios rather than wait in centers outside. Preferably the training should be centered in the barrios and gradually lead the people out into the wider world that has previously rejected them. The problem of disillusionment and despair may be more severe for males than for females. At least women with children and no husbands have no option but to struggle and sacrifice to maintain their families.

But most barrio dwellers are not completely without hopes and aspirations. The difficulty is that their hopes and aspirations are almost entirely centered on their children. At least, this is difficult for those attempting to plan adult education programs to supplement regular day school programs for children. There is one aspect of the dreary picture which does offer hope. There is very high motivation on the part of poor mothers for their children to have a chance at education. Education is clearly perceived as a route to success, and although circumstances intervene to frustrate parents' good intentions, the motivation is there and indisputable. This is particularly apparent among mothers who have no adult male living in the home. These mothers must cope and they do, including making the sacrifices necessary to guarantee education for their children.

The attitudes of barrio mothers toward education should carry a cautionary note for the development of adult education programs, just as they give a note of hope for the possibility of success of day school programs for children. The women believe in education for their children. With proper preparation and information it is possible that the women may see advantages in basic education and training for themselves. But the education and training must be appropriate to their needs. And it must be good. A bad adult education course is often worse than no education at all because it destroys hope with bitter experience.

When the adult illiterate is lured out to an educational program his or her self-esteem is horribly exposed. One can recall the deep embarrassment shown by Indian peasants in Guatemala or urban slum dwellers in Nicaragua as they struggled laboriously through the childish language of a first literacy primer. The adult sweats and blinks and grins with nervousness as he pushes his finger along the line and laboriously sounds out the letters and makes them into words and sentences. If he is in a bad program in which bad materials and poor instructional methods delay his mastery and prolong his agony, he will sense farce, a farce in which he is the butt, and his resentment will be terrible. Many of the men and women in the Guayana barrios have already been through this experience, some of them several times. Whatever programs are tried must work well from the outset. The men and women will not wait. They have houses to clean and labor to perform and in their limited worlds the opportunity costs of training are high.

There is no question of the need for adult education courses in Guayana. The literacy figures demonstrate the need. There is somewhat less clear an indication of the content of programs that would meet with success. On the basis of the study of Guayana families and their circumstances and attitudes, these guidelines should be set for developing adult education courses:

1. Pure literacy courses, that is, conventional programs in reading, writing, and arithmetic, probably would have small payoff, despite the apparent need.

Among women in poorer families, where illiteracy is most severe, there is
scarcely time to spare from the struggle to meet daily pressures of gaining a
livelihood.

2. Basic education courses have attraction for the younger age groups, men
and women from twenty to forty-five. It is doubtful they would have either
attraction or payoff for the groups that are older. The priority age groups are
those under forty-five and perhaps even under thirty-five. Older age groups
present more serious problems pedagogically and have fewer years of active
work life to apply and sustain their literacy.

3. The programs should be basic education, that is, literacy with content
useful for home management and skill acquisition for job performance. There
are, and will continue to be, large numbers of women who must earn a living to
support large families in Ciudad Guayana. These women should have first
priority in selection into skill training courses for women.

4. If the courses provide both basic literacy and skill training, they must be
supported at a level sufficient to secure some meaningful outcome. It is doubtful
that education of any value can be given for the costs and in the time that has
been set by some of the organizations working in literacy and basic education.

5. Inasmuch as there is still an inadequate basis for the design of the content
of courses in Ciudad Guayana, it would be wise to make a detailed study of
existing projects rather than to launch massive campaigns. If present programs
are inadequate, it is more sensible to cooperate with INCE and ODEA in the
design of pilot projects which have the appropriate features. A bad program in
literacy or basic education is worse than no program, as it sets up unrealistic
expectations which will be frustrated.

6. Basic education should continue to work out of the neighborhood school
in the evenings, just as the education of children takes place in the school for the
daytime hours. The essential concept is that the school serve the total family. An
ideal program would put a social worker or basic education specialist in every
school. This specialist would know the economic and social problems of the
local community so well that the resources of the school could be marshaled to
improve the lot of the entire family. The chief targets of the programs should be
the mothers and the children. Male basic education and skill training could take
place at more remote centers that have special facilities for such programs.

7. It is only practical to note that in the beginning the schools must take the
initiative in providing adult education and in encouraging adults to take
advantage of it. There may, in view of past neglect, seem to be considerable

apathy on the part of adults for their own education and training. Hence, it is not likely that adults will at the outset take initiative in the management of school-community programs. It is essential, however, that the barrio adults be involved in the management of such programs just as soon as there are any signs that they are ready to do so, and from the outset in those situations where there is high motivation. The most likely sequence is that the programs first be designed to provide what the barrio adult needs. If the programs do accomplish this, they will become what the barrio adults want and ultimately what they make in an effort to provide for themselves. There are barrios where parents have organized to provide facilities for their children. In these barrios it is reasonable to hope that adults could do the same for their own programs. There are hard-core barrios, however, where this would not work at first.

The program could begin modestly by encouraging existing teachers to obtain a more intimate knowledge of the communities which surround their schools. As relationships develop, teachers could begin to form specific educational programs with home management, home improvement, and planning as basic content, and women's vocational training as a later stage. The advantage of such a program is that women who would not be likely to come to more remote centers could be reached in their neighborhoods. The school assumes a more central role of service to the entire family. The content must be intimately related to community requirements and have as an essential component the possibility of strengthening the family. Programs have not yet been running long enough in Ciudad Guayana to reveal whether or not they are reaching the hard-core cases. More likely the most eager and motivated have come into the centers. Reaching the others will get proportionately more difficult. Space does not permit a detailed description of a program at this point, but the essential concept described should be embodied in any program attempted in Ciudad Guayana. Running the program in schools, because they are available, is different from programing them in schools to serve the surrounding communities. This is an important feature to incorporate in new programs.

Skill Training Programs

A second type of program is best described as prevocational training. These are day programs in the construction trades for young, unskilled adults. Table 12.1 describes programs operating in 1966. To date the programs are at too low a level to guarantee entry-level skills. The obvious signal should have been to expand the programs to 1,600-hour programs in the construction trades.

TABLE 12.1
Enrollment Capacities of Informal Training Programs, Ciudad Guayana, 1967–1975

Programs / Years	Existing 1966	Probable 1967	Required 1967	1968	1969	1970	1971	1972	1973	1974	1975	Total Enrollment 1967–1975	Total Graduates 1967–1975
I. Basic Adult Education													
A. Alternative One (low)	1,800	2,000	2,000	3,000	3,000	4,000	4,000	4,000	4,000	4,000	4,000	32,000	24,000
B. Alternative Two (high)			3,000	3,000	4,000	5,500	5,500	5,500	5,500	5,500	5,500	43,000	32,250
II. Prevocational Training													
A. Industrial	855	195											
1. Alternative One (low)			250	300	450	600	700	700	800	900	900	5,600	4,200
2. Alternative Two (high)			350	500	800	1,000	1,150	1,250	1,350	1,450	1,550	9,400	6,900
B. Commercial	60	60											
1. Alternative One (low)			100	150	250	300	350	550	550	600	650	3,500	2,600
2. Alternative Two (high)			250	250	350	350	450	700	800	900	1,000	5,050	3,800
C. Feminine Technical	120	120											
1. Alternative One (low)			200	300	400	600	900	1,100	1,300	1,500	1,700	8,000	6,000
2. Alternative Two (high)			400	600	900	1,200	1,500	1,700	1,900	2,100	2,300	12,600	9,540
III. Formation Training													
A. Industrial Formation	—	400	600	775	900	900	980	980	980	980	980	8,075	6,460
1. Forge-Metallurg. Trades		330	330	380	380	380	380	380	380	380	380	3,370	2,696
2. Foundry Trades				50	50	50	100	100	100	100	100	650	520
3. Electrical Trades		70	70	70	70	70	100	100	100	100	100	780	624
4. Construction Trades			200	200	200	200	200	200	200	200	200	1,800	1,440
5. Automechanic Trades					125	125	125	125	125	125	125	875	700
6. Large Equip. Operation				25	25	25	25	25	25	25	25	200	160
7. Maintenance/Installation				50	50	50	50	50	50	50	50	400	320
B. Commercial Formation	—	—	—	600	600	600	600	600	600	600	600	4,800	3,600
C. Feminine-Tech. Formation	—	—	—	—	—	—	—	—	400	400	400	1,200	960
D. Paramedical Formation	—	—	25	75	100	150	200	275	300	400	500	2,025	1,520

TABLE 12.1 (continued)

Programs	Existing 1966	Probable 1967	Required 1967	1968	1969	1970	1971	1972	1973	1974	1975	Enrollment Total 1967–1975	Total Graduates 1967–1975
IV. Perfeccionamiento Training													
A. Industrial Perfeccionamiento													
1. Forge-Metallurg. Trades	—	240	235	365	395	395	395	395	395	395	395	3,365	2,860
2. Foundry Trades	—	200	200	200	200	200	200	200	200	200	200	1,800	1,530
3. Electrical Trades	—	—	—	40	40	40	40	40	40	40	40	320	272
4. Construction Trades	—	40	35	35	35	35	35	35	35	35	35	315	268
5. Automechanic Trades	—	—	—	75	75	75	75	75	75	75	75	600	510
6. Maintenance/Installation	—	—	—	—	30	30	30	30	30	30	30	210	178
	—	—	—	15	15	15	15	15	15	15	15	120	102
B. Commercial Perfeccionamiento	—	—	—	150	150	150	150	150	150	150	150	1,200	1,020
C. Feminine-Technical Perfeccionamiento	—	—	—	—	—	—	—	—	150	150	150	450	380
V. Apprenticeship Training													
A. Intensive Apprentice Training	280	335	350	420	490	560	630	670	710	750	800	Not Applicable because courses are 3–4 years in length	1,200 (approx.)
1. Forge-Metallurg. Trades	170	205	205	235	245	255	275	285	290	290	300		450
2. Foundry Trades	—	60	—	—	20	40	60	60	70	80	80		120
3. Electrical Trades	60	60	60	70	70	70	80	80	90	100	100		150
4. Construction Trades	—	—	15	25	45	65	95	105	110	120	120		180
5. Automechanic Trades	—	—	—	—	10	20	20	20	20	30	40		60
6. Maintenance/Installation	30	30	30	50	60	70	70	80	90	90	100		150
7. Other Trades	20	40	40	40	40	40	40	40	40	40	70		90
B. Introductory Apprentice Training	500	800	800	900	1,100	1,300	1,400	1,700	1,900	2,200	2,400	13,700	13,000

TABLE 12.2
Pertinent Features of Required Informal Training Programs, Ciudad Guayana, 1967–1975

Programs	Organization Responsible	Course Duration	Features Graduation or Promotion Rates To Be Maintained	Locales by Order of Preference
I. *Basic Adult Education*	1. ODEA 2. INCE	1. Regular primary education for children is 7,700 hours. 2. ODEA: 1,300–1,400 hours. 3. Past, INCE: 1,000 hours. 4. Present, INCE: 560 hours. 5. Recommended: 500–1,000 hours.	0.75 (per year)	1. Schools 2. Community Centers 3. Factories
II. *Prevocational Training*	1. ODEA 2. INCE	200–500 hours (day or night).	0.75	1. Facilities of technical secondary schools at night 2. Community centers at day 3. Primary schools at night 4. Specially constructed centers (day and night)

III. *Industrial Formation*	INCE	1,600 hours (day).	0.80	1. Specially constructed INCE shops
				2. On-the-job
				   a. large equipment operation
				   b. maintenance/installation

IV. *Commercial Formation*	INCE	1. One course of 800 hours. 2. One course of 1,600 hours (day).	0.75	1. Specially constructed INCE center
V. *Feminine Technical Formation*	INCE	1,600 hours (day).	0.80	1. Specially constructed INCE center
VI. *Paramedical Formation*	1. INCE/and 2. Local hospitals	1,600–2,000 hours (day or night).	0.75	1. Hospitals (on-the-job)
VII. *Industrial Perfeccionamiento*	INCE	300 hours (night).	0.85	1. Center used for industrial formation
VIII. *Commercial Perfeccionamiento*	INCE	300 hours (night).	0.85	1. Center used for commercial formation

Continued on next page.

Types of Clientele that should Enter Program	Skill Level at Which Course Should Work	Required Investment (Buildings and Equipment)	Required Current Cost per Enrollee	Student/Teacher Ratio Required (Upper limit)
Adults, aged 14–45	Not Applicable	None to very little. Perhaps central coordinating office will be needed. This would cost about Bs. 350,000.	Bs. 350	15/1
1. Adults, 14–45 2. Unemployed 3. Unskilled 4. No labor force requirement	Unskilled	1. None to very little if locales 1, 2, and 3 are used. 2. Considerable if locale 4 is used. If large center is used, cost would be about Bs. 1,500,000; with small center, cost would be Bs. 500,000.	?	20–25/1
1. Adults, aged 18–30 2. Men 3. Unskilled to semiskilled 4. Unemployed or employed 5. Member or potential member of labor force	Semiskilled	1. INCE center with 450 day places would cost about Bs. 3,000,000. 2. On-job training requires no investment cost.	Bs. 2,500 to Bs. 3,500	15/1
1. Adults, aged 18–30 2. Men or women 3. Unemployed 4. Unskilled to semiskilled 5. Member or potential member of labor force.	Semiskilled	Unknown, but for a center with 600 day places, from Bs. 1,500,000 to Bs. 2,000,000.	?	15/1
1. Adults, aged 18–30 2. Women 3. Unemployed 4. Unskilled to semiskilled 5. Member or potential member of labor force	Semiskilled	Unknown, but for a center with 400 day places, investment costs would range from Bs. 1,500,000 to Bs. 2,000,000.	?	15/1
1. Adults, aged 18–30 2. Women 3. Employed 4. Unskilled to semiskilled	Semiskilled to skilled	None or very little.	?	10–15/1
1. Adults, aged 20–40 2. Employed 3. Semiskilled to skilled	Skilled	None.	Bs. 1,700 to Bs. 2,300	15/1
1. Adults, aged 20–40 2. Employed 3. Semiskilled to skilled	Skilled	None.	?	15/1

TABLE 12.2 (continued)

Programs	Organization Responsible	Course Duration	Features Graduation or Promotion Rates To Be Maintained	Locales by Order of Preference
IX. *Feminine-Technical Perfeccionamiento*	INCE	300 hours (night).	0.85	1. Center used for feminine-technical formation
X. *Intensive Apprenticeship Training*	Factory or firm, in accord with INCE law	6,000–8,000 hours (day, 3–4 years).	0.75 (over 3- to 4-year period)	1. Factory facilities, on-the-job 2. Special center on factory grounds
XI. *Introductory Apprenticeship Training*	Factory or firm	20–400 hours.	0.95	On-the-job

Instead it appears that INCE will abandon the construction trades courses in order to open the metal trades center courses. This is a surprising move in the face of the demand for skilled construction workers that exists now in the Guayana work force. A more sensible plan would be to lengthen the construction courses, using the shop capacity and equipment that will exist for some time in the present INCE center. The demand for workers in the metal trades is not now as serious as in the construction trades and will not be for two or three years.

Also needed are long apprenticeship courses. Similar programs with very small classes have been operating in the steel mill. The courses should be scheduled for rapid expansion. The same should be done with the shorter courses for the training of operators or semiskilled workers in industry. The law guarantees that these apprenticeship programs will increase rapidly, but it does not guarantee that they will be well run. Supposedly the self-interest of the establishment should ensure this and the experience of INCE should make it even more likely. Still it would be well to make a more detailed study of the plans for these programs.

Table 12.1 shows the required enrollment capacities in informal education and training programs through 1975. This represents an expansion of the existing programs as well as the development and expansion of new programs which are described in Table 12.2.

The recommendation would be to combine basic education with rudimentary vocational training, especially for women. The length should be 1,800 to 2,000 hours and the material should cover acquisition of learning skills (reading,

Types of Clientele that should Enter Program	Skill Level at Which Course Should Work	Required Investment (Buildings and Equipment)	Required Current Cost per Enrollee	Student/Teacher Ratio Required (Upper limit)
1. Adults, aged 20–40 2. Employed 3. Unskilled to semiskilled	Skilled	None.	?	15/1
1. Adults, aged 18–25 2. Employed 3. Unskilled to semiskilled	Skilled	1. With locale 1, none or very little. 2. If locale 2 is used, considerable.	?	10–15/1
1. Adults, 14–45 2. Employed 3. Unskilled to semiskilled	Unskilled to semiskilled	None to very little.	?	10–15/1

writing, arithmetic), home-family management (nutrition, consumer education, dressmaking, home decoration), and for working women rudimentary skill training for commerce and personal service occupations. The current cost per person enrolled will rise over present cost as shown.

Group III, Table 12.1, describes a new kind of informal training program for Guayana. The first experience with this kind of program will come when the new metals and machine trade center is opened by INCE in an expanded center in Ciudad Guayana.

Group III also covers training for women in commercial and business fields and for the female service occupations (cosmetology, fashion and dressmaking, and so forth). A third group covers preparation for supporting technicians in the health fields. This field will grow very large in Venezuela and Ciudad Guayana and there are no existing formal training institutions. The higher technicians could be trained in the Technological Institute but there is a need for lower level medical support people (practical nurses, attendants, therapists).

Group IV lists the high skill training for improvement of workers already at semiskilled jobs in industry. The grouping follows more or less the same breakdown as III.A, except that large equipment operators will be omitted. This is a borderline case even in III.A. Group IV also has improvement courses for women in the same areas as Group III.

Group V lists the long-term apprenticeship training which presently exists in the three major industries in Guayana but will be expanded to cover other manufacturing and mining establishments, as well as the larger construction firms. Output is low because of the length of the courses.

In total the informal training output which is scheduled in Table 12.1 will, when combined with the output of technical schools, meet the requirements for skilled craftsmen listed in Table 2.3. In the case of *perfeccionamiento* training, it will also help to give the technical-industrial school graduates further training after they enter the work force. The output of these courses may very well be much larger than that shown in Table 12.1.

TABLE 12.3
Steps That Should Be Taken in Expanding and Improving Informal Training Programs of Ciudad Guayana, 1967–1975

Required Steps	Year
I. Expansion and improvement of basic adult education programs.	1967 and 1967–1975
II. Establishment of paramedical formation program with a capacity for 25 students, and expansion of this program as required through 1975.	1967 and 1967–1975
III. Expansion and improvement of prevocational training programs.	1967 and 1967–1975
IV. Construction of INCE industrial formation shops for metal-forge and electrical trades with capacity for 450 students; establishment of INCE perfeccionamiento programs for these trades, with a capacity for 235 students.	1967
V. Construction of INCE industrial formation shops for construction trades, with a capacity for 200 students, and establishment of INCE perfecciona-miento program for these trades, with a capacity for 75 students.	1967
VI. Construction of INCE industrial formation shop for foundry trades, with a capacity for 50 students and establishment of INCE perfeccionamiento program for these trades with a capacity for 40 students.	1968
VII. Establishment of INCE industrial formation on-the-job training programs for large equipment operation and maintenance/installation personnel, with a capacity for 75 students.	1968

The large number of blank spaces in Tables 12.1 and 12.2 should serve to alert planners that the surface has not even been scratched in the programing of informal education and training. Much detailed analysis remains to be done and must be done before major investments are made in further training courses. Table 12.3 should not suggest that there is sufficient information to launch the programs listed. It should be used only to give a rough approximation of priorities and possibilities.

The informal education and training program, even in broad outline, implies a large investment and critical one. The planning of it should not be lightly or superficially done. It will require the services of a variety of highly specialized technicians. The time has come when further remote and "general" planning may only serve to lay out a clear course of mistakes.

13
A Plan for Implementation of Programs

All of the previous chapters serve no purpose if not followed by a proposal for implementing the strategy and programs described. The mechanism which has been proposed to facilitate improvement of the human resource development institutions of Ciudad Guayana is the Center for Educational Research, Planning, and Services. This center might also be named the Human Resource Development Center to indicate that its functions would transcend those usually associated with "education," that is, with formal, academic schools. Instead of being concerned just with schools, this Center would coordinate the activities of all human resource development institutions in the city, or work to create organisms which could provide that coordination. It would plan the development of future institutions or the expansion of existing ones or assist institutions in planning their expansion. It would advise existing agencies, public and private, with respect to their activities in Ciudad Guayana. It would offer or create services for existing and future institutions.

No such organization exists in Venezuela today, or in any part of the world as far as is known, although the concept itself is not new. Because there are no extant models and because Venezuela, and especially the Guayana, is in a state of rapid change, it is difficult to offer precise descriptions of the legal structure to support what is proposed. For example, at this time it might appear well advised to establish the Center as a dependency of the Ministry of Education, preferably under the direction of the Office of Educational Planning (EDU-PLAN). Authority and financing would come from the Ministry. But the Ministry itself is carrying out a self-study which is bound to result in dramatic changes in its organization. It is possible that an arrangement under the auspices of the Ministry would not be possible given new procedures in the Ministry. It is possible that EDUPLAN would not be the proper supervising department. Furthermore, even if established under the Ministry as it is now or might be in the future, the Center would require a number of extraofficial connections (for example, relationships with private industry) which would exceed the legal authority of the Ministry.

Given the difficulty of anticipating change in national agencies, it seems best to divide the development task into three parts. One part of the task of creating a human resource development system in Ciudad Guayana would involve creation of the organizations which would carry out the functions of the larger system, even if the system itself were never realized. That is, one part of the task involves creation of organizations to provide in-service training to teachers, guidance and counseling for students, development and production of instructional materials, improved planning and administration within formal school levels, and other services. These organizations could come into existence without the establishment of a system linking all levels and kinds of human resource development institutions in the city. It is believed, however, that individual projects would not function efficiently unless linked in a complete system.

A second part of the task involves creating systematic arrangements among elements of the formal educational establishments of Ciudad Guayana. Primary schools can be brought to coordinate their activities, programs, and purchases. Middle-level schools can share facilities, ideas, and materials. And primary and middle-level schools can work together much more effectively than they do at present. This too could be achieved without linking the formal academic system to other agencies in the city responsible for human resource development. However, it is believed that the formal schools would be more attuned to community needs if they were linked to industry, commerce, and other training institutions.

The third part of the task, then, involves linking all human resource development agencies and relating them to the users of human resources, that is, industry, commerce, and the community in general.

The proposal made here describes a set of steps for attaining the first goal, creation of the basic organizations for a human resource development system. It also contains the initial steps for creating a formal school system and a community human resource development system. However, failure to attain the latter two goals should not prejudice the viability of the component organizations. Given this plan it should be possible to improve the efficiency and relevancy of schools and other training institutions to some degree, even if the legal or political structures necessary for building a system cannot be obtained. And even if the Center for Educational Research, Planning, and Services is never established, the human resource development institutions in the city can be improved in efficiency and relevancy.

Component Organizations for a Human Resource Development System

Described briefly in this section are the organizations or institutions which would be established if the plan proposed here were to be implemented.

1. *Administration*. A central administration for all formal schools would be established, following the model described in Chapter 11. This plan for school administration differs from present arrangements in the following significant ways:

There would be a chief school officer with authority over all levels.

There would be a centralized purchasing office for all levels.

Supervision would be carried out by curriculum area instead of by level.

System-wide specialists would provide services to all levels.

Planning would be done for all levels locally, instead of nationally within each level.

To implement this plan it would be necessary to convince the various subsystems (primary, academic secondary, technical, and commercial schools) of the advantages of coordination. This could be done locally without much difficulty; nationally it would mean changing the structure of the Ministry of Education or treating Ciudad Guayana as an experimental area. This plan calls for an increased investment per student enrolled. However, it was shown that costs per graduate in each subsystem would decline as the system offers more services more efficiently. The professionals described in the plan probably do not now exist and would have to be trained.

2. *Quality of Instruction*

A. An in-service teacher training section would be established in Ciudad Guayana. At the present time, most in-service training of teachers takes place in Caracas, under the auspices of the Instituto de Mejoramiento Profesional of the Ministry of Education. The Instituto recognizes the need to establish local facilities, both to provide greater response to local needs and to reduce costs to teachers.

B. As part of the training section or as part of the planning section, school authorities and planners would carry out regular assessments of need for training. Their planning statements would also be based on developments in the instructional materials center. As new materials are developed teachers would have to be trained in their use.

3. *Extra-Instructional Services to Students*

A. A guidance department would be established to offer vocational counseling to upper primary and early secondary students, and to candidates for informal technical training programs. Guidance at the ministerial level is now controlled by the División de Orientación Vocacional, which has a small staff and budget. The Ministry is committed to increase the competence of this group. This will require training, more staff, and the development of psychological and pedagogical tests for vocational counseling. Discussions are now taking place with respect to establishment of a "branch" in Ciudad Guayana. The guidance department would necessarily have relations with the fledgling employment service (run by the Ministry of Labor) now operating in Ciudad Guayana. This service will provide employment information and may also develop instruments for vocational placement. The guidance department would also be related to the industrial hiring agencies which have both information and developed selection procedures. The technical education committee to be described must be functioning before the guidance department can operate effectively.

B. In addition to vocational counseling, schools would also offer academic counseling to students. This office would identify students who are not succeeding in school and assist them to overcome their familial or learning problems. This kind of activity is now being developed within schools in Ciudad Guayana and has Ministry approval. However, the professional training of teachers in methods of identifying and assisting failing students is limited. Because teachers do not or cannot maintain regular contact with the families of their students, it will be necessary to provide either visiting teachers or social workers to investigate home situations. It is likely that this can be financed by assigning one teacher within each school to this task, relieving him of classroom responsibilities. This would mean only a slight increase in class size and would give schools a direct link to the community. These teachers would be trained by a professional at the central administration level.

C. In addition, there are plans to establish a placement service for graduates of terminal programs. This might function out of the guidance department and be linked to the technical education committee, the employment service, and industry hiring offices.

4. *Sensitivity and Response to Community Needs*

A. A technical education committee would be established as an extra-official arrangement between all technical training groups and industry. The former include, at present, the Technical-Industrial School, the Instituto Nacional de Cooperación Educativa (INCE), the Commercial School, and the Colegio La Salle. Industry-commerce groups include the steel mill, the Orinoco Mining Company, the Iron Mines Company of Venezuela, the aluminum plant, and the small business association. Also involved will be the industrial unions and the employment service.

With the assistance of planners from the Center for Educational Research, Planning, and Services, this committee would determine the city's present and future needs in manpower training by pooling responsibility and dividing up the task. There is some precedent for this kind of arrangement in Venezuela—a human development committee exists in Valencia and has functioned well. No legal or political difficulties are expected once the committee is formed, though actual formation might be difficult because these groups are not accustomed to working together.

Most likely the committee would remain a policy group. Actual data-gathering and planning would be done by other groups (for example, the employment service and the Center). The existence of relationships among the various training and industry groups will provide a number of spin-off benefits as both sectors increase their understanding of each others' problems.

B. A school planning group would be formed as part of the central administration or as part of the Center for Educational Research, Planning, and Services if the central administration does not materialize. This group would be responsible for the planning of all school construction. It would provide information to the in-service teacher training section with respect to staff needs. It would service the technical education committee with information about feed from schools. It would rely on industry, the employment service, and other data-gathering groups for information necessary in planning buildings and programs. It would assist the instructional materials center in planning its operation.

C. A community services department would be established if the central administration is developed. If not, two separate agencies would be developed.

1. A preprimary education center would take on the responsibility of

organizing, establishing, and supervising public preprimary services. The kind of service which would best seem to meet the needs of the city at present is a form of day-care center in which both children and mothers participate. Participation of mothers would provide them with home management and cultural development training, as well as enhancing their ability to enter the labor force. The day-care center would provide children with medical and nutritional services better than many families in the city can now afford. The center would also prepare children for entrance into primary schools. Administrative and financial arrangements for such a program are under study, as well as less complex and less expensive kinds of facilities which would partially meet the needs of families. There are no legal problems or difficulties expected.

2. An adult education section would coordinate all programs which do not include technical training. INCE and ODEA tend to duplicate each other and there is good reason to believe that the two agencies could coordinate their activities. Local adult education personnel are already working with school people and such an arrangement could be increased in scope, bringing adults in even more contact with schools. Needed at present is an assessment of the two institutions to determine the need for new courses or expansion of present programs. This section would work closely with the instructional materials center, with the guidance section (especially counseling for students), and with the technical education committee. It would use information collected by the planning section.

5. *Content of Education.* An instructional materials section in Ciudad Guayana would be responsible for providing teachers with a wide range of teaching aids, few of which are now available. The instructional materials section would promote the expansion of school libraries both to include more schools and students, and to serve the reading needs of the adult community. This would bring adults into schools, and would back up the adult education program. The section would provide a film library which would distribute and show educational films in the various primary and middle-level schools and in community centers. It would train teachers in the development and production of audiovisual aids at the classroom level as well as providing materials for system-wide use. It would provide the Ministry of Education in Caracas with information and materials to be included in textbooks being prepared at the national level.

The instructional materials section would provide one means for influencing curricula designed at the national level, by providing the materials used by teachers to teach the curricula. In the absence of a central administration, the instructional materials center would serve as a central school purchasing agent for school supplies now bought at retail prices by each school.

There appear to be no legal problems here, and local school people would welcome this kind of service. The Ministry of Education has indicated support for greater local participation in the development of instructional materials, though it seems to wish to maintain its control over what is mass-produced.

Special Emphasis of the Center for Educational Research, Planning, and Services

1. In the planning of curriculum and teacher training programs, early emphasis of the Center will be on the areas of physics, chemistry, biology, and mathematics. This emphasis of the Center is necessary because it fits the most pressing needs of the Ciudad Guayana schools and is consonant with the necessity for emphasizing physical sciences as a background to the programs in technical training which are of primary importance in an industrialized setting such as Ciudad Guayana. For this reason one of the first staff members assigned should be a specialist in the planning of programs in the physical sciences and mathematics.
2. The planning of programs in technical and skilled trade fields for industry will be a second major focus of Center activities. This will include working with the Guayana schools, INCE, and the industries in the development of medium-term and short-term skill courses to prepare technicians and skilled workers for the industries of Guayana. Because the planning of in-school and in-industry related programs is so central to the mission of the Center, the chief specialist of the Center for the first two years should be an expert in the planning and administration of informal educational programs in technical fields.
3. The long-range planning for the Technological Institute should begin even in the first year of the Center's operation. The specific and detailed planning, however, would not get underway until the second year. A consultant specialist in postsecondary technical education could be made available to the project from the outset and he would become a resident in Ciudad Guayana when the planning reached the stage at which his full-time presence was required.
4. A considerable amount of research and planning has already been done for Ciudad Guayana and in order not to lose the benefit of this and to preserve continuity, one of the full-time resident specialists in the Guayana Center should be a person already familiar with the area and the research and planning accomplished to date.

The Center proposed here is a unique one that will attempt to combine research, planning, and services in a form that has not heretofore been tried. No one organization or agency could support all of the research or services that might be based in the Center. The expectation is that local, state, and national resources would be turned to the enormously expensive task of education in the Guayana.

Part Three

Implementing
Human Resource
Development Plans
in a Regional
Development
Agency

14
The Process of Human Resource Development in Guayana

The first draft of this book was written during the summer of 1966. Much has happened in Guayana since that time, and one of the difficulties in capturing the essence of a developing city or region is that the subject will not stand still during the portraiture. For the writers, Ciudad Guayana represents a happy difficulty: many aspects of the educational institutions of Ciudad Guayana have shown significant improvement between the first and last draftings of this manuscript. This last chapter calls attention to these phenomena, which form a part of the description of Guayana as a developing region by demonstrating the special flavor of the city and the character of its people. This final chapter also allows the reader to evaluate, admittedly over a short period of time, the validity of projections made in December 1964 and again in September 1966. Planners are fallible prophets. In this case, we are happy to be so. We took a conservative position in the original projections, hoping to encourage greater attention to the problems of the city. That attention was forthcoming, and it is this result which counts. This chapter, finally, describes and evaluates efforts to implement some of the recommendations made in this study.

Recommendations on paper do not build institutions. However, by reviewing the process and its consequences, something can be learned about the development of education in a regional context.

Changes in Ciudad Guayana

The city has grown and is now filling out the skeleton of roads and highways originally cut by the engineers. There have been minor modifications in the highway plan, but in general one would recognize the city as corresponding to the planners' maps made in 1962 or 1963. In fact, the city from the air looks very much like the planners always said it would.

There has been some unanticipated growth of the city on the eastern, or San Félix, side. Barrio settlements have multiplied along the far edge of the city. This is planned growth now, for the municipal council's housing agency assigns people to parcels laid out along dirt streets cut through the brush. It is, one might say, a planned squatters' settlement, and for this reason much better than the slum barrios along the riverbanks which formerly typified so much of the low-income areas of the city. These new developments occurred chiefly because of some delays in the provision of low-income housing and a larger than expected flow of rural migrants unable to find employment in the city.

Unemployment levels remain around 15 percent. The labor force had grown to about 25,000 in 1967, most of that growth in the services sector, with small merchants expanding services into new housing areas. There are two bus lines now, innumerable taxis and *por puestos*, many barbershops, and several open-air markets in the poorer sections. The employment picture will change again in 1969, as both the steel mill and the Orinoco Mining Company create new jobs. The mining company is establishing a new ore reduction process that will require several hundred new employees, and the steel mill is going to build a flat products plant. The arrival of the aluminum company, now in production, apparently did little to help reduce unemployment. Many of the workers were hired on the outside.

Employment in construction continues to be high. Ciudad Guayana is still very much in the making, as evidenced by the rumble of earth movers and clouds of dust drifting across the fields of houses and apartment buildings in the first stages of construction. The major highway linking the villages making up the city is almost completed; Avenida Guayana is clearly visible now, and when completed next year will re-route traffic around Dalla Costa and through the barrio sections of El Roble.

Some projects have been finished, but not yet opened. For example, the new hospital stands alone on the hill overlooking the Dalla Costa side of the Caroní, unused for lack of personnel. But a new park on the Cachamay Falls of the Caroní draws capacity crowds on weekends. The residential high school and primary school built by the CVG for a religious order is now open. Ground is being cleared for a large sports stadium-playground complex near Punta Vista. Ciudad Guayana continues to boom.

Developments in Education

The educational establishment is booming also. There are (in 1968) thirty-three primary schools operating in Ciudad Guayana and an enrollment of 21,000 children, compared to the twenty schools and 14,000 children of 1965. Some 450 teachers work in the schools now. There has been a comparable increase in secondary enrollments and numbers of schools. Table 14.1 offers a comparison of the present enrollments by grade in primary schools and those projected in the summer of 1966.

TABLE 14.1
Comparison of Projected and Actual Primary School Enrollment

Year		1	2	3	4	5	6	Total
					Grade			
1965–1966	Actual	3,435	2,774	2,473	2,024	1,600	1,232	13,538
1966–1967	Projected	4,132	3,374	2,722	2,410	2,041	1,556	16,235
	Actual	3,431	3,138	2,837	2,417	1,920	1,463	15,216
1967–1968	Projected	4,957	4,021	3,326	2,712	2,379	1,970	19,365
	Actual	4,128	3,930	3,622	3,018	2,393	1,784	18,875
1968–1969	Projected	5,813	4,756	4,049	3,307	2,777	2,331	23,033
	Actual	5,048	3,927	3,982	3,562	2,768	2,115	21,402

The student population of the city has increased pretty much as expected. Enrollments are slightly lower than projected for two reasons. First, only half the new schools have been built that were called for in the plan. Litigation and delays in construction are responsible. Second, the Ministry of Education decided in 1966 to devote its efforts to retention of older children in schools, that is, to reduce dropouts. As a consequence, the rate of increase of new enrollments declined. In Ciudad Guayana this meant that actual enrollments in third and fourth grade were higher than those projected, whereas enrollments in first and second grades were lower.

One consequence of the failure to build schools as rapidly as called for is that the city's schools now enroll a *smaller* proportion of the school-age population than they did in 1965. A city-wide school census carried out in May 1967 showed that 22 percent of the school-age population was not attending school, as compared with 20 percent in June of 1965. Class sizes continue to be large also, as would be expected. However, the number of unitarias has been sharply reduced. There are now only six unitaria schools in Ciudad Guayana and they enroll a scant 160 children.

Over-all, the numerical aspect of primary and secondary education in Ciudad Guayana has not improved, and it may be a bit worse than previously. But quantity is not quality, and there is reason to believe that the quality of education has improved. Proportionately, Ciudad Guayana services no more children today than three years ago, but it may be providing that proportion a better education.

Perhaps the most significant change in primary education is that most of the public school children now have textbooks. The school library program, recommended in the 1964 plan, jointly financed by the CVG and the Ministry of Education, and run by the Banco del Libro, has not only provided the seven largest schools with libraries, but also textbooks for all of their children. In addition, the program trained teachers in the use of textbooks as well as in the preparation of audio-visual aids. A good portion of the training program was spent training teachers how to write daily lesson plans. A follow-up evaluation by the Banco del Libro indicated some significant changes in instructional practices. Furthermore, students from the morning sessions now voluntarily come to the school in the afternoon, and vice versa, to read. Adults from the community also drop in from time to time. But the most significant of this program's accomplishments is that it has served as a model for the whole country. Under Presidential Decree 567, penned after a visit of the President to the school libraries in Guayana, all children in Venezuela will eventually receive free textbooks.

About half the primary schools in the city now use a standardized objective test as a diagnostic instrument in the lower primary grades. As far as can be determined, this is not done anywhere else in Venezuela. Teachers seem fairly satisfied with the procedure, and there are hopes that the practice will be extended.

Teachers are more careful about the evaluation of children. At the end of the first semester they must submit to the primary supervisor a list of all those children in their grade that they expect to fail the year. If the proportion of children exceeds 25 percent, the teacher must propose a plan, to be worked out in detail with the supervisor, for helping failing children. As a consequence of this program, and the emphasis placed on the negative consequences of failure by the Banco del Libro training program (using material from the study reported in this book), failure rates in Ciudad Guayana have decreased sharply. No doubt some teachers have merely lowered their standards. But there is reason to believe, and hope, that many teachers now recognize the school's responsibility to make sure that as many children pass as possible. A survey of teachers' attitudes carried out in March of 1968 provided data on this point, as well as on others.

There is also more initiative from school directors. Several schools open their libraries at night for adults. Others have established health services for their students, an uncommon practice in Venezuela outside of the big cities. The directors meet regularly and are planning common extracurricular activities. For example, there is now an inter-school sports program. There is also a small pilot program in operation to train new directors before they take on their assignment. The candidates work with the supervisor and become familiar with the area in which their school is located. People who have known the schools in Ciudad Guayana for awhile are impressed with the steady improvement of confidence and enthusiasm shown by teachers and directors alike; they are beginning to see how much they can do by their own efforts. The city's schools now receive visitors from Caracas and other cities who have heard about events in the Guayana and want to learn more in order to improve their schools.

At the middle-school level there are few changes. The major activities have been the formation of an Association of Professors of Science and Mathematics, and establishment of a Technical Education Committee bringing together representatives of training and educational institutions and industry. These activities are described in this chapter.

Much of what has happened in Ciudad Guayana is directly attributable to the local school people. They have carried the brunt, and many of the ideas have been theirs. However, it is also true that the presence of a group of technical advisors working in education has had its impact. The Center for Educational Research, Planning, and Services described in Chapter 13 was not established as planned, that is, with the potentiality of carrying out all the necessary tasks. The Ministry of Education was not able to provide staff counterparts for the Center. However, Center advisors did work in the city, beginning in late 1966. Their presence has its consequences. The rest of this chapter describes the history of attempts to work with national and local agencies to build a functioning school system in Guayana.

Nation, Region, and Locale: Links for Implementing Human Resource Development Plans

Underdeveloped countries suffer from ineffective communication and execution links among nation, region, and locale. This is in the nature of the brute beast underdevelopment: communication up and down the line is delayed; so is execution, and a fearful demurrage exacted. Life is lived and the battle is fought and problems occur out on the regional and local line, at the periphery; but resources are gathered in and the power of decision resides in the national capital at the center. This is certainly true of human resource development in Venezuela. The two major human resource development activities, formal and informal education, are controlled by highly centralized bureaucracies with headquarters in Caracas; but the problems of education and training that plague Ciudad Guayana and jeopardize its future development must be confronted and solved in the city and the development zone itself.

It is the task of a regional development agency, such as the Corporación Venezolana de Guayana, to mediate between the local problem-demand situation and the national agencies which have the power and resources to contribute toward solutions. Perhaps in no other area is the problem of mediation more sensitive than in the implementation of human resource development planning.

In this chapter the emphasis is not so much on technical problems of human resource development planning as on the mediational role that a regional planning and development agency must play in implementation. The regional planning agency must always be aware of the difficulties of bringing centralized decision making and resources to bear on local problems. It must be linked at both ends of the development chain. The agency must be anchored in the locale so that its investigators sense issues before problems reach crisis proportions. At the same time, the regional agency must have strong links to the center of power in the national capital where the money and the power of decision lie, for without access to the "court" it does little good to know what the local needs and problems are. At the local level the regional planning and development agency must exercise caution that it does not get so involved in daily problems that it has no time or reservoir of good will to spend on long-range problem resolutions.

Before 1965 the Desarrollo Humano Section of CVG was not firmly linked at either end of the development chain. It had no resident staff members in education in Guayana: there was a foreign resident anthropologist monitoring social problems locally, but this was inadequate coverage of educational problems. On the other hand CVG had little contact with the major educational organizations in Caracas. The Ministry of Education was the main agency in formal education and INCE was the main agency working in informal education. On a smaller scale there were private schools and training programs run by and in the industries themselves.

The Ministry of Education dominates formal education in Venezuela at the primary and middle school level and is moving with increasing power and assurance into postsecondary education. A dependency of the Ministry, ODEA, also plays an important role in adult education but the major activity in informal education, the preparation of adults and young people through programs of basic education, skill training, and apprenticeship, is controlled by INCE with headquarters in Caracas. CVG, as a regional development agency, faced the task of stimulating the educational efforts of the Ministry and INCE and coordinating them so that resources, human and fiscal, could be effectively brought to bear on the resolution of human resource development problems in Guayana.

Local Institutions for Human Resource Development

The human resource development situation in Guayana in 1965 can be briefly reviewed. There was a high existing demand for skilled workmen to man established and new industries and to fill jobs in the construction and services which supported the industries. There was no pool of educated and trained workers in Guayana, although there were large numbers of unemployed, unskilled adults. The unemployment rate probably ran from 12 to 20 percent during the years 1963–1966. The projected demand for skilled workers for the years 1965–1975 was very high. Immigration was no longer a potential source of educated and trained workers. Migration promised little because Guayana could not compete with other equally prosperous, but more attractive, areas and cities in Venezuela.

In the face of all this, what was the education and training situation in Ciudad Guayana in 1965?

1. ETI, the public industrial secondary school, had not even opened in early 1965. It was an empty shell, completed by the Ministry of Public Works, but not accepted by the Ministry of Education. It would take four years to build toward adequate enrollments.

2. La Escuela Artesanal La Salle, the private trade training school, was operating at far below capacity and its programs were catering mainly to pre-industrial training, giving entry-level skills in the building trades to boys twelve through fifteen in grades four to six. Most La Salle artisanal graduates were too young to enter the work force even if they had the skills. There were discussions

of the possibility of using La Salle facilities for work-study programs to be run jointly by the school and industry, but in 1965–1966 there was no specific program proposal.

3. Orinoco Mining Company (U.S. Steel) had run many short courses in orientation, plant safety, and introduction to new processes and practices, but it offered no systematic long courses or apprenticeship program. Iron Mines Company of Venezuela (Bethlehem) did about the same, but slightly less of it.

4. SIDOR, the government steel mill, had an apprenticeship program in the machine trades which was complete and well supported, but very small. A foreign training mission was assisting SIDOR and a specific and fairly well-equipped area had been set aside for the training. At the same time this small effort was going forward, the loss due to worker incompetence was very severe and labor turnover extremely high.

5. INCE programs were basic literacy and education supplemented with some vocational training in the building trades to prepare young men to enter the work force as construction helpers. The programs were for young adults, fifteen through nineteen, and the major purpose was to teach youngsters how to learn. Local construction companies, then supporting skilled workers from outside the zone, stated that INCE- and La Salle-trained workers had insufficient skills at graduation to function as helpers in the building trades. This may have reflected prejudice or ignorance, but it indicated in some measure that existing Guayana training programs were held in low repute by potential employers. With construction beginning to boom the companies had to bring in equipment operators and other semiskilled men from outside. Skilled jobs were going begging in all of the industries. At SIDOR labor costs were high as the government-owned steel mill struggled with human and technological problems to bring its output up to 50 percent of capacity.

With demand high and clear, and supply woefully short, what prevented the mobilization of Guayana agencies to meet such a compelling need? Furthermore, what could CVG as a regional development agency do to get local industries and training institutions working to solve the obvious problem?

A Strategy from a Regional Development Agency: The Plan

With need so apparent and response so weak, it scarcely seems sensible that the first step in a human resource development strategy for CVG would be to make a precise estimate of the manpower requirements for the region, beginning in the base year 1965 and running to the target year 1975. But this indeed was the first step taken, as the early chapters of this book detail and as following sections of this chapter explain. The next move was to analyze the output of the schools and training institutions and to compare requirement targets with output estimates. The comparison, in all educational and training categories save the very lowest, indicated a substantial deficit of educated and trained people. On the basis of the estimated deficit a human resource development plan, complete with current and capital cost estimates, was prepared for Guayana. The question then became what to do with this plan.[1]

Prior to 1964 CVG had no stated policy or formal strategy for assisting human resource development. Judging from its actions, or lack of them, its hopes in the area could be summarized:

1. Hope that the problem of human resource development through education would be solved by the migration of educated and trained people and by spin-off in the industrialization process itself. This was the most desirable of all possible eventualities for CVG, inasmuch as it would cost nothing and not even require explicit attention from CVG planners. By early 1964 it was apparent that this pleasant dream would not be realized and that CVG had to do something.

2. Hope that other agencies would solve the problem of human resource development in Guayana.

a. The Ministry of Education would handle formal education, as it was required to do under law.

b. Industries would run in-service apprenticeship and training programs.

c. INCE would handle informal training and cooperate with the industries in apprenticeship programs.

d. Private organizations, mostly Catholic teaching orders, would establish schools and training facilities that would contribute powerfully to the solution of the problem. CVG officials believed that Catholic institutions would attract higher grade professionals to Guayana because they would be interested in private education for their children. The belief that Venezuelan professionals would not want anything but private, religious education for their children was based partly on facts from the accidents of Venezuelan history. In the past, upper-middle-class parents preferred private education because public education had been systematically deprived of sufficient support to guarantee minimal standards of quality. Given equal facilities there would be less reason for Venezuelan middle-class professionals to prefer private education.

At the outset, CVG officials felt that the private educational alternative would entail small outlays. They soon learned the contrary. Private organizations did not flock to the new city to found schools. CVG had to provide land, then capital outlay for buildings, then money for equipment, and finally in 1964 CVG had to furnish temporary budgetary support to cover current expenses. The CVG assistance policy offended Ministry of Education officials and citizens who supported public education and some powerful politicians and government administrators. Most serious of all, private education showed not the slightest capacity to meet the vast education and training burden in Guayana.

3. By early 1964 CVG officials realized that private education would not solve the problem of education in the Guayana and the hope was that the Ministry of Education would rise to the occasion if they were informed of how important the Guayana zone was to the development of the country, how critically necessary educated and trained people were to development in Guayana, and how inadequate current educational and training programs were in meeting manpower requirements. Presumably the plan would show all this, and once Ministry officials had the plan they would respond to the needs it outlined. The plan was presented in 1964.

The Response of the Ministry: Stalemate. The Ministry responded by insisting that CVG assume responsibility. Even with huge resources there are strict limits on how rapidly an educational system can expand. No amount of money creates instant teachers, and the dictator's people had dealt sly but devastating damage to the teacher training institutions. It is no wonder that the Ministry sought easement from any part of the crushing burden of education in Venezuela.

The CVG, by Venezuelan Ministry of Education standards, did have large resources—the annual budget of the CVG in 1964 was almost half that of the Ministry of Education. It seemed obvious that CVG should take over a major share of support of education in Guayana. But the fact was that CVG (until 1965) allocated not one bolívar to public education, which it felt was a Ministry problem, but instead allocated whatever money it did spend on education to private Catholic schools. At the same time the CVG exhorted the Ministry of Education to increase its allocations to public education in the zone.

The Ministry of Education allocated just about as much to schools in Guayana as it did to schools in any part of Venezuela outside of Caracas. This does not mean that public schools in Guayana were well supported. Data in other sections of this book indicate the contrary. In Guayana, Ministry efforts were inadequate to build and run schools or to educate a work force for a highly demanding industrial complex.

In late 1965 the Ministry of Education-CVG stalemate persisted. At headquarters in Caracas there was no communication between the Ministry and CVG officials in Human Development Section. In the field there was only sporadic contact between local school teachers and directors and occasional CVG visitors. These visitors asked questions, wrote down names, raised hopes, but went away not to be seen again.

Hence, in formal education the task for CVG human resource development planners was more than merely to provide a fillip to Ministry effort in the Guayana schools. The first order of business was to establish communication at local, regional, and national levels. Second, it was vital to create mutual trust among functionaries of the Ministry and CVG. In addition to communication and trust in basic motives, it was also necessary to demonstrate the competence of those working in human resource development in CVG. This was a case of proving the Venezuelans' ability to themselves; in development planning foreign advisors sometimes win a reputation for competence more readily than capable nationals. The fact is that technicians in both CVG and the Ministry were competent.

The difficulties between CVG and Ministry functionaries were also exacerbated by presumed political and religious differences. CVG functionaries were viewed as rightist and ultraconservative and Ministry officials as leftist and radical. These descriptions were exaggerated and often incorrect on both sides, but with a breakdown in communication it was the legend and not the fact which had weight.

Beyond demonstrating competence it was necessary for CVG to demonstrate interest through some significant earnest of purpose that would contribute to public education in Guayana. Ministry officials felt, and with justification, that CVG officials were attempting to call the tune without having paid the piper. Only after trust could be established and competence and interest demonstrated would it be possible for the Ministry and CVG to cooperate in planning and implementing educational programs in the Guayana. Many of the problems of establishing harmonious working relationships between a national ministry and a regional planning agency might be characteristic of any developing country. Relationships have not always been harmonious between SUDENE and the

Brazilian national Ministry of Education, or the state secretariats of education
in the northeast states. Some of the problems in Guayana, however, were unique
to Venezuela and its history and peculiar to the development zone and the
CVG policy of aiding private education exclusively.

Breaking the Stalemate: CVG Provides Earnests of Purpose in Public Educa-
tion. Even before presenting the first plan to Ministry officials, foreign advisors
assisting CVG in planning human resource development for the Guayana
attempted to convince CVG officials that the mere presentation of a plan would
be insufficient to stimulate the Ministry to give special attention to education in
the Guayana. Because of the history of Ministry-CVG relationships, Ministry
officials were adamantly opposed to giving any special consideration to Guayana. They felt that CVG was favoring private education with public funds
which should have gone to public education. If anything, Ministry officials were
disposed to do less in Guayana than elsewhere. Foreign advisors maintained
that before Ministry officials could be convinced of CVG sincerity or, in fact,
before the advisors themselves could be convinced, the CVG would have to
make some contribution to public education which would serve as an earnest of
purpose of their intent to help public education in Guayana. CVG officials
stated that they were not opposed to aiding public education, but stated that it
was necessary to have a plan which specified needs in public education before
they could make a sensible investment. The plan outlined in the first strategy
report, then, had a number of very specific proposals for allocations of CVG
funds to public education.

From the list of possibilities CVG chose to assist the following projects:

1. *Textbooks.* CVG provided funds to Banco del Libro so that a basic
library and textbook loan collections could be set up in seven public schools in
Ciudad Guayana. Under the textbook program Banco del Libro lent text
books to poor children who otherwise would have had no book or an unsuitable
one. As previously mentioned, this program proved of national significance: the
model for the program set up in Guayana so impressed President Leoni that a
decree was issued generalizing the program to all of Venezuela. The program
has not been extended to all areas and schools in Venezuela yet, but at least the
intent and the decree exist; CVG and the Banco del Libro were credited with the
model program.

2. *School Construction.* CVG provided funds to build six primary schools in
Ciudad Guayana. Again this was a wise program. The schools were badly

needed and the result highly visible. Construction involved a one-shot invest-ment for CVG and had no continuing fiscal obligations.

3. *Assorted Goods and Services Provided to Specific Schools.* CVG provided a number of small donations of goods and services to individual schools. It provided milk and lunch funds to the technical-industrial school as well as some stock and equipment. CVG provided some services, such as transportation, to directors, inspectors, and teachers. CVG continues to provide some textbooks, curriculum materials, playground equipment, and building materials. None of these contributions was large, but they were strategically placed and won good will for CVG.

4. *Technical Advisory Services to the Guayana Schools.* CVG provided a variety of technical services to school officials and teachers in Guayana. CVG helped the primary school inspector of Guayana in the design and management of the first school census. This provided useful and important results which were used to justify program expenditures with the Ministry and to convince CVG directors of the need for school construction. CVG also helped the technical school with some advice on equipment and programing. Regular CVG contri-butions in this area came with the establishment of the Guayana Center for Educational Research, Planning, and Extension Services, described later in this chapter.

5. *Other CVG Activities in Public Education.* Not all the activities which CVG attempted had any useful result. CVG attempted to provide assistance for in-service teacher training programs in the public schools. By and large these projects never came to fruition because of intra-ministry political squabbling. There were other such failures which need not be described.

6. *CVG Assistance to INCE.* CVG always had fairly close relationships with INCE, at least with the higher echelons in Caracas. In Guayana there was no close cooperation, although CVG did provide some assistance in planning and establishing the INCE Metal Trades Training Center.

7. *CVG Assistance to Private Schools.* CVG did not need to establish its generosity to private schools inasmuch as it had made very heavy contributions, on capital and current account, to almost all the private schools in Guayana. CVG assisted materially two elaborate parochial schools and gave heavy capital assistance to the La Salle Artisanal School. It also helped with equipment and at one point carried a share of the La Salle current budget. CVG provided advisory and technical services to La Salle from the Guayana Center in order to

assist La Salle in developing other sources of support for its programs. CVG also made a very large capital grant for the construction of a private boarding school. However, after 1965, CVG was searching for ways of reducing its capital contributions and continuing obligations to private education in Guayana. This was not easy to do. Private school authorities, mainly out of desire to serve the poorer classes with free education and training, had little enthusiasm for adopting the fee structures which would make them self-supporting. Religious educators had not come to Guayana to serve the affluent. They wanted to run CVG-supported programs for the poor children. Hence CVG's original policy of assisting private schools which would serve the middle class did not work out exactly the way it was designed, and varied according to the social welfare objectives of groups and individual religions.

Establishment of the Guayana Center for Educational Research, Planning, and Extension Services

The Center described in Chapter 13 was established in skeleton form in the fall of 1966. After its establishment the locus of CVG human resource development activities shifted to Ciudad Guayana. Prior to this, CVG had maintained one professional technician in education on site in Guayana, but the bulk of planning and research activity had been accomplished in Caracas with occasional visits to "the field" for research and project inauguration. The move to Guayana had been strongly urged by the foreign advisory group. After two years of assistance to the CVG Desarrollo Humano Section, largely in Caracas, the foreign advisors insisted on two fundamental conditions for continuing the advisory program:

1. The locus of activity would be in Guayana and not Caracas. CVG officials agreed with this, although it was not as easy for them to shift Venezuelans out of Caracas as it was to assign foreigners to Guayana.

2. The Guayana Center for Educational Research, Planning, and Extension Services, although launched with CVG and foreign human and fiscal resources, had to accept the Ministry of Education as an equal partner and had to work with all agencies, public and private, in human resource development in Guayana. Again CVG agreed to this condition readily and proposed signing an agreement with the Ministry under which CVG would furnish support for Ministry officials seconded to the Center and would pay the salary of the director named by the Ministry. After two years of Center operation the agreement between CVG and the Ministry of Education is still unsigned and a

Venezuelan director has not been appointed. This situation influenced markedly the three main activities carried out by the foreign advisors in the Guayana Center.

Activities of the Guayana Center for Educational Research, Planning, and Extension Services

The original notion of the Guayana Center was that it would provide a location for all activities in educational planning, research, and special services, and that CVG technicians residing in the Guayana, foreign advisors from Harvard-CSED or elsewhere, Ministry officials residing in the Guayana and specialists visiting and working there temporarily, all would have working space in the Center. This objective was realized in part despite the fact that no formal protocol was ever signed with the Ministry of Education. The district primary supervisor and the ODEA promoter have offices in the Center. The Center has carried on a variety of research and planning services, among which were the design and management of a second school census, a revised manpower analysis and plan for Guayana, various surveys of primary school building needs in the short run, surveys of secondary-level programs in technical education, and in some cases specific advisory service on the development of curricula in technical-industrial education programs.

Major fields of activity at the Center fall under three rubrics: (1) informal education and training (especially adult literacy and basic cultural extension); (2) science and mathematics education, mostly at the middle school level; (3) technical education. Harvard-CSED assigned three advisors to the Guayana Center, and each one had as his principal task one of the three specific activity areas. Each advisor also had general duties which were shared. For example, all worked on the school population census. None of the three advisors had a Venezuelan counterpart at comparable level and this was one of the weakest aspects of CVG support and Ministry cooperation, as well as violation of a cardinal principle dear to the hearts of international technical assistance theorists. It also reflected a general peculiarity of foreign technical assistance in Venezuela where there were always more resources to launch and support programs than Venezuelans to man them. This is unique to Venezuela, and the opposite of most development projects in developing countries.

The Plan, first published in 1965, was a relatively useless exercise until implemented, and in the first stage the three activity areas seemed to be of paramount importance. A fourth activity area, the reorganization of primary

education in Guayana, was probably even more important, but had to be
approached much more circumspectly and treated over a much longer time
span. All three of the major activities of the Guayana Center illustrate the
importance, albeit the difficulty, of the technical-mediational role which a
regional agency such as CVG must play in implementing human resource
development planning.

Activities in informal education and science and mathematics education will
be described briefly, but more attention will be given to activity in the area of
technical education because this was the most complicated of the three, insofar
as it involved working with the largest number of independent agencies and
institutions. Activity in technical education was also the most successful, in the
sense of reaching a more developed stage in implementation and having some
stable organizational form to show at the end of the working period of the
foreign advisor.

Science and Mathematics Education. The teaching of science and mathematics
goes on in a number of separated schools in Ciudad Guayana. As asserted
earlier, there is no primary education system in Ciudad Guayana. Much less are
there formal links among the middle schools which in 1966 included a public
commercial school, two public liceos, four private liceos, one public technical-
industrial school, and one private artisanal school. One of the major activities
of the science education advisor attached to the Guayana Center was the
organization of an Association of Professors of Science and Mathematics. The
Association was designed to provide a source of information to local professors,
a forum for analysis and discussion of problems in science and mathematics
instruction, and a pressure group to ensure adequate continuing support for
science education activities in the Guayana schools. The Association was
conceived as possibly providing impetus to formation of links among middle
schools.

The science advisor spent a great deal of time in the beginning building
personal relationships with science and mathematics teachers in the schools.
After personal relationships had been established, it was necessary to demonstrate that science-mathematics instruction was a problem and that the problem
could be solved without necessarily discovering a new treasure trove of resources. School officials and teachers in Guayana, as elsewhere, were willing to
admit that there were problems. The shortcomings of the programs were
apparent enough. But teachers attributed all problems and difficulties to lack of
resources and support. With more money, the problems would be solved, the

educators said. To get the analysis a step beyond this classic implication, so much beloved by educators the world over, it was necessary to make a detailed study of science-mathematics instruction in the Guayana schools. Little was known about middle education generally in Ciudad Guayana, and a study seemed a necessary first step.

Here the mediational role of CVG was critical but deficient. The foreign advisor in science and mathematics needed CVG help to gain access to study the public and private secondary schools of Guayana. The key individual, the state supervisor of secondary education, had to be directly courted by the foreign advisor because CVG neither had entry at the state level nor sufficient power at the national level to guarantee access. The advisor made his own contacts at the local level, secured the information, and prepared a report for science-mathematics teachers. Concurrently, the advisor organized the Association and the first meetings were held during the end of academic year 1966–1967.

In its early stages the Association appeared promising. Several meetings were held, and all the conventional but necessary activities to improve a curriculum area were generated. New science-mathematics instruction materials were presented to the teachers and discussed. A small curriculum library collection was begun. Scholarships for vacation period training were provided to Guayana science teachers. Plans were made for a program of in-service teacher training in Guayana. A proposal was made that a Venezuelan be appointed to carry on the work of the foreign advisor.

Then the growth and development of the Association stopped abruptly in 1967–1968, after a school vacation had interrupted developments. Programs and conferences were planned only to be canceled after the vacation; momentum was never regained. Attendance at the Association meetings dwindled. No Venezuelan counterpart to the foreign advisor was appointed.

What had been accomplished? In 1967 some materials had been distributed; some professors had been sent out for training in short courses; some ideas had been exchanged; a model professional organization had been tried; but there was no observable improvement in science-mathematics teaching in Guayana, nor was there any institutionalized means to ensure future progress. CVG was unable to secure cooperation and direction from the national level. Within the Ministry of Education in Caracas there was mixed support. The directorates of the relevant middle education programs cooperated to a certain extent, but the Ministry planning office, EDUPLAN, and the Division of In-Service Teacher Training ignored the Association. CVG and the foreign advisors were unable to stimulate local professors to make the sacrifices necessary to guarantee high quality programs. Finally, it came down to statements that if CVG could provide funds to attract high-quality teachers and funds to hire supervisors and funds to purchase equipment, then science-mathematics education could be improved in the Guayana. So the project turned full circle and at the end was about where it was in the beginning—the basic problem was lack of resources and the basic solution was provision of resources, human and fiscal. This, though discouraging, is a classic *tour de frappe* in development planning and technical assistance.

Informal Education: Literacy and Basic Education. A second major activity area for the Guayana Center was informal education, that is, literacy and basic education, rather than technical and vocational training. The two organizations in this field, INCE and the Ministry of Education Office of Adult Education, ODEA, have already been described. The lack of coordination between the two organizations, both with headquarters in Caracas, has also been mentioned (Chapter 5).

Adult education, divided between two powerful Caracas-based agencies, proved more difficult to coordinate institutionally than science-mathematics education, which required working with many individual teachers scattered in public and private schools. In the science-mathematics situation there was no powerful hierarchy interposed between the individual teachers and the advisors in the Guayana Center. Each individual was on his own and effective work depended on personal contacts between the foreign advisor-promoter and the individual teachers. Only when it came to arranging programs through the Ministry of Education In-Service Training Section did the problem of relationships among agencies become important in science-mathematics; and coordination failed.

In informal education, because of overlapping responsibilities and organizational ambiguity, institutional coordination was difficult from the outset. At the local level the foreign advisor attempted to bring together INCE and ODEA educational workers in Guayana. There was one meeting and no further contact after that. At the national level it would have been imperative for CVG to intercede at the top. This CVG did not choose to do in adult education although, as will be seen, it did use its good offices unstintingly with INCE in the technical and industrial education area. No cooperation was effected between INCE and ODEA in adult education programs. INCE looked askance at the poorer quality programs of ODEA, and some ODEA officials felt that INCE should not even work in general adult education. There have been indications that INCE and ODEA might work together on joint research, but this is only a remote possibility for the future.

Informal education was to have had a large research component. The intent of Guayana Center advisors was to make a complete and detailed study of the objectives, curricula, costs, instructional staff, clientele, and results of all informal education programs operating in the Guayana. To this end, the preliminary form of a questionnaire was developed. This first approximation of an evaluation instrument was applied prematurely to an inadequately designed sample and the numerical results were of only scant validity and interest. Despite its technical shortcomings, the survey may have established some good will and increased receptivity among INCE and ODEA functionaries. During the term of the foreign advisor in the Guayana Center several rather conventional descriptive reports of informal education programs were prepared and circulated. There is presently in progress a much more complete and adequate study of informal education in Guayana.

In the informal education area, CVG and foreign advisors requested that INCE and ODEA station a responsible planner-coordinator in Guayana. ODEA, with highly constrained resources, was unable to provide such a person and its programs continue to be planned and coordinated, insofar as they receive any over-all direction, from Caracas. In the case of INCE, where CVG had closer relations, it proved possible to get a planner and supervisor assigned to Guayana. In exchange CVG helped INCE establish a Guayana training center in commercial and service jobs.

Over-all, then, the Guayana Center was unable to get better coordination of local programs in basic education, although it was indirectly instrumental in getting INCE to station a local planner and program coordinator in Guayana. At the national level the Center advisors were unable to bring INCE and ODEA together and unable to get CVG to assist in effecting coordination. CVG continued to have good relationships with INCE and mediocre relationships with the Ministry of Education. In research the first field investigation was handled hastily and inadequately. Much-improved research has been developed and is now being applied in Guayana. In planning, some rather conventional reports, describing local programs, were prepared.

Technical Education: Formal School and Informal Programs. Coordination of technical education was a formidable task. Of the three major activities of the Guayana Center, technical education presented the most difficult problems in research, planning, or extension services. Responsibility for technical education, formal and informal, was shared by the largest number of agencies, public and private. The two major agencies, the Ministry of Education and INCE, have been amply described, both in their programs and with respect to their relation-ships with CVG. Within the Ministry the chief agency was DARINCO, the Department of Artisanal, Industrial, and Commercial Education.

The locus of DARINCO activity in Ciudad Guayana was ETI, the Technical-Industrial School. The senior resident official of DARINCO in the Guayana was the director of ETI. The director of ETI, as is customary in Latin American schools, has considerable autonomy in all matters relating to the internal management of the school, but very little latitude in dealings with organizations and institutions outside. Caracas guards its authority zealously and permits little local initiative in establishing and maintaining relationships with outside agencies at the local level. To make any commitment the ETI director had to be cleared by one of the national supervisors or even the Director General of DARINCO. Some matters might even go to EDUPLAN, the Ministry over-all planning office, or to the Minister's office.

At the local level there was no one person in charge of the four major INCE programs in technical education. INCE activity in all four areas, as well as INCE activities in basic education, were under a regional coordinator who reported directly to the INCE president and executive board in Caracas. The headquarters of the regional coordinator were in Puerto La Cruz, about two hundred miles away from Ciudad Guayana.

Private efforts in technical education were represented by Colegio La Salle, operated by the Christian Brothers. The director of La Salle had complete autonomy in dealing with any group on any problem relating to technical education in his school. He needed no permission or approval from his superior in Caracas.

Private industry is best represented by the Orinoco Mining Company, which had in 1967 the largest work force of any single, private industry in the zone, and conducted various short training programs for its workers. Orinoco Mining is the oldest of the large industries in Guayana and has operated there since the opening of the Cerro Bolívar mines in 1954. It operates with almost complete autonomy from its parent organization, U.S. Steel. The president of the com-pany has a home in Ciudad Guayana.

ALCASA, Aluminium de Caroní, S.A., is one of the newest industries of the zone and began its operations in 1967. It is jointly owned by Reynolds

International and CVG; it is a medium-sized industry with large training problems but insufficient scale to make an independent training program worthwhile. The ALCASA president lives in Ciudad Guayana.

Public industry was represented by SIDOR, Siderurgica del Orinoco, the government-owned steel plant, which was the largest employer in Ciudad Guayana. SIDOR also had the largest manpower problem, and a training program with four hundred apprentices enrolled in 1967. Production has been limited because of the shortage of skilled production workers in the steel plant. From the plant general manager on down, SIDOR officials showed strong interest and support for improving technical training in Guayana. Although offices are maintained in Caracas, many important managers of SIDOR live in the Guayana.

With so many different organizations and agencies having a stake, either as producer or consumer or both, in technically trained workers, the coordination problem in technical education was destined to be delicate.

First Step in the Center. The first activity in technical education of the Guayana Center was a study of the problems in Guayana. It was not difficult to discover and identify a host of special and general problems, although classifying them so that a concerted attempt at solution could be devised was, as always, not easy. The problems have been listed: there was high current demand, a low pool of skills, indications of a rapidly increasing demand, and low capacity of existing institutions to meet future demand. These were only the most obvious problems.

Programs in Guayana were not only deficient quantitatively, they were of inadequate quality. The programs of INCE, ETI, La Salle, and even the in-industry courses either aimed too low and failed to produce workers with sufficient skill level for the jobs available, or were so inefficient and ineffective that wastage was appallingly high and the skill level of the few who did graduate too low. Instruction in both formal and informal courses was poor because teachers were poorly trained, poorly paid, and scarcely supervised at all. Curriculum objectives seemed reasonable on paper, but the means to attain them were not made available because labs, shops, classrooms, equipment, and stock were not adequately provided.

In addition to the specific shortcomings of existing programs, there were no coordinated plans or consistent response to local needs in technical training. There was duplication in programs, but also very large gaps. The agencies based in Caracas did support technical training in Guayana, but the programs often consisted of the automatic application of national program plans and standards with little attempt to adapt them to the specifics of the local situation. Attention also came in fits and starts and was not always maximized in accord with peak local needs. At the very time there was a critical shortage of construction workers in Guayana, evidenced by the importation of skilled workers in the building trades from abroad or from other parts of Venezuela, INCE, because of an internal jurisdictional problem between Caracas and Guayana, closed its Guayana courses in the construction trades. Not that these courses were adequate either in level or numbers of graduates, but the fact of the closing is illustrative of the general lack of coordinated local request and adequate Caracas response.

At the local level it might still have been possible to harmonize plans and programs, whatever the separation among Caracas-based agencies, but the situation in Guayana was chaotic. Schools and programs were raw and new. So were staff. There was no time to plan ahead. Needs were pressing from the outset and response and support were always spotty. No one had time to coordinate his program with anyone else's. The store was open and customers streamed in and there was no time to get the kinks out of the staff or the bugs out of the plant and equipment.

There were some problems, common to developing countries, which Guayana did not have to face. There was no shortage of funds. CVG had sufficient funds to support programs of merit, and this fact afforded a powerful means to lever innovation or reform. INCE programs in industrial training were of fair quality and well supported. The private industries had large resources and efficient and high caliber management to employ them. SIDOR, representing as it did an initial investment of 350 million dollars and outlay of many more millions during the attempt to get the plant into full production, would scarcely scrimp when it came to supporting a program to enhance productivity over both the short and the long run.

There was, in addition to funds, powerful and influential support for technical training in Guayana. The connection between education and production was never so apparent as in the technical training area. There was no question of providing resources to some general fund which might or might not respond immediately to the training requirements of the organizations furnishing the funds. At issue was a technical training program, located in the Guayana, run by residents of the Guayana for the industries of the Guayana. This fact was to exert a powerful influence on the outcome of activities in the technical education area, as opposed to other areas of education and training.

So much for advantages. Back to problems. A final difficulty was that there was no tradition of local cooperation in the Guayana. The leaders of private industry did not meet, nor did representatives of public or private education. Each agency and company went its own way and although there was no open enmity or competition, as in the INCE–ODEA situation in basic education, there was no knowledge of other programs or interest in informing and sharing. One of the major problems then was that cooperation had to be stimulated and created where there was no tradition for it, and where such tradition as existed had a powerful and determining influence on what was possible. In Hirschman's terms, communication and cooperation at the local level for the purposes of concerted attempts to solve common problems were "traits" that did not exist in the society, and any project which attempted to solve the problems of technical education in Guayana would have to take into explicit account the absence of these traits and the need to create or "make" them.[2] Still, Guayana had special advantages in this regard. Its very newness and rawness made the force of tradition less than in older sites.

Research and planning activities in technical education ran through several stages:

1. Reconnaissance, to identify organizations and individuals involved either as users or producers of technically educated and trained people. The result of this activity was the identification of the organizations and schools previously mentioned.

2. Study of the problems and resources of technical education in the Guayana and in Venezuela generally, so that whatever the solution proposed it would be based on knowledge of needs and resources. The result of this study was the development of reports and plans on manpower development in Guayana. Many of these reports and plans had been prepared originally by former CVG and foreign planning advisors. The major contribution of the technical education advisor was to present the information in a form that was meaningful and usable for local users and producers of trained manpower and to see that these local officials studied and discussed the information. This is no mean contribution to the implementation of planning.

3. Development of personal contacts at the local level with people and organizations concerned with technical training. Identification of organizations

and individuals. The result of this was the formulation of reports and a list of potential institutions and individuals for membership on the Technical Education Committee. A set of criteria for determining membership on the Technical Education Committee was also devised.

4. Organization of a committee made up of persons representing institutions which produced and employed technically trained manpower. This was the major activity of the Guayana Center advisor in the area of technical education. The committee was organized and the first three meetings were held between August and November of 1967.

5. Committee deliberation and planning in the early meetings gave indications that it could fulfill the mission envisaged, that is, the coordination and planning of technical education in Guayana. Only a few examples need be cited. The private school and one of the industries jointly planned a work-study program in the electrical field. INCE and one of the industries began jointly to plan an apprenticeship program. There was a proposal to use this program as a model for other INCE-sponsored apprentice programs in other industries. The committee proved to be so interesting that DARINCO-Caracas decided to study it as a model to be used in other regions of the country. In short, the committee began to accomplish what it was designed to do.

6. Evaluation of the creation, organization, and action of the Technical Education Committee. An evaluation can best be based on the concluding comments of the final analysis prepared by the advisor who organized the Technical Education Committee in the Guayana:

Conclusions and Recommendations
Looking back over the year's labor in Ciudad Guayana what has been learned about education and development in Guayana? More important, what has been learned in Guayana that would be applicable in other developing countries? The lack of cooperation between industry and the education and training establishment is a powerful negative influence in development. Committees which promote this communication and cooperation can make an important contribution to human resource development. The Technical Education Committee of Guayana contributed to the development of the region by performing the following tasks:
1. Informed members mutually about pressing problems.
2. Stimulated suggestions for solution.
3. Effected cooperation in the analysis of the problem and the proposal for solution.
4. Contributed to comprehensive solutions rather than partial ones.
5. Contributed to continuity in efforts toward solutions by tying local problems to national resources.

The problems of education are found at the local level, as always, in the Guayana region. But resources and the power of decision are concentrated in the capital, as in the Ministry of Education in Caracas. *The link between local schools and national officials is the supervisor or similar middle-level administrator.* It is this office that offers the potential for communicating the national plan to the sub-regions of the country. The person holding this office is in a position to understand how local problems can be communicated to Central authorities where decisions are ultimately made. This will allow Central planning authorities to modify their programs in response to local conditions. Middle-level administrators usually have sufficient experience to define local problems and to propose proper solutions to senior officials. It is crucial to identify this position when organizing local or regional committees. *Any committee set up to stimulate communication and cooperation between the local schools and the national officials must recruit the key middle-level administrators and work closely with them.*

The identification of these key administrators at the middle level and in the middle positions between the immediate local problem and the national and centralized command center, and effective work with them, was the major component in the successful work with the technical educational committee.[3]

The organization of the Technical Education Committee, despite the number of organizations involved and the complex and sensitive relationships implied, proved to be one of the most successful of the Guayana Center's efforts in planning implementation.

The Guayana Center as an Autonomous Agency. The model which the Guayana Center represents has its critics. For example, Hirschman has criticized the autonomous agency, which CVG was, and which its creature, the Guayana Center for Educational Research, Planning, and Extension Services even more certainly was. Hirschman states,

The administrative device embodying this intermediate solution is the autonomous authority and agency, which is designed to insulate the project from the country in general and from the rest of the public sector in particular. . . . The real limitations and hazards faced by such an agency go largely unnoticed. . . .[4]

CVG was set up as an autonomous agency specifically charged with coordinating all development activities in the Guayana. It was set up partly to ease coordination problems across the many sectors and areas that would be represented by government ministries, private agencies, and institutions. Development problems do not divide themselves up neatly and fall into place according to government ministries or economic sectors. CVG, however, was also set up for the reason Hirschman criticizes, to create a small paradise in a dirty developing world, to avoid the corruption and inefficiency sometimes found in the older line bureaucracies. If this was not the purpose in establishing CVG, it was one of the reasons why CVG functionaries stayed in their enclave in the early days of human resource development planning. The CVG officials did not accuse functionaries of other government agencies of corruption, but CVG officials did feel that the others were less efficient and often wrong.

The Guayana Center in turn was a special-purpose local autonomous agency. Its special purpose was human resource development in the Guayana. It was created by a nationally constituted autonomous agency. As the local spawn of a national autonomous agency, the Guayana Center should have had all of the problems which Hirschman attributes to such agencies. But it did not.

From the outset there was an attempt to break the Guayana Center out of its enclave by providing for a director who would be responsible to the Ministry of Education but paid by the CVG. There was a determined effort to get the Ministry to recognize the existence of the Center by signing an agreement to support it jointly with CVG. Under the rigid laws which governed education, the Ministry could launch such a project if the Guayana educational system were declared an "experimental" area. It was precisely this tactic—which permits operation by decree—that allowed the Ministry to set up Oriente University. In the first two years of its existence the Ministry did not sign the agreement and a director of the Guayana Center was not appointed. Yet, all activities sponsored by the Guayana Center did not suffer the classical ailments Hirschman attributes to autonomous agencies.

Concluding Evaluation of Regional Plan Implementation in the Three Main Activities of the Guayana Center

In implementing the human resource development plan through the Guayana Center, activity in technical education was more successful than activity in science-mathematics, which in turn had more success than literacy and basic education. There were, of course, individual differences in the maturity, competence, and personal style of the foreign advisors charged with the specific activities in the three areas. There were also idiosyncratic differences in the confidence and competence of the Venezuelan institutions and individuals with whom advisors worked. Apart from these, what contextual differences seem to account for success in the technical education area, as opposed to the partial or complete failure experienced in the other two activity areas?

A partial accounting is possible:

1. *Middle-level managers*

   The advisor in technical education cited the importance of working with middle-level managers who are close enough to the action to see the problems, but sufficiently highly placed to get something done about solving them. "Middle level" may be inappropriate, but we can think of no better term. These managers must be resident in or near the region and have sufficient power to make decisions in most cases or to get a complete hearing and timely decisions from above in other cases.

2. *Economic motivations uppermost for participants on committees*

   In technical education, as opposed to basic education-literacy and science-mathematics education, there was an obvious and direct connection between the training of workmen and their subsequent job performance, and economic return to industries. The managers of industry and the officials in the education and training establishments were undoubtedly affected by this powerful economic motivation. For the industrial managers a contribution to better programs would yield better trained workers, enhanced productivity, and higher profit; for the educators the motive was to secure increased support for their programs. Hence, in the technical education area rewards were not long run or deferred as in literacy and science education. This probably accounted for the greater willingness of organizations and men to contribute time and energy to the Technical Education Advisory Committee.

3. *Cooperation did not involve direct confrontation of two strong, nationally based organizations*

   In the area of informal education two strong protagonists, INCE and the Ministry of Education, represented by ODEA, would have had to cooperate, despite their rivalries. It is small wonder that the effort failed. In the technical education area the same organizations were involved, but their interests did not compete or conflict directly, and there were many other organizations also involved. In the case of science-education, there were no organizations at all involved as such, merely a group of individual teachers from various unconnected middle schools, public and private. However, the number of organizations involved in technical education did not seem to complicate the matter.

4. *Complementary interests among participants*

   In technical education there were complementary interests between the several suppliers of educated and trained manpower and the several potential users. In both informal education and science and mathematics the participants were all suppliers and in some cases competitors.

5. *Mix of private, autonomous, and public agencies*

Technical education had a mix of private, autonomous, and public organizations and, though one would expect this to complicate matters, it did not seem to work that way. Informal education involved public and autonomous agencies and science-mathematics involved public and private organizations. A mix of all three seemed to be best.

6. *Support and authorization (legitimization) at both national and local level*

Success depended on support and certification at both the national and local level. At the local level the problem had to be certified as genuine and pressing. At the national level there had to be authorization by higher decision makers. This happened only in technical education. National backing was lacking in science-mathematics and local cooperation was lacking in informal education.

7. *Activity involved a minimal amount of trait making*

It is perhaps trivial to state that the activity worked best when, in Hirschman's terms, a minimal amount of "trait making" was required. In technical education most of the administrators, whether of private, autonomous, or public organizations, had been trained or exposed to foreign models and methods. These managers had observed situations where people cooperated when it was in their interest to do so. In some cases the participants were representatives of foreign firms where cooperation for long-term self-interest was well established. This was not the case in science-mathematics where individual teachers were so oppressed by problems of immediate self-interest that no long-range view was possible. It was not the case in informal education where organizational competition was without cost to the participants, and cooperation would have brought no reward. The foreign advisor in technical education could naturally be more effective in dealing with an area involving quasi-foreign traits.

8. *Something, even if only information, is given at the outset*

From the outset the advisor in technical education was in possession of considerable useful information which he could provide to potential participants as bait for further activity. This was not the case in the other two areas. In science, data had to be collected and this took time and dissipated energy which might have gone to organizational or operational activity. In informal education vast amounts of energy were expended just to get positioned to collect the data. Little information was furnished to participants in these latter two activities.

9. *Activities worked better if they promised some organizational reward*

The appeal in technical education was largely organizational, that is, some return to the organization. In science-mathematics the return, as it seemed to be perceived, was personal and individual (something in it for the teachers as individuals). Because the activity could not sustain a sufficient level of individual "goodies" for rewards, its appeal tended to fade. It would be hard to identify any reward in informal education except the promise of increased efficiency. The participants probably had no great interest in this in the first place.

10. *Activities worked better if they did not jeopardize autonomy and prerequisites*

Activities were more successful if they did not entail any threat or hint of infringement on autonomy. This was the case in technical education. The committee did not jeopardize anyone's interest or freedom, and each organization was a member without risking any of its freedom. This was not true in the area of informal education. Presumably, better planning and coordination and reduction of duplication would mean infringement on some organization's freedom to waste resources. In science and mathematics the individual teachers had to submit to another organization and its regimen, but sacrifice of autonomy was not great. The area was perhaps neutral.

Epilogue

This is Ciudad Guayana in its seventh year, in the Year of Our Lord 1968. Mills are abuilding, the city is growing, schools are rising and people are attending them. In too few cases they attend with profit. On this much rests. If the schools and training establishments can contribute powerfully to enabling the people of Guayana to live and work in creative concert, the vision of industrial development and urban amenity can be realized at the confluence of the Orinoco and Caroní. Education and training alone and unaided cannot make Guayana, but a failure to provide them can be a powerful contributor to breaking it.

This study has limned the human prospect, and it appears most fair. People are arriving in large numbers. Some are equipped by education, training, and experience to live in the city and man its industries; most are not. Those not equipped by education, training, and experience must be helped to acquire it. Presently Ciudad Guayana has the rudimentary structure of an educational and training establishment attempting to cope with a problem which is known only in its lineaments. But the structure can be filled out to bear weight and the details of the problem filled in.

The people of Guayana, even the poorest and most underprivileged in the barrios, have the capacity to learn. They have faith that learning will help. At this point in time their hopes are concentrated on their children. This is no mean thing, for Guayana is a city of the next generation. But faith in themselves can be restored to the present generation of adults if the school will sally. Education and training must be brought to the people of the barrios. It cannot wait for them to seek it. This education and training must serve the total family of the barrios. If the education and training is what the barrio people need it will become what they want, and if it becomes what they want it will become what they provide for themselves.

There are clear signs that the barrio families have been bestirred to get an education for themselves, or at least for their children. Barrio parents have organized to provide rudimentary educational facilities for their children. The study showed that women of very limited means made relatively large financial sacrifices to send their children to school. Prospects for the next generation are bright. But the present generation cannot be written off the demographic ledger. Education and training must be provided for these Venezuelans who presently suffer from the neglect of a human resource development policy in the past— "policy of reinforced concrete" it is sometimes called, because so much attention was paid to highways and monuments and so little to people. This will not be an easy provision to make.

Still Venezuela has the resources and, in Ciudad Guayana, Venezuela has demonstrated the will to employ them. The physical infrastructure is there in its roads, ports, bridges, and buildings. The mills are there. The people are there. It is only necessary to prepare them to husband their patrimony so that they may enjoy it by increasing it. The great investment has been made in exploiting Guayana's natural and physical resources; the next great investment must come in developing its human resources. This will be done in large measure through education and training. There are no apparent constraints. There is will, resource, and basic capacity, and the only problem is in harnessing them. The traces will chafe but the wagon will roll.

We hope to go down to the Guayana in the days of the 1980's to see the mills and the city and the schools that now are only partly transformed from paper to reality. In our mind's eye it is a fine sight, and a likely one.

Appendix A
Method

The data necessary to plan the educational system of Ciudad Guayana came from many sources. To begin to anticipate both economic and social needs of the city and its people it was necessary to work with economists planning the industrial complex, with demographers studying migration, with urban planners laying out the form of the future city, with officials from various ministries, especially Education, and with a host of other persons, the activities of all of whom contribute to making a city viable now and in the future. This chapter discusses only those procedures used to gather major sources of data. The presentation is intended more as an illustration of the complexities of investigating a newly born city than as an exegesis of procedures which could be transferred to other situations. No brief is made here for the universal desirability of these procedures. In most cases circumstances dictated the method used, and it is realized that some of the data are not fully adequate. But none other could be obtained.

A necessary first step in the investigation was the establishment of estimates of minimal demand for educated and trained workers in the city's labor force in 1975. By comparing demand figures with output potentials of schools and training institutions, an evaluation could be made of the feasibility of certain economic goals. The last step of this analysis is represented in the tables of Chapter 2.

Employment in the future labor force was estimated by calculating expected productivity-per-worker indices for each industry sector and then dividing these indices into production goals established in the economic plan.[1] The economic plan provided estimates of increases in productivity by year until 1980, so that the growth of the labor force could be plotted yearly. Estimates of labor force participation rates, and unemployment, were applied to yield a yearly population estimate for the coming years. From estimates of population were calculated numbers of children eligible to enroll in schools. Population growth was also estimated on the basis of a study of migration into the city, yielding similar results.[2]

Employment within industries can be distributed according to expected occupations and corresponding educational levels. Guesses are made as to what level of education or training workers should have to meet productivity targets fixed by the planners. These are educated guesses: the planner consults statistics from similar industries in the same country and others, visits factories to study work patterns, consults with training experts. In the Guayana case, feasibility studies had been done for certain industries which provided reliable data on numbers of workers to be employed and the desirable occupational mix. Some of these studies were detailed enough to facilitate setting educational levels for the various occupations. For other industries the data are more speculative.

William Charleson of the CSED of Harvard University ran an analysis designed by Russell Davis of the more than 6,000 applications for employment in the steel mill which had accumulated over a five-year period. These applications contained information on age, education, previous work experience, and point of origin of the prospective worker. The analysis provided insights into occupation-education relationships and migration flows.

Charleson also directed a survey of industrial and commercial establishments in the city, covering half the known labor force. This provided the basis for an estimate of the present labor force and its characteristics. Some of these workers will retire or die before 1975. The difference between the work force of 1966, wasted by death and retirement, and the work force of 1975 (as produced by projections) represents the demand for educated and trained people which must be filled by migration or the output of Guayana schools and training establishments.

All of these data had to be produced, they were not available in Venezuela at that time. The Ministry of Labor did not run regular labor force surveys in any part of the country. Special analyses of the National Census of 1961 were soon made obsolete by virtue of the rapid growth of the city.

The process used to describe educational characteristics of the future labor
force is something less than precise, and is fraught with assumptions and
guesses.[3] Furthermore, it provides only an estimate of minimal demand for
trained labor. What part of this demand the schools can supply was estimated
by projecting the effect on numbers of graduates at the various levels which
could be produced by improving the system. The total number of graduates of
schools is assumed to enter the labor force, although it is known that some will
not, especially women. At present there are no adequate means of estimating
this number. Further, because the shortfall of the supply of graduates is so
large, this correction would not make much difference in policy recommendations.

A second problem with the technique is that one cannot know with accuracy
how efficacious improvements in schools will be with respect to increasing
numbers of graduates. In all instances the most modest assumptions were
chosen.

To study characteristics of the institutions which would supply the labor
force, that is, schools and training institutions, it was also necessary to collect
basic data. At that time (1964) the Ministry of Education could provide only a
list of the facilities operating in the city, it had no information on capacity or
condition. Davis and Charleson designed and directed a study of all the educational facilities in the city, public and private, graduate and unitarias. First, it
was necessary to locate them physically—no location map was available, and
supervisory officials did not know the locations of all the schools.

The school plant survey collected information on the age and condition of the
school, number of students, teachers, classrooms, shifts per day, books, maps,
bathrooms. The study described the budget available to each school director and
how he spent it. It investigated relations between schools, and contact of schools
with Ministry officials.

The study revealed the complete absence of any sort of school system, and the
inability of individual school directors to upgrade their schools, much less
maintain them physically or qualitatively. At that time support from the
national Ministry offices was almost nonexistent. Schools existed isolated from
each other and from developments in other regions of the country. And the
Ministry in Caracas was equally ignorant of the needs of the schools.

The school plant study provided the basis for a set of recommendations to the
CVG for immediate, impact contributions to the educational system. It also
revealed that the total economic plan would probably fail, through shortage of

skilled manpower, unless extensive investment were made in the educational and training systems.

The School Record Study

Few of the schools in the city maintained permanent record files for their children in 1965, and data on individual children are still not available from the Ministry of Education. Information was needed to determine attendance rates and patterns in the city, to begin the construction of school districts necessary for planning of future schools, and to identify areas of the city particularly plagued by nonenrollment.

Each year schools require students to register, and the child's representative or teacher fills out a card with the student's name, age, sex, birthplace, residence, previous school attended, grade level, and previous mark. From these cards information was taken about all the first-, fourth-, and sixth-grade students in the city. An attendance map was made showing that 90 percent of the students attend the school closest to their home, that only 5 percent of the students attend a school, public or private, more than 1 kilometer from their home. The data also gave more precise information about repeater rates by grade and school than was available from Ministry of Education sources. It provided a crude index of the size of the school-age population in the various parts of the city, and information about marks given by public and private schools, in three grade levels. The study also permitted an analysis of double enrollment, and minor analyses on characteristics of students enrolling late in the school year and those withdrawing from school. These data were the basis for projections of the output of graduates in the future, assuming no changes in the educational system. They also suggested questions to be investigated in the research on attitudes toward education.

Data of this sort are relatively easy to collect, for schools keep attendance cards for the entire year and are eager to have someone use them. School directors reacted enthusiastically to the request for cooperation and were gratified by the feedback provided, one of the few opportunities they have had to get some overview of the educational problems of the city. Not all of the schools use the same card format. A standard format combined with a sampling design would permit the rapid collection of information which could advantageously be used to pinpoint overcrowded schools or to study increases in student population by area of the city.

The School Census of June 1965

The good will built up by earlier contacts with the school directors and the district education supervisor, plus the knowledge amassed with respect to the school system, prompted the supervisor to ask for assistance from the CVG in the design and execution of a school census. As far as is known, no census of the school-age population had ever been carried out in the city, and few of the teachers or directors had participated in censuses in other areas.

The census was designed to describe the school-age population of the city in terms of physical location and attendance at school. The census schedule was deliberately simplified as much as possible to facilitate data collection and analysis. Census takers enumerated all children between the ages of six and fourteen living in the city (six was used as a bottom age to allow projection to the following school year). The schedule provided data on the age and sex of these children, which ones attended school, reasons for nonattendance, and location in the city.

Primary school teachers in the city served as the enumerators. As it was not possible to train the teachers, sessions were held with school directors explaining in detail purposes and procedures of the census. Each director was given a map of the city which delineated the area his teachers would cover and the subareas to be assigned to individual teachers. Most of the teachers could not read maps, and many did not know the areas well enough to find them on the basis of a verbal description; directors and CVG personnel helped the teachers begin the census.

Teachers marked each house visited with chalk, the census supervisor toured all the areas of the city checking for coverage; in some instances areas had to be re-enumerated because some houses had been missed. The city was covered in three days, in late June. Data were analyzed by hand and a census report distributed to the schools by 1 September 1965.

Comparison of the census results with those obtained from sample surveys indicates that the census covered at least 95 percent of the residences in the city. Some children were missed because their families were out of town for the day, or because the person answering questions did not name all the school-age children in the house, or because the residence was not counted. But school directors and planners felt the investment of time well rewarded; as a result of the census the CVG decided it must build public schools in the city. The district supervisor carried the census report to his superiors in the state of Bolívar, and to Caracas, to make a strong and supported plea to the Ministry of Education for more schools in the city. The CVG planning staff now had reliable data on which to base plans for locations of future schools.

The Education and the Family Survey

Sample Design. Data from the school census provided a list of the population of school-age children in the city. From this could be drawn a sample which would fairly represent all such children. The survey would get at parental attitudes toward education and information about the child which parents alone could supply, given the sorry state of school records. The sampling unit of the survey would be mothers or female guardians of children of school age. Women respondents were chosen because a significant number of families had no adult man present, and because there was reason to believe that mothers could give better information about the child than could fathers. As it turned out, the survey results confirmed these expectations and also demonstrated that mothers are more relevant than fathers for the child's success in school.

The sample was stratified on three variables. The census showed that attendance at school varied according to the area of the city and according to age. Assuming that children not attending school at the time of the census would be more likely not to have attended in the past, attendance in June 1965 was used as the third stratification variable.

The population list obtained through the census was divided by area of the city (excluding Puerto Ordaz, as almost all children attend school there), and then by age, and then by attendance of the child at time of the census. This produced thirty-two lists of children. Within these lists a sample was drawn taking every nth child, n based on a ratio of the length of the area-by-age-by-attendance list to the number of children to be included in the sample group. All groups were oversampled, as experience in the pretest indicated that it would not be possible to find in November about 35 percent of the cases counted in June of 1965. The groups of nonattending children were oversampled more than the attending children, as experience had indicated that these children were more likely to have left the city. For purposes of analysis the sample was drawn to yield equal numbers of children in each of the four areas of the city (San Félix, El Roble, Dalla Costa, Castillito), in each of four age groups (7–8, 9–10, 11–12, 13–14), and the groups of attenders and nonattenders. The effect was to produce a sample which could be weighted, using the sampling ratios, to represent the total population (see Table A.1). In drawing the sample, care was taken not to include more than one child per family. The child's name

TABLE A.1
Sample Design and Rate of Completion of Interviews with Mothers of School-Age Children

Area	Age	Attend	Population	Selected	Interviewed	Not Completed
San Félix	7–8	Yes	1,162	30	20	7
		No	498	40	21	15
	9–10	Yes	1,220	30	20	7
		No	140	40	20	11
	11–12	Yes	1,080	30	20	8
		No	100	40	20	16
	13–14	Yes	858	30	20	8
		No	102	40	20	18
El Roble	7–8	Yes	606	40	21	12
		No	383	40	21	7
	9–10	Yes	651	40	21	10
		No	98	40	20	16
	11–12	Yes	648	30	20	5
		No	60	40	20	14
	13–14	Yes	502	30	21	8
		No	70	40	22	16
Dalla Costa	7–8	Yes	223	30	21	5
		No	272	40	20	13
	9–10	Yes	220	30	20	3
		No	124	40	20	7
	11–12	Yes	238	30	20	7
		No	78	40	21	14
	13–14	Yes	174	30	20	9
		No	80	40	20	20
Castillito	7–8	Yes	388	40	23	12
		No	269	50	20	13
	9–10	Yes	456	40	21	9
		No	88	50	20	23
	11–12	Yes	400	40	20	16
		No	60	50	20	21
	13–14	Yes	316	40	20	9
		No	53	50	20	30

and age were noted, as well as his representative's name and address (which in about 30 percent of the cases amounted to nothing more than the name of the neighborhood).

The total sample list included 1,220 children. Of these, 1,042 were actually used (a random replacement procedure within each of the thirty-two sublists was employed), indicating that 37 percent of the drawn cases were not interviewed. Interviews were completed with 653 respondents, of which 640 (20 x 32) were used in the analysis.

TABLE A.2
Reasons for not Completing
Interviews with Mothers

Moved out of city	18.7%
Moved within city	10.6
Not at home	3.8
Person unknown at address	34.0
Address not found	32.2
Overt refusal	0.7
	100.0%

Interviewers noted reasons for noncompletion of interviews, represented in Table A.2. "Moved out of the city" was tallied when neighbors told the interviewer that the respondent had left the city *and* when they named a specific destination. Moves within the city were listed only when a specific neighborhood was named. "Not at home" refers to cases in which neighbors or family reported that the interviewee was not available at that moment. In all cases these were working women available only in the evening, when interviewers would not work. Some of these women were interviewed on the weekend.

The largest reason for noncompletion, "person unknown at address," reflects the instability of the city. Not only do people move within and without the city a good deal, but persons living in an area are often not known to their neighbors. Therefore, interviewers were unable to determine, on looking for a person by name, whether that person was still living in the area or to where he had moved. This reason for incompletion and that of "address not found" occurred most frequently in the most transient areas of the city, but there were no cases incomplete for these reasons in the stable, older sections of the city. It is possible, of course, that included in this group are some persons who did not want to be interviewed and who did not identify themselves to the interviewer. This number is probably not large; Venezuelans are usually quite open about expressing their desires or lack of them, and interviewers did check with neighboring houses.

The reason "address not found" also reflects the geographic instability of the city. Half of these cases occurred in Castillito, where (between June and November) a number of ranchos had been destroyed by floods and by the CVG in preparation for new highways. The others occurred only in the areas of the city with unpaved streets. The use of up-to-date maps of the city, even aerial photographs, would have facilitated contacting most of these cases. But the city is changing so fast that there are no accurate street maps. Since carrying out the survey, the CVG together with the city government has begun to name and identify streets.

There were only three overt refusals to participate in the study. Not only were interviewers well trained, they were also from the area and easily identified as *Guayanesas*. Furthermore, the subject of the interview was well received by all; some of the respondents were disappointed when the interviewers denied any connection with the government, for they hoped that their comments would lead to improvement of schools.

The sample design includes several biases. First, it is biased toward inclusion of the more stable elements of the city's population. Families who left the city or who moved within the city between June and November were not interviewed, but these families are more likely to include children not doing well in school or not attending school (as is seen in Table A.1). The sample is representative of people living in the city in June 1965 who were still living there in November 1965 and who had an identifiable address. Therefore, the aggregate statistics describing the population based on this sample give a more encouraging estimate of the frequency of school success than is actually the case.

The sample is also biased in the direction of large families, as there were more opportunities for children from large families to be selected into the sample. However, as there is no obvious or powerful relationship between family size and criterion variables of success in school, this bias is not a matter of serious concern.

It should be remembered that the sample does not include cases of families living in Puerto Ordaz, and is thus intentionally biased toward lower income groups. However, these lower income groups include 90 percent of the school-age population of the city, and almost 100 percent of the children enrolled in public schools in the city.

Reports of sample surveys designed to describe populations usually include an estimate of sampling error to indicate the range of credibility of the population statistics calculated from the sample responses. The population statistics used in this report are intended only to paint in broad strokes the problems facing the educational system; the school census provides enough population data to indicate that this description is accurate. It was not the concern of this study whether median family incomes were Bs. 550 a month or 700 or 900, but rather to show that family incomes for a number of people are low, and that this low income is related to failure in school. Similarly, it is not considered important that the number of students in the cohort who pass six grades of school in six years be considered 20 or 30 or 40 percent of the total. What is important is the demonstration that most children do not go straight through primary school.

Construction of the Interview Schedule. A first step in the design of the survey was to review studies on problems of nonattendance, desertion, and failure done in other areas. Almost all of the available studies dealt with problems in the developed countries and with students at the secondary level. A theoretical model to account for school success and desertion in Ciudad Guayana was developed and hypotheses derived from it. As was seen in Chapters 8 through 10, the model based on results from research in the developing countries was only partially supported by data from Ciudad Guayana.

Noel McGinn spent a month living in Ciudad Guayana, visiting schools, observing classes, and talking with children and parents in various parts of the city. This experience permitted refinements of the hypotheses developed from previous research and also indicated the limits which would be placed on interviews in Ciudad Guayana. For example, it became obvious that interviews could not run more than thirty or forty minutes in length. Mothers have children and no one to look after them; ranchos are hot in the afternoon sun and there are no shaded patios or cooling fountains; hunger and fatigue make distraction and inattention more common than concentration or coherence. The informal conversations with parents also suggested the general directions of the research; theirs was a tale of constant movement and frustration, of loneliness and frequent despair, tempered with an admirable resilience that makes them receptive to any attempt to provide them with conditions for self-improvement.

As a result of the review of the literature and observations in the field, it was possible to construct a model interview which served as the basis for preliminary versions of the questionnaire. The questionnaire itself was then tested in the field on five separate occasions. Interviewers were trained to look for questions that seemed to upset the mothers, or that were easily misunderstood, or that provoked acquiescent responses, or that yielded meaningless information. At the beginning the questionnaire was completely open-ended, interviewers noting verbatim the mothers' responses. With progressive pretesting it was possible to construct a set of alternatives for almost every question which included all responses given during the pretest trials. At the end of a set of three or four interviews, the pretest interviewers discussed each questionnaire, item for item, with Davis and McGinn, indicating problems and suggesting improvements. This procedure was repeated three times, with four interviewers, who together gave fifty-five interviews.

The questionnaire, which at first took sixty minutes to administer, was gradually reduced to thirty minutes. Excluded from use were items such as a brief projective test, in which mothers told a story about a picture in which a child goes off to school while his poor parents, unemployed, suffer at home. For some persons, the picture evoked a good deal of interesting comment about the problems of life in the city, and the importance of education. But most of the mothers could only describe the pictures used, and some refused to answer at all. The procedure took four or five minutes per picture, and did not seem effective with the particular population being studied. Also eliminated were elaborate attempts to describe the daily diet of the child, and the pattern of family spending. Apparently these cannot be recalled accurately without the use of a highly involved set of questions.

The pretest also allowed a translation from North American Spanish to Caracas Spanish to Guayana Spanish. There are no dialect problems here, but the choice of words used in interviews with lower income groups is important in order to maximize rapport. It is quite possible that the Spanish used in the interview was grammatically incorrect or too slangy, but the interviewers' reports indicate that they were talking the language of the people. The pretest interviewers were social workers in the city; their knowledge of the mores and speech of the people of Ciudad Guayana was invaluable.[4]

The pretest experience also allowed an estimation of the rate of noncompletion of interviews, essential in drawing the sample. The length of time necessary to find and complete each interview, important for planning the final phase of interviewing could also be anticipated. Interviewers spent an average of forty-five minutes looking for each address, thirty minutes in actual interviewing, and this even though they were assigned interviews according to geographical contiguity. This fact alone is powerful testimony to the degree of disorganization of the city as it now stands, and to the dedication of the interviewers, who slogged through boiling sun and steaming rain and yet maintained a consummate skill in winning entry to homes.

Procedures in the Field. Once pretesting was concluded and the final form of the questionnaire developed, a professional survey research company located in Caracas was hired to select, train, and supervise interviewers in their administration of the questionnaires to the sample.[5] The field staff from this company spent a number of hours discussing the questionnaire, reviewing each question as to intent and type of answer expected, before preparing their course to train interviewers. They visited the city and all of the areas in which interviews were to be taken, and thus were familiar with the difficulties of transportation and location of members of the sample.

Finally, they interviewed people in Ciudad Guayana who served as a source of information about possible interviewers. Twenty-three candidates for training were chosen, all women between eighteen and thirty-five years of age. None of the interviewers had ever taught in Ciudad Guayana, though some had been teachers in other cities.

All of the women had some high school education, none had ever been to the university. Women interviewers were used because our pretest experience had suggested that access to homes would be much easier; male interviewers tend to be identified as tax collectors or other agents of the government. Eighteen of these candidates were found acceptable after the training period.[6]

The training lasted two days, and offered the interviewers a complete overview of the purposes of the research and the intent of each question. Sample questionnaires were administered by the trainers, and then by the interviewers. After the first interview in the field each interviewer went through each question and answer with a trainer, reviewing problems. Careful training was required because of the closed-end format of the questionnaire. It was hoped that the pretest had exhausted all the possible answers which mothers could give. The closed-end format proved much faster for the interviewers because they could check off a response rather than to write it down verbatim. But the interviewers had to be able to make quick judgments among possible answers to check on the questionnaire form. Their ability to do this was validated by repeating interviews on a few of the early cases which they handled. They seemed to be doing an excellent job.

Interviewers were instructed as to the location of houses, and the manner of introducing the study.[7] No mention was made of the main intent of the study, attitudes toward education, and the questions were so arranged that this realization would not come until those questions which might be influenced by people wanting to say the "right thing," instead of what they really believed, had already been answered. The interviewers were instructed to deny any connection with the CVG or the city government, and to make a vague reference to the "university" if pressed. Pretest results had indicated that many people in the city knew what surveys are, and that some had had unpleasant experiences previously and would be resistant to questioning (mostly out of fear that they would be dispossessed). But almost everyone wanted to be asked their opinion, especially about education and what could happen in the future. Not only were there only three refusals (out of 656 contacts), but many of the women interviewed thanked the interviewer at the end of the "conversation" for the interest which she, the interviewer, had shown in the problems of the neighborhood. As a result of the interview, women visited schools for the first time in their lives, and some tried to enroll their ten- and eleven-year-old children who had never been enrolled before.

When unable to complete an interview by virtue of not contacting the person listed on the questionnaire face-sheet, interviewers went on to another of the set of interviews assigned to them for that day. Each uncontacted case was assigned to another interviewer the following day who attempted to complete the interview, unless it was clear that the interviewee had permanently left the address. When interviews could not be made after two attempts, a random selection procedure was used to draw another case from the area-age-attendance list for the incomplete interview.

Each completed interview was promptly checked by the field staff, who required interviewers to return to the address if questions had been skipped or if the information obtained was confusing or incomprehensible. As a result complete information was obtained for almost all questions; missing information did not exceed 5 percent for those questions (for example, family income, husband's training) which the interviewees could not answer. In addition to checking interviews in the office, the field staff also repeated some of the early interviews to make certain questions were being asked and recorded properly. Further, the field staff continued throughout the ten days of interviewing to contact every fifth interviewee to make sure that in fact she had talked to the interviewer. The results of these checks were negative; there was no evidence that interviewers had at any time "curbstoned," that is, filled out interviews in the cool of their own homes. Interviewers were paid for each completed interview, and the pay rate was sufficiently high to motivate them to great efforts. In addition, the field staff generated feelings of good will such that, on completing the study, some of the interviewers had a party for their employers.

Coding of Questionnaires. Almost all of the questions in the final form of the questionnaire were precoded, that is, a code number had been assigned to each of the possible alternatives which interviewers could check. Coding was done in Cambridge, Massachusetts. Coders checked each other's work to correct errors and improve reliability.[8]

Intelligence Test Data. On completing an interview, the interviewer gave the housewife a slip of paper on which was noted the name of a local school, a day, and an hour, and instructed her that her child (the subject of the interview) was to appear at the school on that day and at that time to take a test. No further explanation was offered, nor did the housewives ask for one.

Of the 653 children slated to appear for examination, 504 actually came, and of these 237 were children included in the study of mothers or female guardians. The other children were either brothers or sisters of the child subject, or children from families in the neighborhood who had heard about the testing, and thought they should be present. The intelligence test scores analyzed in this report, then, do not represent a sample of children of school age in the city. Psychologists administered all the tests collectively, separating children into groups on the basis of age and reading ability (according to the child's statement).[9] Only the Otis Short Form was administered with a time limit, the other three instruments were filled out according to each child's ability. A number of mothers accompanied their children to the tests, and it was difficult to keep mothers from peering over shoulders, encouraging here, and scolding there. As a result, noise levels in the examination rooms were quite high and distraction maximal. Reliability of the test results must be low. This was the first time that intelligence tests (or printed tests of any form) had been administered in Ciudad Guayana, and many of the teachers only knew of the tests but had never experienced them themselves. School teachers and directors were very interested in the procedure and desirous of instituting a regular testing program, if it could be shown to be of use in identifying children who were advanced or retarded in ability.

Appendix B
Questionnaire for Female Heads of House (translation)

1. How old are you, Mrs.———?

Age in Years	N	%
Less than 20	7	1.1
20–24	42	6.6
25–29	101	15.8
30–34	117	18.3
35–39	167	26.1
40–44	77	12.0
45–49	59	9.2
50–54	31	4.8
55–59	23	3.6
60 or more	14	2.2
Not determined	2	0.3
	640	100%

2. Were you born here in Ciudad Guayana? (If *Not*, in what place and state were you born?)

1961 Population of City or Place of Birth	N	%
100,000 or more	7	1.1
50,000–100,000	62	9.7
25,000–50,000	73	11.4
15,000–25,000	15	2.4
10,000–15,000	82	12.8
5,000–10,000	100	15.6
2,000–5,000	125	19.5
1,000–2,000	53	8.3
1,000 or less	109	17.0
Foreign-born	14	2.2

State of Birth	N	%
Federal District	2	0.3
Anzoátegui	50	7.8
Bolívar	161	25.2
Delta Amacuro	72	11.3
Monagas	118	18.4
Nueva Esparta	15	2.3
Sucre	184	28.8
Llanos states	11	1.7
Western Venezuela	13	2.0
Foreign-born	14	2.2

Birthplace Region	N	%
Ciudad Guayana	39	6.1
Bolívar, 5,000 plus	69	10.8
Bolívar, rural	53	8.3
Eastern Venezuela, 5,000 plus	207	32.3
Eastern Venezuela, rural	232	36.3
Others	40	6.2

2b. How long have you been living here in Ciudad Guayana?

Years in City	N	%
Year or less	32	5.0
One–two years	86	13.4
Three–five years	154	24.1
More than five years	329	51.4
Born in city	39	6.1

(ALL)
2c. In what other places have you lived? (List up to three places without including Ciudad Guayana or place of birth.)

Number of Cities	N	%
One	13	2.0
Two	140	21.9
Three	213	33.3
Four	137	21.4
Five	127	19.8
Six or more	10	1.6

Average 1961 Population of All Cities in which Has Lived		
100,000 or more	9	1.4
50,000–100,000	42	6.6
25,000–50,000	72	11.3
15,000–25,000	100	15.6
10,000–15,000	118	18.5

Average 1961 Population of All Cities in which
Has Lived—*continued*

5,000–10,000	112	17.5
2,000–5,000	93	14.5
1,000–2,000	47	7.3
1,000 or less	47	7.3

2d. How long did you live there?

3. In how many different places have you lived here in Ciudad Guayana?

Number of Residences	N	%
One	286	44.7
Two	228	35.6
Three	88	13.8
Four	25	3.9
Five	7	1.1
Six or more	6	0.9

4. What is (or was) the principal occupation of your father (if does not remember or did not know father ask about mother)?

Respondent's Father's Occupation	N	%
Farmer	357	55.8
Non-farmer	181	28.3
Not determined	102	15.9

5. Could you tell me if your father (or mother) knew how to read and write?

Was Father Literate	N	%
Yes	316	49.4
No	270	42.2
Not determined	54	8.4

6. How far did you go in school, Mrs. ———?

Respondent's Education	N	%
None	268	41.9
One year	40	6.2
Two years	73	11.4
Three years	73	11.4
Four years	90	14.1
Five years	23	3.6
Six years	50	7.8
Seven or more years	23	3.6

7. Could you tell me all the persons who live in this house with you? (Note name of person, age, relationship to respondent, if knows how to read and write, and highest grade attained in school. Begin with spouse if present, continue with others over ten years of age.)

Spouse Literate	N	%
Yes	421	65.8
No	84	13.1
No spouse	135	21.1

Education of Spouse	N	%
None	168	26.2
One year	14	2.2
Two years	45	7.0
Three years	65	10.2
Four years	72	11.2
Five years	28	4.4
Six years	87	13.6
Seven or more years	26	4.1
No spouse	135	21.1

Average Education of Adults in House	N	%
None	58	9.1
One year	61	9.5
Two years	138	21.6
Three years	128	20.0
Four years	104	16.2
Five years	77	12.0
Six years	51	8.0
Seven or more years	23	3.6

Age of Student	N	%
Seven	53	8.3
Eight	77	12.0
Nine	87	13.6
Ten	87	13.6
Eleven	76	11.9
Twelve	84	13.1
Thirteen	71	11.1
Fourteen	83	13.0
Fifteen	12	1.9
Sixteen	10	1.5

Does Student Attend School Now?	N	%
Yes	495	77.3
No	145	22.7

Present Educational Level of Student	N	%
None	225	35.1
First grade	126	19.7
Second grade	86	13.4
Third grade	73	11.4
Fourth grade	65	10.2
Fifth grade	34	5.3
Sixth grade	26	4.1
Seventh grade	4	0.6
Not determined	1	0.2

Total Number of Persons in Family	N	%
Two	2	0.3
Three	18	2.8
Four	34	5.3
Five	53	8.3
Six	85	13.3
Seven	106	16.6
Eight	89	13.9
Nine	84	13.1
Ten	62	9.7
Eleven	48	7.5
Twelve	32	5.0
Thirteen or more	27	4.2

(OBSERVATION)

8a. Type of House Construction	N	%
Galvanized sheet metal	170	26.6
Masonite	50	7.8
Used planks	34	5.3
Mud	88	13.7
Plastered mud	84	13.1
Block	58	9.1
Plastered block	156	24.4

8b. Number of Habitable Rooms (Excluding Kitchen)	N	%
Two rooms/person	14	2.2
One room/person	28	4.4
1.5 persons/room	119	18.6
Two persons/room	176	27.5
Three persons/room	150	23.4
Four persons/room	67	10.5
Five persons/room	24	3.7
Six persons/room	20	3.1
Seven or more persons/room	35	5.5
Not determined	7	1.1

8c. Type of Toilet Facility	N	%
None	159	24.8
Latrine	385	60.2
Flush toilet	96	15.0

8d. Does House Have	N	%
1) Electricity		
Yes	424	66.3
No	216	33.7
2) Refrigerator		
Yes	269	42.0
No	371	58.0
3) Washing machine		
Yes	95	14.8
No	545	85.2
4) Radio		
Yes	390	60.9
No	250	39.1
5) Fruit trees, chickens, or pigs		
Yes	215	33.6
No	425	66.4
6) Newspapers, magazines		
Yes	286	44.7
No	354	55.3
7) Books		
Yes	427	66.7
No	213	33.3
8) Kinds of books		
None	213	33.3
Novels	47	7.3
School	331	49.9
Religious	8	1.2
Various	53	8.3
9) Possessions and facilities (aggregate)		
All	44	6.9
Four of five	73	11.4
Three of five	116	18.1
Two of five	116	18.1
One of five	110	17.2
None	181	28.3

Now, Mrs. ——— we are going to talk a bit about the things that you hope for in this life.

9. What are the most important things that you would like to achieve to feel satisfied in your personal life?

Goals	N	%
Health	276	18.1
Better standard of living	407	26.8
Housing	201	13.2
Work	106	7.0
Outside help	37	2.4
Education for children	439	28.8
Material goods	26	1.7
Others	8	0.6
Not determined	21	1.4
	1,521	

9a. Of these things which you have told me, which do you think is the easiest (most likely) to get (to happen)?

Education	N	%
Likely	258	46.6
Not likely	141	22.0
Not mentioned	201	31.4

10. If you or any other person were thinking of moving to another place in Ciudad Guayana, what would be the most important things that you would take into account to choose that place?

Factors Considered Most Important	N	%
Cost	88	13.7
Services available	178	27.8
Nearness to market	36	5.6
Neighbors	158	24.7
Nearness to student's school	134	20.9
Title to land	6	0.9
Able to raise animals (pigs, goats)	10	1.6
Get work	4	0.6
Others	6	0.9
Not determined	20	3.3

Now we are going to talk about your children. Let's talk for example, about (*child named on face-sheet*).

11. What are the things that you desire (or want) that ——— do in the future?

Things Desired	N	%
Health	66	5.5
Work	141	11.6
Help family	104	8.6
Study	381	31.4

Things Desired—*continued*	N	%
Achieve	336	27.7
Have good character	164	13.5
Marriage	15	1.2
Not determined	6	.5
	1,213	

11a. Of these things which you have told me, which do you think is the easiest to get (most likely to happen)?

Here in Venezuela everyone has an option about education. Some say it is worthwhile to study, others say no.

12. What is your opinion? Do you think that education is important in life?

12a. Why?

Reasons	N	%
In order to get work	277	24.8
He that knows nothing is worthless	394	35.3
Make intellectual progress	141	12.6
To gain culture	53	4.8
In order to be a success in life	241	21.6
Not determined	10	.9
	1,116	

13. Do you think that a child that always gets 10 on his report card is very different from one who always gets 19?

Is an Achiever Different from a Nonachiever?

Yes	510	79.7
No	130	20.3

14. Why do you think that some children get good marks and others don't?

Reasons	N	%
Motivation of student	435	39.0
Diligence of student	283	25.3
Attendance of student	112	10.0
Ability of student	192	17.2
Behavior of student	28	2.5
Factors not controlled by student	61	5.5
Not determined	6	.5
	1,117	

Why Respondent Visited School—*continued*	N	%
Went on own initiative	95	14.8
Lives near	7	1.1
Not determined	14	2.2
Child never attended school	43	6.7

20. Another thing, Mrs. ——, do you have time to help with your children's education, to help them with their schoolwork?

20a. How do you help them?

How Respondent Helps Student with Schoolwork	N	%
Does not help	273	42.7
Helps with homework	249	38.9
Reads books	30	4.7
Visits teacher	25	3.9
Various ways	3	0.5
Not determined	17	2.6
Never attended	43	6.7

21. What kind of marks does —— get (did he get) in school?

Report of Student's Marks by Respondent	N	%
10–13	169	26.4
14–16	151	23.6
17 or higher	27	4.2
Child never completed grading period	119	18.6
Doesn't know	174	27.2

22. Does the education of your children cost you much?

Is Education Expensive	N	%
Yes	444	69.4
No	136	21.2
Not determined	17	2.7
Never attended	43	6.7

(These questions if child not now attending school)

23. Do you know the name of the school closest to here?

Does Respondent Know Name of Local School	N	%
Student attends school	495	77.3
No	83	13.0
Yes	59	9.2
Not determined	3	.5

24. Mrs. ———, before you told me that education is important in life. However, your
child doesn't go to school. Why is that?

Why Child Does Not Go To School	N	%
Student attends	495	74.0
Sickness	28	4.2
No space in school	15	2.2
Family can't afford schooling	44	6.6
Motivation of student	24	3.6
School too far from home	12	1.8
Child works	5	0.7
Student doesn't have materials	12	1.8
Motivation of parents	21	3.1
Family moving	4	0.6
Not determined	9	1.3
	669	

25. Have you looked for some way for him to go back to school?

Has Respondent Made Effort To Put Child Back in School?	N	%
Yes	110	17.2
No	31	4.9
Not determined	4	0.6
Student attends now	495	77.3

26. What do you need so that your child can attend school?

What Is Needed To Put Child in School	N	%
Student attends now	495	77.3
Economic help	60	9.4
Space in school	11	1.7
Interest of child	21	3.3
Health	30	4.7
Other	9	1.4
Nothing	10	1.6
Not determined	4	0.6

(ALL)
27. Another thing, Mrs. ———, how far do you think that ——— could go in school?

Educational Level Expected of Student	N	%
Less than six years	37	5.8
Completion of six years	164	25.6
Completion of high school	198	30.9
Completion of university	122	19.1
Not determined	119	18.6

28. When ———— is finished with school, how much do you think he will be able to earn?

Income Level Expected of Student	N	%
Bs. 150/month	24	3.8
Bs. 250/month	25	3.9
Bs. 350/month	23	3.6
Bs. 475/month	29	4.5
Bs. 625/month	45	7.0
Bs. 800/month	52	8.1
Bs. 1,000/month	55	8.6
Bs. 1,250+/month	93	14.6
Not determined	294	45.9

29. Do you think he is going to help you when he starts to work?

Does Respondent Think Student Will Help Family	N	%
Yes	581	90.8
No	51	8.0
Not determined	8	1.2

30. A lot of parents think that even though their children aren't going to help them when they finish school, that they should spend a lot on their education. Why do you think that they think that way?

Why Money Spent on Student that Will Not Help Parents	N	%
Is duty of parent	292	45.6
Is right of child	31	4.8
Parents hope student will help	156	24.4
To give child self-worth	151	23.6
Not determined	10	1.6

31. Some people say that the education of children demands a lot of sacrifice on the part of the parents, while others say that the sacrifice is little. Do you think that the education of children represents a sacrifice for the parents?

Is Education a Sacrifice for Parents	N	%
Yes	482	75.3
No	158	24.7

32. Some parents make many sacrifices and their children go to school, while others make no sacrifices and their children remain uneducated. Why do you think this is?

Why Parents Do Not Sacrifice	N	%
Lack of interest of parents	459	71.7
Ignorance of parents	104	16.3
Lack of resources	54	8.4
Lack of interest of student	15	2.3
Not determined	8	1.3

33. What do you think of the parent who doesn't put himself out so that his children go to school?

Opinion of Nonsacrificing Parent	N	%
Irresponsible	131	14.6
Doesn't love child	188	21.0
Bad parent	154	17.2
Ignorant parent	140	15.7
Low ambitions for child	248	27.7
Too poor	27	3.0
Not determined	7	0.8
	895	

34. What do you think the government should do so that all boys and girls can go to school?

What Action Government Should Take	N	%
Obligate parents to send child to school	106	16.6
Give direct help to parents	243	38.0
Give direct help to child	79	12.3
Build more schools	190	29.7
Not determined	22	3.4

35. Are you a personal friend of a teacher?

Is Respondent Friend of Teacher	N	%
Yes	300	46.9
No	340	53.1

36. Do you think that in general teachers are unpleasant or nice?

Respondent's Opinion of Teachers	N	%
Nice	415	64.8
Indifferent	210	32.8
Not nice	10	1.6
Not determined	5	0.8

Now we are going to talk a little about ———'s health.

37. Does ——— suffer frequently from asthma, diarrhea, weakness, headaches, vomiting, fatigue, dizziness, fever, lack of appetite, chills?

Number of Symptoms Displayed by Student	N	%
None	156	24.4
One	132	20.6
Two	111	17.3
Three	78	12.2

Number of Symptoms Displayed—*continued*	N	%
Four	74	11.6
Five	45	7.0
Six	26	4.1
Seven	14	2.2
Eight	4	0.6

(ONLY IF MALE LIVING IN HOUSE)
38. How long have you been living with your husband?

Age When Most Recently Married	N	%
Less than 15 years	43	6.7
15–16	80	12.5
17–19	107	16.7
20–24	116	18.1
25–29	72	11.3
30 or more	85	13.3
No spouse	135	21.1
Not determined	2	0.3

Spouse's Relationship to Student	N	%
Father	279	43.6
Doubtful if father	17	2.6
Not father	138	21.6
Spouse's from previous marriage	5	0.8
Adopted	12	1.9
Other relationship	52	8.1
Servant	2	0.3
No spouse	135	21.1

Respondent's Relationship with Male Head of House	N	%
Married	293	45.8
Concubine	143	22.3
Abandoned (i.e., no male head)	135	21.1
Other civil state	69	10.8

39. Where is your husband working?

Spouse's Occupation if Employed	N	%
Professional	8	2.0
Administrator	8	2.0
Office worker	15	3.6
Salesman	47	11.4
Agricultural worker	12	2.9
Miner	3	0.7
Transport worker	38	9.2
Skilled	84	20.4

Spouse's Occupation if Employed—*continued*	N	%
Unskilled	157	38.1
Services	38	9.2
Not determined	2	0.5
	412	

Spouse Employment State	N	%
Employed	412	64.4
Unemployed	93	14.5
No spouse	135	21.1

40. What does he do there? (see above)

41. How long has he been doing that?

Time Spouse Employed or Unemployed	N	%
Employed six months or more	270	53.5
Short employed	142	28.1
Short unemployed	62	12.3
Unemployed six months or more	28	5.5
Not determined	3	0.6

42. And before working in that, what did he do?

Spouse's Occupational Mobility	N	%
Up	85	22.8
Stable	206	55.4
Down	81	21.8
Not determined (first employment)	133	—

43. Has your husband received some special training for his work?

Did Spouse Receive Special Training	N	%
Yes	132	20.6
No	368	57.5
No spouse	135	21.1
Not determined	5	0.8

44. How does your husband help you with the rearing of the children?

Spouse's Help in Raising Children	N	%
No spouse	135	21.1
None	22	3.4
Economic help only	104	16.2
Some help	273	42.7
Great help	106	16.6

Appendix C

Summary of Indications[1] from Multivariate Analysis

I. From Factor Analysis

1. Students from favorable cultural, economic, and social background have all-round high performance in school.

2. Income alone does not predict school success in Guayana. There are high-income low achievers and low-income high achievers. In a highly industrializing and urbanizing situation, there are "nouveau riche" who do not show high success.

3. Living standard as measured by amenities—possessions—is a much better predictor than earnings.

4. Cultural level as indicated by mother's and total adult members'—but not father's—education is an even better predictor of school success.

5. Goals and measured aims of educational achievement are related to school attendance and achievement.

6. Social stability, as measured by marital and family stability despite size and lack of income, go with school success.

7. Migration and family instability have a bad effect on both school attendance and school achievement.

8. Cultural contacts, for example, newspaper and radio, go with school achievement, but not alone; they must be accompanied by other economic, cultural, and social advantages.

9. There are poor all-around families and they show the absolutely lowest school achievement.

a. Usually this is a rural migrant with unstable family and past. Even after access to school the child has no success.
b. There are also rural migrants with stable family histories where children succeed well enough after they once gain access to schools.
c. There are very poor urban dwellers—who may or may not be migrants from other urban areas—whose children have done well enough because they have had access to the schools.

10. There is a striver class that is low on cultural background and economic advantages, but mother puts a very high value on educational attainment and hence children reflect it by success even though they suffer many other disadvantages.

II. Findings from Canonical Correlation Analysis

11. Influence of rural background on access to school (measured by age enrolling) is clear, but the influence on later school success is not so clear.

12. An urban opportunity factor is clearly shown.

13. Migration, the moving around to many different places, is not of itself significant if the moving has taken place primarily in urban areas where there are schools.

14. Occupational stability is more important than occupational status in relation to school success.

15. There is some indication that stability in employment is more important than absolute earnings. All stability measures are more important than magnitude of earnings in themselves.

16. There is evidence of the culture of poverty in certain families. Families are rather homogeneous. If one member of the family does poorly, they all do.

17. Occupational mobility showed on factor analysis that it was "different" from other measures of economic, social, and cultural advantage. It was not clear why and how it differed, but it did.

18. Average education in family (educating family) and mother's education (mother influenced) relate highly with success; and father's education much less so. Family education level is most important.

19. Urban life style and contact with the world are important to school success; income and material possessions even more so; family crowding, spouse participation, and marital status are not so high.

20. Male spouse's high participation in child rearing goes with child's lack of success in school.

21. There is agreement between high goals for education of children among barrio mothers and actual performance. When mothers valued education in their own case and that of the child, the child went to school and succeeded.

22. There was also a high agreement between the mother's motivation for education for herself and the child's enrollment, attendance, and achievement in school. The mother with high motivation for education might not always have realized her goals in her own lifetime, but she did accomplish them through her children. Mothers with high educational attainment aspirations for themselves and their children enrolled their children early, kept them in school, and encouraged them to succeed, at least in primary school.

23. High expressed preference for rewarding rather than punishing the child went with school attendance, enrollment, and success.

III. Multiple Regression Analysis

24. Possession of goals, especially educational goals of mothers, is the best predictor.

25. The family with few adults (small, nuclear families of young parents) has very positive influence on the child's school performance. (Stability of home.)

26. Mother married. (Stability of home.)

27. Average adult education is high. The educating family. Clustering or halo effect.

28. Family has lived in large cities. Urban effect.

29. Male spouse's education is low. Almost perverse effect of spouse on child.

30. Income and possessions have very strong effect. Affluence and education.

31. Mother rewards rather than punishes. Goes with high school achievement of child.

IV. Multiple Discriminant Analysis

The following go with school success:

32. Mother born in large city. Urban influence goes with school success.

33. Importance of goals and expectations (expects to educate child and does).

34. Attends church frequently. (Used only in this set, but shows importance of general contacts and culture.)

35. Subject born outside region. Probably urban, because San Félix rural in those days. Urban.

36. Subject has more education than spouse. Importance of wife and mother on child; not spouse.

37. Subject is child-oriented on achievement. Reward and reinforcement.
38. High contact with the world. Culture and communication.
39. *Negative go with failure*
   a. Spouse education high.
   b. Low motivation. Motivation goals and realism.
   c. Low status occupation.
40. Family education better predictor of success than income.

First Factor Analysis

A principal components analysis and an image covariance factor analysis were run on the intercorrelations of the complete set of forty-eight variables. The image covariance analysis showed eight roots with values greater than one; these roots had a cumulative percent of trace of slightly less than 75 percent. The results on six factors are shown in Table C.1.

The first factor was "high success"; loadings were high on all measures of success—income; possessions; education of wife (R), husband, and adult members generally; high contact with the world; and high occupational status. All these fortunate circumstances, not surprisingly, went with high success on all measures of school performance.

The second factor was "slightly less successful" on all antecedent measures but very unsuccessful on educational achievement. Although it was obvious that favorable economic-cultural circumstances of the family contributed materially to school achievement, there were substantial numbers of students who did not show successful school performance despite fairly favorable economic circumstances. The most startling difference between Factor One and Factor Two is the education of the woman of the house. It is much lower for the unsuccessful grouping of Factor Two, although both are well off on income. There is also a marked difference of material comforts. This shows that possessions are more important than income. The second factor differed markedly from Factor One on the "motivational" or "goal" variable loading. Factor Two had negative expected educational attainment.

The third factor had quite low loadings on family possessions and favorable circumstances, fairly high loadings on measures of family stability (marriage, spouse participation in child rearing), and insignificant loadings on educational success. Family size had a high loading. This seems to represent the performance of children from large, poor, and stable families who do reasonably well in school, despite adverse material circumstances.

TABLE C.1

Forty-eight Variables Used in Multivariate Analysis and the Subset of Twenty-five with High Loadings on a Factor Analysis

VARIABLES[a]		
Number	*Name*	*Direction*
1	Age of respondent	Less than 20 to 60 or more
2	Size of city of birth	100,000+ to less than 1,000
3*	Average size of other cities	100,000+ to less than 1,000
4	Number of cities	1 to 7
5	Residences in Ciudad Guayana	1 to 6
6*	Respondent's education	None to 7 or more years
7*	Spouse's education	None to 7 or more years
8	Average adult education	None to 7 or more years
9	Total number adults	1 to 6 or more
10	Percent adults literate	100 percent to none
11*	Total persons in family	2 to 13 or more
12*	Rural-urban living style	Rural to urban
13*	Possessions	All of 5 to none of 5
14*	Crowding: persons per room	2 rooms per person to 5 or more persons per room
15*	Monthly income per person	Less than Bs. 25 to Bs. 1,000 or more
16*	Respondent's goals for self	Wants and expects to educate child, to does not want to educate child
17*	Respondent's goals for child	Low motivation to educate child to high
18	Expected educational attainment	Less than 6 years to university
19*	Number of symptoms	None to 9
20	Marital state of respondent	Married to abandoned
21	Time spouse employed	Employed for long time to unemployed for long time
22*	Spouse participation in rearing child	No spouse to high participation
23	Frequency of church attendance	Daily to never
24	Region in which respondent born	San Félix to foreign-born (distance from Ciudad Guayana)
25	Spouse-wife education	Spouse has more to wife has more
26*	Migration scale	Low mobility to high
27*	Respondent's personal goals	Production to amenities
28*	Desired if move	Improvement to no personal improvement
29*	Goals for child	Long to short
30*	Why education is important	Work to cultural improvement
31*	Reasons for grades	Controllable to uncontrollable

[a] The variables included in the set of twenty-eight are starred. They are independent measures, that is, not included as part of another variable.

TABLE C.1—*continued*

Number	Name	Direction
32*	How treat nonachieving child	Reward to punish
33*	How respondent knew school and teacher	Self-initiated to teacher-initiated
34*	Opinion of nonachieving parents	Child-oriented to parent-oriented
35*	Role of government	Direct aid to child to direct aid to parents
36	Spouse occupational mobility based on present and past job	Up to down
37	Income-housing-toilet facilities— presence of housing—crowding	Low on all variables (in poverty direction) to high
38	Housing-income-possessions	Low on all variables to high
39*	Contact with world—radio, newspaper, church attendance, associations	High contact to low
40*	Occupational status	Low status occupation (for example, no husband, or unemployed) to high status
41	Age of student	7 years to 16
42*	Average education of children	None to 7 or more years
43	Percent children attending	None to 100 percent
44	Number of years enrolled and not completed	None to 6 or more
45*	Age at first enrollment	6 to 12 or older
46*	Success-failure scale	Successful to unsuccessful
47*	Academic history scale	Never enrolled to always passed
48	Age-grade scale	2 years ahead in school according to age to 5 or more years behind

FACTORS

	1	2	3	4	5	6 . . . Cum.
L Roots	6.68	2.45	1.94	1.78	1.69	1.34
% Trace	26	10	8	7	7	5 6

$$\sum \% = 630$$

Variable Loadings
Antecedent Variables

	1	2	3	4	5	6
4. Number Cities Lived	0.13	− 0.03	− 0.28	0.40	0.53	0.26
6. R's Education	0.56	0.11	− 0.15	− 0.13	0.25	0.26
7. Spouse's Education	0.48	0.28	− 0.34	0.04	0.08	− 0.37
8. Avg. Adult Educ.	0.64	0.13	− 0.20	0.13	0.10	− 0.42
11. Family Size	− 0.01	− 0.07	0.45	0.33	0.22	− 0.30
12. Urban Life Style	0.59	0.14	− 0.13	0.07	− 0.09	0.21
13. Possessions	0.72	0.16	0.02	0.09	− 0.13	− 0.06
14. Living Space	0.38	0.14	− 0.23	− 0.12	− 0.25	0.26

TABLE C.1—*continued*
Variable Loadings
Antecedent Variables

15. Income	0.58	0.27	− 0.14	− 0.13	− 0.17	0.16
18. Educational Goals	0.43	− 0.31	− 0.01	0.00	− 0.05	− 0.01
20. Marital Status R	0.40	0.12	0.49	− 0.15	0.20	− 0.05
21. Employment	0.46	0.21	0.19	− 0.03	− 0.12	0.10
22. Spouse Participation in Rearing S	0.38	0.20	0.46	− 0.14	0.24	− 0.03
26. Migration Scale	0.09	0.04	− 0.31	0.42	0.59	0.29
37. Affluence Scale 1	0.70	0.27	0.07	− 0.10	− 0.12	0.18
38. Affluence Scale 2	0.69	0.23	− 0.09	0.02	− 0.09	0.23
39. Sophistication-Contact	0.56	0.16	0.00	0.13	− 0.07	− 0.05
40. Occupational Status	0.52	0.29	0.38	− 0.11	0.06	0.01

Criterion Variables

42. Avg. Ed. of Children	0.48	− 0.38	0.02	0.35	− 0.24	0.04
43. % Children Attend	0.41	− 0.36	0.07	0.06	− 0.04	0.02
44. Years Completed Sch.	0.27	− 0.36	− 0.10	− 0.43	0.06	0.07
45. Enrolled Young	0.33	− 0.36	0.00	0.12	0.08	− 0.09
46. School Success	0.40	− 0.54	0.05	0.08	− 0.22	0.03
47. Academic History	0.52	− 0.64	− 0.12	− 0.30	0.15	− 0.03
48. Regular Age for Grade	0.50	− 0.64	− 0.12	− 0.30	0.15	− 0.03

The fourth factor was loaded high on migration and number of cities in which the family had previously lived; school performance showed high loadings on a late start, and many incomplete years. Quite clearly school attendance is jeopardized by migration and instability of residence.

The fifth factor was even more highly loaded on migration and number of cities, but the effect on school performance seemed different. In the fifth factor the loading on uncompleted school years was lower and age for grade was more regular, but academic success loadings were negative. This was the effect of migration and instability on school achievement.

A varimax rotation of the factors provided no additional information or explanation, but merely emphasized the indications of the original analysis. The rotation did tend to show even more marked lack of school success on Factor Two and greater school success on Factor Three.

A principal components analysis was run on a set of variables reduced to twenty-eight from the original forty-eight. The table of roots, trace, and loadings will not be shown. The major indications by factors were:

Factor One. This was the success factor again, high on economic and material antecedents, high on sophistication and contact, and high on academic achievement and school success.

Factor Two. This was a factor showing rather high material and economic well-being, but low motivation for education, fairly low family (husband-wife) education, lower sophistication and contact with the world, and quite low school success and achievement.

Factor Three. This factor showed quite low on material and cultural antecedents and the very lowest on school success and achievement. This is the "poor all-around" factor.

Factor Four. This was the large family, poor, crowded, rural, and uneducated, but with stability and medium success and achievement in school, after access to a school was secured in the first place.

Factor Five. This appeared to be the urban, migrant, small, but poor family that had access to the schools for the children earlier because of urban background, but had scant success in school over time.

Factor Six. This shows moderate loading on material antecedents, low on family education, but very high on the economic value placed on education, and moderately successful in school and academic achievement.

Biquartimin Rotation. The biquartimin rotation on the original principal components analysis was not helpful. It merely made the classes more pronounced and polarized educational achievement and nonachievement so that it was more difficult to relate school performance to antecedent variables.

Multiple and Canonical Correlation Analysis

Analysis through canonical correlation was performed in order to relate sets of "pseudo"-predictor or independent variables with sets of dependent variables. The term "pseudo" is used advisedly because canonical correlation is a technique for estimating the relationships between two sets of transformed variates. As does any correlation technique, it deals with relationship rather than causality, and the designation of the academic success set of variables as "dependent" is a mere convention.

In the first canonical analysis the attempt was to assess the relationship between a set of variables relating to migration and rural-urban background and a set of variables relating to enrollment, attendance, and achievement in Guayana schools. The fact that there is a highly significant canonical correlation between a transformed variate in the rural-migration set and the school attendance achievement set suggests interesting interpretations which are offered in the text, but does not establish causality. These comments hold for each successive set of background variables which through canonical correlation will be related to the school enrollment, attendance, achievement set of variables.

First Set Comparison: Migration and Urban Residence Compared to School Success

Urban Migration Antecedents	*Academic Success* (All scales >, positive)
Var. No.	*Var. No.*
1. Average size of other cities lived in	1. Age-grade scale (regular age for grade)
2. Size of city of birth	2. Academic history
3. Migration scale	3. Success
	4. Average education of children
	5. Age, first enrolled
	6. Number years uncompleted in school
	7. Percent of children in family who attend school

Not surprisingly, the multiple correlations between sets and some individual variables were significant (see Tables C.2 and C.3).

TABLE C.2
Multiple Correlations Between Migration Variables and Academic Set

	1	2	3
Multiple R	0.21	0.19	0.13
F Ratio	4.05	3.22	1.50
Probability <	0.0002	0.002	0.16

The relationship of urban background to educational success is clearly shown. Migration has a much less marked relationship perhaps because the city is so heavily populated with migrants, of both rural and urban origins, and varying levels of education and income.

TABLE C.3
Multiple Correlations Between Academic Variables and Migration-Urban Set

	1	2	3	4	5	6	7
Multiple R	0.19	0.12	0.13	0.15	0.14	0.12	0.12
F Ratio	7.52	3.11	3.91	4.57	4.35	3.13	3.35
Probability <	0.0001	0.03	0.009	0.004	0.005	0.03	0.02

Age-grade pattern and age at first enrollment are the most highly related to urban-migrant background. This is obviously so because rural migrants often come from places where no school existed and children could not enroll at the legal entry age. The influence of this late enrollment on other indicators of school success is also suggested.

In both sets canonical variables were derived by component analysis and compared. A high degree of relationship exists between them, that is, urban background is highly related to school success and achievement.

Wilks Lambda for total set = 0.9224338
Chi-square for total set = 51.15 $d.f.$ = 21   Probability < 0.0003
Rao's approximation   Probability < 0.0003

Chi Square Tests
With one root removed   Probability < 0.04
With two roots removed   Probability < 0.15

The significant relationship is between "urban" rather than "migrant" antecedents.

TABLE C.4
Canonical Correlation: Urban-Migrant and School Success Variables

	1	2	3
Canonical R's	0.21[a]	0.15[b]	0.11
Betas			
Academic			
1	0.66 (0.91)	− 0.14 (− 0.61)	
2	0.34 (0.33)	0.23 (0.79)	
3	− 0.12 (− 0.23)	0.70 (0.02)	
4	− 0.59	− 0.22	
5	0.28	− 0.05	
6	0.07	0.28	
7	0.03	0.55	

[a] $p < 0.01$
[b] $p < 0.05$

In the first canonical, which is highly significant, loadings on the size of city lived in (small) and size of the city in which the subject was born (small) both go with school retardation reflected by older age in grade (which comes from late enrollment due to rural deprivation of opportunity) and low average education attained by all children in the family. The influence of rural background on educational opportunity in Venezuela is clearly shown. The influence on school success is not so clearly shown.

In the second set the loading goes the other way, toward having lived in large cities, but with a rural birthplace for the mother. This goes with fairly successful school performance by the child, but a low percentage of children in the family attending school. Fairly high migration in the first canonical shows some tendency to go with lack of educational opportunity but not necessarily with school failure.

Second Set Comparison: Material and Economic Conditions and School Success

In the second canonical analysis a set of variables describing economic and material status of the barrio family is related to the same set of school enrollment, attendance, and achievement variables used as pseudo-dependent variables in the first analysis.

Material-Economic Conditions	*School Success*
1. Poverty-affluence scale (composite)	1. Age-grade scale (regular age for grade)
2. Occupational status	2. Academic history
	3. Success
3. Monthly income	4. Average education of children
	5. Age, first enrolled
4. Occupational mobility	6. Number years uncompleted in school
5. Occupational stability (time employed)	7. Percent of children in family who attend school

The multiple correlations between individual variables and opposing sets were again highly significant, as expected (see Tables C.5 and C.6).

The component analysis of the material and economic conditions set (Table C.7) showed a rather interesting contrast on loading between the first two factors, which accounted for about 73 percent of the variance.

TABLE C.5

Multiple Correlations Between Material Condition Variables
and School Success Set

	1	2	3	4	5
Multiple R	0.29	0.16	0.23	0.16	0.20
F Ratio	8.44	2.50	5.05	2.48	3.86
Probability <	0.0001	0.02	0.0001	0.02	0.0005

In the material conditions set, the poverty-affluence scale,
which actually was a composite of some of the other variables,
showed a highly significant relationship with the academic
opportunity and school performance set. Monthly income was
also highly related. A more interesting relationship is the one
between occupational stability and the school success set of
variables. Occupational stability is more highly related to
school success than occupational status.

TABLE C.6

Multiple Correlations Between School Success Variables and Material Condition
Set

	1	2	3	4	5	6	7
Multiple R	0.21	0.24	0.16	0.24	0.13	0.14	0.20
F Ratio	5.85	7.74	3.42	7.60	2.26	2.72	5.19
Probability <	0.0001	0.0001	0.005	0.0001	0.05	0.02	0.0002

On the academic opportunity and school success side, academic history and
average education of the children came out highest. These variables reflect access
over some period of time to adequate education.

TABLE C.7

Factor Analysis of Material and Economic Condition
Set (First Two Factors Only Shown Here)

		Factor 1	Factor 2
Latent Root		2.54	1.10
% Trace		50.81	21.91
Variable Loadings	*Scale Direction*	*Factor 1*	*Factor 2*
1	>	0.79	− 0.35
2	>	0.80	− 0.01
3	>	0.71	− 0.41
4	>	0.36	0.82
5	<	− 0.80	0.36

Factor One is the material success background and it is higher on all success variables except occupational mobility (4), which is loaded high in the second factor. The second factor shows much less affluence.

The derived canonical variates were then compared, with these results:

Wilks Lambda for total set = 0.8586391
Chi-square for total set = 96.40 *d.f.* = 35   Probability 0.0001
Rao's Approximation   Probability 0.0001

Chi-square Tests
With one root removed   Probability 0.13

The test with one root removed indicates that interpretation of the second factor is tenuous. Nonetheless it is interesting enough and sufficiently in accord with the situation demonstrated in later simpler tests to have been worth noting.

The canonical analysis (Table C.8) shows a high relationship between general affluence and school attendance.

TABLE C.8
Canonical Correlation: Material Condition and School Success Variables

	1	2	3	4	5
Canonical R's	0.31^a	0.16	0.12	0.08	0.05
Betas					
1	0.01 (0.81)	0.39 ($-$ 0.43)			
2	0.59 ($-$ 0.36)	0.56 (0.25)			
3	$-$ 0.53 (0.24)	$-$ 0.21 (0.20)			
4	0.37 (0.01)	$-$ 0.49 (0.85)			
5	0.13 ($-$ 0.40)	0.32 (0.05)			
6	$-$ 0.47	0.01			
7	0.08	0.38			

[a] $p < 0.001$ (all other canonicals not near significance).

Third Set Comparison: Educational Level in Family and School Success of Child

Educational Level Family	*School Success*
1. Average adult education in family	1. Age-grade scale (regular age for grade)
2. Respondent's (mother's) education	2. Academic history
	3. Success

3. Spouse's education

4. Average education of children
5. Age, first enrolled
6. Number years uncompleted in school
7. Percent of children in family who attend school

TABLE C.9
Multiple Correlations Between Family
Education Variables and School Success Set

	1	2	3
Multiple R	0.25	0.25	0.16
F Ratio	9.66	6.10	2.43
Probability $\leqslant$	0.0001	0.0001	0.02

The multiple correlations between the individual family education variables and the set of school success variables were highly significant. Spouse's education had the lowest relationship.

TABLE C.10
Multiple Correlations Between School Success Variables and Family Education Set

	1	2	3	4	5	6	7
Multiple R	0.26	0.29	0.22	0.27	0.17	0.16	0.23
							$d.f.\ 1 = 3$
F Ratio	15.19	19.30	11.00	16.26	6.45	5.27	12.19
							$d.f.\ 2 = 636$
Probability $\leqslant$	0.0001	0.0001	0.0001	0.0001	0.001	0.002	0.0001

The multiple correlations between the academic success variables and the family education set were all highly significant.

TABLE C.11
Factor Analysis of the Family
Education Variables

	1	2	3
L Root	2.17	0.56	0.27
% Trace	72.4	18.6	9.1
Loading			
1	0.91	− 0.05	− 0.41
2	0.80	0.57	0.19
3	0.83	− 0.49	0.26

The first factor had high positive loading on all three variables. The second factor was low negative on average education of the family, fairly high positive on mother's education, and fairly high negative on spouse's education.

Wilks Lambda for total set = 0.8619359
Chi-square for total set = 96.40 *d.f.* = 21   Probability < 0.0001
Rao's approximation   Probability < 0.0001

Chi-square Tests
With one root removed   Probability ≤ 0.06

The negative contribution of spouse's education, despite fairly high positive loading on mother's education, is a phenomenon that recurs throughout.

TABLE C.12
Canonical Correlation: Family Education and School Success Variables

	1	2	3
Canonical *R*'s	0.33[a]	0.14	0.11
Betas			
1	0.43 (0.91)		
2	0.49 (0.16)	(other two nonsignificant)	
3	0.06 (− 0.38)		
4	0.62		
5	0.07		
6	0.22		
7	0.37		

[a] Significant < 0.01.

High positive family education and fairly high negative spouse's education went with families in which children enrolled early and the family attained high average education. The general level of education of adults in the family is most closely related to school success and the education of the male spouse (not necessarily the father) may be inversely related.

Fourth Set Comparison: Material and Cultural Conditions of Family and School Success of Child

Material and Cultural Conditions
Variables   *School Success*
1. Urban life-style of family   1. Age-grade scale (regular age for grade)

2. Contact with world (press, radio, etc.)
3. Housing-income and material possessions
4. Marital status of R
5. Material possessions of family
6. Crowding in housing (persons per room)
7. Spouse participation in rearing of child

2. Academic history
3. Success
4. Average education of children
5. Age, first enrolled
6. Number years uncompleted in school
7. Percent of children in family who attend school

TABLE C.13
Multiple Correlations Between Culture-Material Variables and School Success Set

	1	2	3	4	5	6	7
Multiple R	0.29	0.29	0.32	0.21	0.39	0.24	0.14
F Ratio	8.56	8.16	10.33	4.15	15.78	5.47	1.82
Probability $\leqslant$	0.0001	0.0001	0.0001	0.002	0.0001	0.0001	0.10

Urban life style, contact with the world, housing, income, and possessions, and uncrowded homes were all highly related to the total set of school success variables. The marital state of R was less highly related but still significant. The participation of the spouse in the rearing of the child had no significant relationship.

TABLE C.14
Factor Analysis of the Culture-Material Conditions Variables

	1	2	3	(four other factors not shown because of low latent root)
L Root	3.11	1.60	0.85	
% Trace	44.38	22.87	12.11	cumulative % = 79.4
Loading	Scale Direction			
1	> 0.74	0.40	0.38	
2	< − 0.66	− 0.02	− 0.24	
3	> 0.84	0.28	− 0.27	
4	< − 0.48	0.79	0.08	
5	< − 0.86	− 0.12	− 0.02	
6	< − 0.48	− 0.23	− 0.75	
7	> 0.46	− 0.81	0.02	

Factor One showed high loadings on urban life style of family, contact with world through media. Income and material possessions were very high. The marital status of the respondent, family crowding, and the spouse's participation in the rearing of the child were much less highly correlated with school success.

Factor One shows high loadings, all in a favorable direction (the signs vary in directional significance as indicated). Spouse participation is low and in a favorable direction.

Factor Two is unfavorable or low on amenities and culture, but there are two high loadings that should be noted. The high loading of unstable marital status shows the unfavorable influence of unsettled marital state which goes along with poverty and lack of cultural contacts. The high loading toward spouse non-participation reflects the fact that either the union is unstable or there is no spouse.

The third factor shows a pattern of poverty and crowding.

Wilks Lambda for total set = 0.7591017

Chi-square for total set = 174.05 $d.f.$ = 49.0   Probability < 0.0001

Rao's approximation   Probability < 0.0001

Chi-square Tests

With one root removed   Probability < 0.01

With two roots removed   Probability $\leqslant$ 0.12

There are two distinct factors, "success" and "family instability."

TABLE C.15
Canonical Correlation: Culture-Material and School Success Variables

	1	2	3	
Canonical R's	0.41[a]	0.19	0.15	(other four not close to significance)
Betas				
1	− 0.05 (0.23)	0.32 (− 0.07)	− 0.48 (0.54)	
2	0.41 (− 0.28)	0.31 (− 0.17)	− 0.62 (0.14)	
3	0.48 (0.10)	− 0.46 (− 0.58)	− 0.13 (− 0.63)	
4	0.63 (− 0.44)	0.27 (0.45)	0.45 (− 0.07)	
5	− 0.02 (− 0.73)	0.11 (− 0.64)	− 0.01 (0.10)	
6	− 0.42 (− 0.23)	0.60 (0.11)	0.16 (− 0.53)	
7	0.15 (− 0.26)	− 0.39 (0.07)	− 0.38 (− 0.01)	

[a] $p < 0.01$.

The first canonical set shows the high relationship between school success and favorable material and cultural conditions in the home and family. On the material-cultural side the high contributors are amenities and possessions (0.73), high marital stability (0.44), and fairly high contact with the world (0.28). Again there is the effect of spouse participation: low participation goes with success.

On the school achievement side there is high average education of children (0.63), success in school (0.42), and successful academic history (0.48).

Fifth Set Comparison: Mother's Goals and Attitudes and School Success of Child

Mother's Goals and Attitudes	*School Success*
1. Expected educational attainment for child ($\genfrac{}{}{0pt}{}{>}{+}$)	1. Age-grade scale (regular age for grade)
2. Educational motivation of mother ($\genfrac{}{}{0pt}{}{>}{+}$)	2. Academic history
	3. Success
3. Mother has long-term goals for child ($\genfrac{}{}{0pt}{}{<}{+}$)	4. Average education of children
	5. Age, first enrolled
4. Mother rewards child rather than punishes ($\genfrac{}{}{0pt}{}{<}{+}$)	6. Number years uncompleted in school
5. Mother has production goals for herself ($\genfrac{}{}{0pt}{}{<}{+}$)	7. Percent of children in family who attend school
6. Mother has improvement in mind if she moves ($\genfrac{}{}{0pt}{}{<}{+}$)	

TABLE C.16
Multiple Correlations Between Mother's Goals Variables and School Success Set

	1	2	3	4	5	6
Multiple R	0.51	0.24	0.13	0.16	0.15	0.07
F Ratio	31.73	5.74	1.66	2.33	2.20	0.45
Probability $\leqslant$	0.0001	0.0001	0.11	0.02	0.03	0.87

The multiple correlation of the goal and attitude variables with the school success set showed a highly varied pattern. School success variables showed highly significant correlations with the mother's specific goals for educating her children. The mother's own motivations toward education, as expressed verbally, also correlated highly with the child's performance at school, although it did not always match mother's actual educational attainment. There is also a high relationship (significant < 0.02) between school achievement and whether or not the mother uses reward or punishment to stimulate the child's performance in school.

The analysis of goals and attitudes set shows three factors of interest in Table C.17.

TABLE C.17
Factor Analysis of the Goals and Attitude Variables

		1	2	3	
L Root		1.67	1.04	1.00	
% Trace		27.78	17.26	16.59	Cumulative % = 61.6
Loading Scale					
Variable	Direction Loading				
1	> 0.43		− 0.22	− 0.44	
2	> 0.84		− 0.06	0.14	
3	< − 0.59		− 0.03	− 0.16	
4	< − 0.06		0.87	0.27	
5	< − 0.17		− 0.45	0.80	
6	< − 0.62		− 0.16	− 0.21	

TABLE C.18
Canonical Correlation: Mother's Goals and Attitudes and School Success Variables

	1		2	
Canonical R's	0.53[a]		0.21 (other four not close to significance)	
Betas				
1	0.63	(0.95)	− 0.48	(0.23)
2	0.13	(0.17)	− 0.43	(− 0.72)
3	0.01	(− 0.05)	− 0.50	(0.13)
4	0.58	(− 0.24)	0.02	(0.03)
5	− 0.16	(− 0.01)	− 0.09	(− 0.58)
6	− 0.36	(0.02)	0.35	(− 0.28)
7	0.31		− 0.45	

[a] $p < 0.001$.

The first factor is loaded very high on educational motivation for self (0.84) and child (0.43), on long-term goals (0.59), and on the necessity of improvement (0.62). The second factor is very high on punishment as a means of stimulating school achievement (0.87) and has a high loading (0.45) on production-oriented goals, that is, "get things done."

Wilks Lambda for total set = 0.6713720
Chi-square for total set = 251.81 $d.f.$ = 42.0   Probability < 0.0001
Rao's approximation   Probability < 0.0001

Chi-square Tests
With one root removed   Probability ≤ 0.07

Interpretation of the second factor is marginal.

The first canonical is highly significant. There is very high loading on mother's expected educational attainment for children (0.95) and fairly high (0.24) on preference for reward, rather than punishment, for stimulating children's success in school.

The second canonical shows very low educational motivation of mother (0.72) going with general lack of enrollment, attendance, and school success in the family.

Multiple Regression Analysis

In this analysis, forty antecedent variables (family education, material circumstances, origins, and so forth) were run against school achievement measured by the variables age-grade standing. The variables that directly correlated high with school success are shown in Table C.19.

TABLE C.19
Simple Correlations of Antecedent Variables with School Success Criterion Variable

Rank	Correlation	Variable No.	Variable Description
1	0.40	18	Educational level mother expects child will attain
2	0.23	8	Average adult education in family of child
3.5	0.22	13	Material possessions of the family
3.5	0.22	6	Respondent's (mother's) education
5.5	0.21	37	Composite scale of income, housing, possessions
5.5	0.21	12	Urban life style of family
7	0.20	38	Housing-income-possessions of family
8.5	0.18	3	Family has lived in large cities
8.5	0.18	20	Child of stable marriage. Respondent married
10	0.16	10	Mother has high goals for child
11.5	0.14	2	Child born in large city
11.5	0.14	15	High monthly income per person in family

Table C.19 expresses the direct or simple relationship between antecedent variables and the criterion. However, antecedent variables are themselves interrelated and this interrelationship affects the simple relationship with the criterion shown in Table C.19. To account for this interrelationship and to assess the best set of multiple predictors, a multiple stepwise regression analysis was performed. The stepwise procedure selects a subset of variables which best predict to the criterion, school success. In stepwise regression the best predictor is selected and partialed out of the correlation matrix; then, the next best predictor is selected, and so on. Each predictor is tested by an F-ratio and the program stops when this ratio falls below a critical value.

The best set of multiple predictors appear in Table C.20. The stepwise regression analysis does produce some changes from the set of original variables that correlated most highly with the criterion on a simple basis.

TABLE C.20
Predictor Variables Resulting from Multiple Stepwise Regression Arranged According to Critical Ratio Test of the Regression Coefficients (Betas)

Beta Ratio	Rank	Variable No.	Variable Description
11.2	1	18	Educational level mother expects child to attain
3.45	2	9	Family has few adults living in house
2.78	3	20	Respondent (mother) is married
2.45	4	8	Average adult education is high in family of child
2.43	5	3	Family has lived in large cities
2.35	6	7	Spouse has low educational attainment
2.33	7.5	37	Composite scale of income, housing, possessions
2.33	7.5	32	Mother rewards nonachiever rather than punishes

Multiple $R = 0.52$ $R^2 = 0.27$

Multiple Discriminant Analysis of Family Income, Education, and Children's School Success

The subjects were divided into eight groups according to their positions on two antecedent variable measures (family income and educational attainment of the family) and the variables relating to school enrollment, attendance, and achievement. A median split was used for the division into high and low categories. The division into eight groups would be as schematized in Table C.21.

Table C.21 reflects the income-family education-child's school performance characteristics of the sample of 640 mothers of school-age children in Ciudad Guayana. The descriptive facts of Table C.21 tell some things about the sample. The most frequent (126) category was low on all three measures (income, family education and school performance). The next highest category was high on all measures (117). Large numbers of Guayana families, however, departed from this pattern. The largest variant group (96) was composed of families in which income was high, and family education and child's school performance

TABLE C.21
Three-Way Classification of Subjects by Income, Family Education, and School Performance

		Income of Family				
		Low		High		
		Education of Family Members				
		Low	High	Low	High	N
School	Low	L–L–L	L–H–L	H–L–L	H–H–L	
		126	23	96	65	310
Success	High	L–L–H	L–H–H	H–L–H	H–H–H	
		86	50	77	117	330
	N	212	73	173	182	640

both low. The next largest group (86) was low on antecedents but high on school performance. This group had a frequency in the sample of 65. The lowest frequency of all was the group which had low income, high educational level in the family, and low school performance.

All of these things merely characterize the sample which by design was weighted toward the low education and low school performance families of Ciudad Guayana. (Appendix A describes the sampling procedure and lays out the limitations of generalizations that may be based on the sample.) The objectives of multiple discriminant analysis were:

1. To test the way family income, family education, and school performance serve as bases for constructing groups according to positions above or below the mean on these variables.

2. To test the extent to which these groups are mutually exclusive and non-overlapping.

3. To test the extent to which, knowing a subject's position on one or both of the antecedent variables, it would be possible to assign the subject a position on the performance variable.

4. To observe the extent to which exceptions on the grouping patterns could be attributed to the influence of other variables.

Two variant groups were of particular importance:

The groups which were low on both family income and education. What are the factors which distinguish between those with successful children, and those without?

The groups which were high on both family income and education.

The over-all discriminant analysis provided two clear-cut components which accounted for over 80 percent of the trace. There was the faint outline of third and fourth components, but the analysis did not make these combinations clear beyond the fact that high antecedents went with high performance and low antecedents with low. The two major functions were

TABLE C.22
Centour and Probability Matrix of the Discriminant Analysis Applied to the Eight Groups[a]

		L–L–L 1	L–H–L 2	H–L–L 3	H–H–L 4
Centour	Group 1	0.0000	6.7089	2.2012	10.3396
Probability	Group	0.7993	0.0049	0.1633	0.0023
Centour	Group 2	5.0964	0.0000	6.6285	4.3824
Probability	Group	0.1669	0.3711	0.0477	0.1227
Centour	Group 3	2.0749	7.3185	0.0000	6.8860
Probability	Group	0.3555	0.0045	0.6163	0.0165
Centour	Group 4	8.3296	6.3884	4.8690	0.0000
Probability	Group	0.0234	0.0107	0.0810	0.7733
Centour	Group 5	3.7469	6.7726	5.8658	16.9913
Probability	Group	0.1033	0.0040	0.0220	0.0001
Centour	Group 6	7.7185	4.1339	8.9694	9.0639
Probability	Group	0.0137	0.0143	0.0045	0.0036
Centour	Group 7	7.4894	7.3531	5.7647	14.2676
Probability	Group	0.0186	0.0035	0.0271	0.0003
Centour	Group 8	15.0256	10.9452	10.9628	8.4197
Probability	Group	0.0004	0.0005	0.0017	0.0050

[a] Probability refers to the likelihood that an individual case will be included in the group given his scores and the derived discriminant function. The centour represents the distance of the cases

a. High on parent education, many possessions, high expectations for education, average education of children, early enrollment, and high percentage of children attending.
b. Low parent education, few adults, large family, but early enrollment and high average education of children.

The centour scores and probabilities shown in Table C.22 give an indication of the extent to which the groups in Table C.21 were mutually exclusive and nonoverlapping. Table C.23 gives the percentage of "hits" or correct assignment to groups as a function of applying the equations built by the analysis. The extent to which frequencies occur along the diagonals reflects how well the groupings can be predicted from knowledge of other variables. The over-all

TABLE C.22—*continued*

		L–L–H 5	L–H–H 6	H–L–H 7	H–H–H 8
Centour	Group 1	7.2282	17.6742	9.8039	11.9958
Probability	Group 1	0.0228	0.0001	0.0046	0.0027
Centour	Group 2	11.7831	5.1854	8.1988	6.6423
Probability	Group 2	0.0062	0.1534	0.0272	0.1049
Centour	Group 3	13.2170	18.2540	10.5413	13.4201
Probability	Group 3	0.0014	0.0001	0.0040	0.0017
Centour	Group 4	21.8383	11.3829	11.1963	5.9897
Probability	Group 4	0.0000	0.0049	0.0043	0.1024
Centour	Group 5	0.0000	5.4211	3.4099	7.4543
Probability	Group 5	0.7117	0.0430	0.0939	0.0220
Centour	Group 6	4.5525	0.0000	5.0880	2.7155
Probability	Group 6	0.0707	0.6258	0.0393	0.2280
Centour	Group 7	2.3346	5.3522	0.0000	6.8495
Probability	Group 7	0.2592	0.0521	0.6044	0.0349
Centour	Group 8	13.6924	4.1351	5.7782	0.0000
Probability	Group 8	0.0007	0.0791	0.0278	0.8850

making up a group from another group. The greater the distance, the more dissimilar or unique are the groups in question.

TABLE C.23
Hits and Misses Table of Eight Groups Formed by Median Splits on Income, Education, and School Performance

		Predicted Cases								
	1 Lo Lo Lo	2 Lo Hi Lo	3 Hi Lo Lo	4 Hi Hi Lo	5 Lo Lo Hi	6 Lo Hi Hi	7 Hi Lo Hi	8 Hi Hi Hi	*N*	% Hits
1 Lo Lo Lo	84	1	17	2	13	2	3	4	126	67
2 Lo Hi Lo	2	8	2	3	1	3	2	2	23	35
3 Hi Lo Lo	26	0	55	8	1	0	4	2	96	57
Original 4 Hi Hi Lo	3	2	5	46	0	1	1	7	65	70
Cases 5 Lo Lo Hi	10	0	1	1	56	3	14	1	86	65
6 Lo Hi Hi	0	2	2	1	5	31	3	6	50	62
7 Hi Lo Hi	2	0	3	0	14	1	48	9	77	61
8 Hi Hi Hi	3	0	0	8	2	8	4	92	117	80
	130	13	85	69	92	49	79	123	640	66

percentage of hits was 66, indicating that it is possible to predict to the pattern of family income and education and success of child in school about two times out of three.

The most predictable group is that with high score on all three grouping variables, that is, high income, education, and school success. This group was predicted with 80 percent hits. The next most predictable group is that with high scores on income and education but with low school success; this was predicted with 70 percent hits. The two next most predictable groups are those with low scores on income and education, and low or high scores on success in school.

The group means on the variables used in the predictive equation were scanned to determine differences between groups with similar income and education levels, but differing educational outcome scores. The *successful* low income and education group differs from the unsuccessful low income-education group in the following variables:

Low income-education but educational success group has higher means on

Variable number	Variable description
10	Size of family—large
12	Number of possessions—more
16	Expected educational attainment for child—higher
26	Desired if move—improvement
31	How respondent knew school and teacher—self-initiated

The successful group *high* on income and education differed from the unsuccessful group with the same antecedents on the following variables:

High income-education but educational success group has higher means on

Variable number	Variable description
1	Age of respondent—older
8	Number of adults—more
12	Number of possessions—more
16	Expected educational attainment for child—higher
17	Number of symptoms—fewer
18	Marital status of respondent—married
19	Time spouse employed—short time
21	Frequency attend church—high
35	Contact with world (media use, associations)—higher

No test of significance was applied to these differences, and no claim is made here that they would emerge on an analysis applied to a different sample. But there are strong similarities between the types of variables that are related to academic success when differences in income and education levels are controlled, and those emerging from other analyses reported in this book. For the poor group, it is mostly motivation which distinguishes between successful and unsuccessful education of children. The successful children from low income and education families have mothers with higher aspirations for the child who act on those aspirations. This motivation for improvement affects the children to some degree. Family size probably reflects more the presence of other adults, and perhaps a husband, who can act as models for the child as well as alleviating the effects of temporary economic crises. The larger number of possessions indicates either economic good fortune at some point or stronger middle-class values.

For the more fortunate group, in this sample high on both education and income, the pattern that distinguishes between success and failure in education of children seems to be more a function of family stability and occupational mobility. The successful group seems more integrated into the community. These families have more possessions, greater contact with the world through the mass media and voluntary associations, say they attend church more frequently, and are married. These may also be older families, with housewives more experienced in family management and more able to weather the crises which affect citizens of Guayana. The number of symptoms that the mother reports in describing her child is lower, suggesting better health conditions despite equal income and education. The short time that spouse has been employed can be interpreted as representing those who have recently changed jobs, although there is no indication that it necessarily reflects upward occupational mobility.

Notes

Chapter 1

1. For a recent review of research and comment, see Richard M. Morse, "Urbanization in Latin America," *Latin American Research Review*, Vol. 1, No. 1 (Fall 1965), pp. 35–74. Also helpful is Philip M. Hauser (ed.), *Urbanization in Latin America* (New York: Columbia University Press, 1961). A useful collection of research reports on social correlates of industrialization is Joseph A. Kahl (ed.), *La Industrialización en America Latina* (México: Fondo de Cultural Economica, 1965).
2. William L. Flinn, "Rural to Urban Migration: A Colombian Case," (Madison: Land Tenure Center of the University of Wisconsin, Rp. July 19, 1966); J. Matos Mar, "Migration and Urbanization: The Barriadas of Lima" in Hauser (ed.), *Urbanization in Latin America*, pp. 170–189; Gino Germani, "Inquiry into the Social Effects of Urbanization in a Working-Class Sector of Greater Buenos Aires," in Hauser (ed.), *Urbanization in Latin America*, pp. 206–233.
3. Russell G. Davis, "Basic Education in Nicaragua—Report on Present Status and Six-Year Plan for Development" (Managua: United States Overseas Mission, October 1961).

Chapter 2

1. A description of some of the factors involved in the selection of the Guayana as a development region is contained in John Friedmann, *Regional Development Policy: A Case Study of Venezuela* (Cambridge, Mass.: The M.I.T. Press, 1966).
2. For a more detailed description of economic goals for the Guayana, see Corporación Venezolana de Guayana, *El Programa Económico de Guayana: Clave del Desarrollo de Venezuela* (Caracas, 1966).
3. For an analysis of the role of oil in the Venezuelan economy, see Edwin Lieuwen, *Petroleum in Venezuela; a History* (Berkeley: University of California Press, 1954). Also, Edwin Lieuwen, *Venezuela*, 2nd ed. (London: Oxford University Press, 1965), Chapter 4.
4. Alexander Ganz, "La Lógica Económica del Programa," *Desarrollo Economico*, Vol. 2, No. 2 (1965), pp. 12–16.
5. Alfred Marshall, *Principles of Economics*, 8th ed. (London: Macmillan, 1961).
6. Theodore W. Schultz, *The Economic Value of Education* (New York: Columbia University Press, 1963).
7. Jacob Mincer, "On-the-Job-Training: Costs, Returns, and Some Implications," *The Journal of Political Economy*, Vol. 50, No. 5 (Supplement, October 1962).
8. Gary S. Becker, *Human Capital: A Theoretical and Empirical Analysis, with Special Reference to Education* (New York: National Bureau of Economic Research, 1964).
9. Carl S. Shoup, *The Fiscal System of Venezuela. A Report of the Commission to Study the Fiscal System of Venezuela* (Baltimore, Md.: The Johns Hopkins Press, 1959).

10. Robert M. Solow, "Technical Change and the Aggregate Production Function," *Review of Economic Statistics*, August 1957, pp. 312–320.
11. John W. Kendrick, *Productivity Trends in the United States* (Princeton, N.J.: Princeton University Press, 1961).
12. H. S. Parnes, *Forecasting Educational Needs for Economic and Social Development* (Paris: Organization for Economic Cooperation and Development, 1962).
13. See H. S. Parnes (ed.), *Planning Education for Economic and Social Development* (Paris: Organization for Economic Cooperation and Development, Mediterranean Regional Project, 1963), and The Mediterranean Regional Project, *Education for Economic and Social Development* (Paris: Organization for Economic Cooperation and Development, 1965). The latter includes country reports for Greece, Portugal, Italy, Spain, Turkey, and Yugoslavia.
14. Corporación Venezolana de Guayana, "Estrategia para el Desarrollo de los Recursos Humanos de la Zona de Guayana: Análisis Preliminar y Recomendaciones," mimeo (Caracas, May 1965). A more complete plan based on revised and updated information is Noel F. McGinn and Russell G. Davis, *Human Resource Development in Ciudad Guayana, Venezuela* (Cambridge, Mass.: Harvard University, Center for Studies in Education and Development, Occasional Paper No. 2, April 1967).

Chapter 3
1. There are several sources for additional material on the urban plan for Ciudad Guayana. See Lloyd Rodwin, "Ciudad Guayana: A New City," *Scientific American*, Vol. 23, No. 3 (September 1965), pp. 122–132, for a summary of the plan and planning process. For a detailed analysis, one may consult the ninety-odd working documents produced by the staff of the Harvard-M.I.T. Joint Center for Urban Studies, 66 Church Street, Cambridge, Mass.
2. For another analysis of the CVG role in the development of the region, see John R. Dinkelspiel, "Administrative Style and Economic Development: The Organization and Management of the Guayana Region Development of Venezuela" (Harvard University, Department of Government, unpublished Ph.D. dissertation, 1967).

Chapter 4
1. John S. MacDonald, "Migration and the Population of Ciudad Guayana," mimeo (Caracas: Corporación Venezolana de Guayana, February 16, 1966).
2. Flinn, "Rural to Urban Migration: A Colombian Case"; Matos Mar, "Migration and Urbanization"; Germani, "Inquiry into the Social Effects of Urbanization"; Jose Francisco de Camargo, "Exodo Rural No Brasil" (Sao Paulo: Faculdade de Ciencias Económicas e Administrativas, Boletim No. 1, 1957).
3. MacDonald, "Migration and the Population of Ciudad Guayana."
4. John S. MacDonald, "Population Redistribution and Urbanization in

Guayana," mimeo (Caracas: Corporación Venezolana de Guayana, no date), p. 3.
5. *Ibid.*
6. Lisa Peattie, "La Movilidad Social," *Desarrollo Economico*, Vol. 2, No. 3 (Tercer Trimestre, 1965), pp. 25–30. Peattie points out that there is almost no assistance to or opportunity for those without jobs, training, or resources. The beginning of a poverty culture, perpetuating itself through generations, is possible in Guayana, but many look on schools and training for the young as a way to break the chain. This shines through in the school study.
7. *Ibid.*
8. This and following statements are based on an analysis of interviews in Ciudad Guayana which form part of the study *Conflictos y Consenso* carried out by the Center for Development Studies (CENDES) of the Central University of Venezuela in 1963.

Chapter 5
1. The steel mill and the Orinoco Mining Company have already established such a standard for new employees.
2. These requirements are clearly recognized by Latin American educators and planners. See Departamento de Asuntos Educativos, *Corrientes de la educación primaria en America Latina 1934–1962* (Washington, D.C.: Unión Panamericana, 1964).
3. For a description of education in Venezuela, see George I. Sanchez, *The Development of Education in Venezuela* (Washington, D.C.: Office of Education, Department of Health, Education, and Welfare, 1963). For a general review of education in Latin America, see I. N. Thut and Don Adams, *Educational Patterns in Contemporary Societies* (New York: McGraw-Hill, 1964), pp. 355–386.
4. Data are taken from an unpublished survey by Celia Germani of CSED.
5. For a description of the curriculum and those of other Latin American countries, see M. B. Lourenco Filho, *Primary School Curricula in Latin America* (Paris: UNESCO, Educational Studies and Documents No. 24, 1957). See also Ministerio de Educación, *Programa de educación primaria*, 6 vols. (Caracas: Ediciones Venezolanas de Divulgación Educativa, no date).
6. There is little published research on teachers in Venezuela. See Orlando Albornoz, *El maestro y la educación en la sociedad venezolana* (Caracas: Distribuidora de Publicaciones Venezolanas, 1965). A detailed study of teachers in Ciudad Guayana is now being carried out by CSED.
7. These salaries seem high by comparison with those paid teachers in other Latin American countries. However, Venezuela's cost of living index, inflated by the easy money of oil, is the highest in Latin America, and Ciudad Guayana is among the most expensive cities in the country. Middle-class three-bedroom apartments rented for Bs. 750 ($165) a month in 1965. Milk sold for two bolivares ($.44) a liter. Beef varied between seven and ten bolivares a kilo ($.77 to 1.10 a pound).

8. For a more detailed review of these ailments, see Thut and Adams, *Educational Patterns in Contemporary Societies*; Walter V. Kaulfers, "Latin American Education in Transition," *The Educational Record*, Vol. 42, No. 2 (April 1961), pp. 91–98; Thomas B. Davis, "A Survey of Elementary and Secondary Education in Latin America," *Journal of Inter-American Studies*, Vol. 3, No. 1 (January 1961), pp. 97–120; Robert J. Havighurst and Jayme Abreu, "The Problem of Secondary Education in Latin America," *Comparative Education Review*, Vol. 5, No. 3 (February 1962), pp. 167–174.

9. There was some criticism of Venezuela's slavish copying of the Brazilian model, and supposedly whole sections of law with small application in Venezuela were copied directly from Brazil. An examination of current laws and regulations does not show this and INCE works well.

Chapter 6

1. Division Desarrollo Humano, "Estimación del costo anual de una escuela primaria graduada de doce aulas, en Ciudad Guayana," mimeo (Caracas: Corporación Venezolana de Guayana, July 1967).

2. Robert J. Alexander, *The Venezuelan Democratic Revolution* (New Brunswick, N.J.: Rutgers University Press, 1964).

3. This school was eliminated in 1966 by construction of a twelve-room school building in the vicinity.

4. All of the six-year schools in Ciudad Guayana had lunch programs in 1965, supported by the government. In the public schools these handle about one of every six children who need the service. Parents fight to get their children enrolled in the lunch program, and some children who would not come to school otherwise do so to get the free meal. But many others go to school after a breakfast of coffee and *cassava*, or bread and Coca-cola in the more urbanized families. None of the public schools was visited by nurses or doctors in 1965–1966.

5. Consejo Federal de Inversiones, *La Deserción Escolar en la Argentina: Su Evolución y Situación Presente* (Buenos Aires, 1964).

Chapter 7

1. MacDonald, "Migration and the Population of Ciudad Guayana."

2. *Ibid.*

3. An analysis of a subsample drawn in Ciudad Guayana for the study *Conflictos y Consenso* in 1963 shows that residents of Guayana rank teachers first as "those who are doing the most for Venezuela," ahead of doctors, priests, politicians, and others. This study was carried out nationally by the Centro de Estudios del Desarrollo of the Central University of Venezuela.

4. For a critical analysis of primary education in Venezuela, see Gladys de Acosta Saignes, *Investigación Sobre Materiales de la Escuela Venezolana* (Caracas: Universidad Central de Venezuela, 1965). Dr. Acosta Saignes demonstrates that the chief problem with primary school teachers is that they do not teach fundamentals but rather more advanced skills. Teachers in the

second grade, in her study, spent more time on materials which the curriculum in language indicates should be dealt with in the higher grades than on those basics supposed to be covered in the second grade.

Chapter 8
1. For a description of family housing in Ciudad Guayana in 1963, see Anna Maria Sant'Anna, "Situación Habitacional en Santo Tomé de Guayana, 1963," working paper (Caracas: Corporación Venezolana de Guayana, August 1964).
2. Families in Ciudad Guayana in 1963 were consuming an average per person of 1,410 calories per day, whereas requirements were defined at 2,300 calories. Calorie consumption was lower in Ciudad Guayana than any other sampled region of Venezuela, even though per capita family incomes were higher than in most regions. Caloric intake in San Félix averaged at 1,285, whereas residents of Puerto Ordaz consumed an average of 2,210 per day. Diets in Ciudad Guayana excluding Puerto Ordaz were considered to be deficient in intake of protein, calcium, phosphorous, iron, vitamin A, thiamine, riboflavin, and niacin. Dietary deficiencies were particularly marked in children under five. See Instituto Nacional de Nutrición, "Encuesta de Nutrición," mimeo (Caracas, May–June 1963).
3. Eduardo Hamuy, *El Problema Educacional del Pueblo de Chile* (Santiago: Editorial de Pacífico, 1961).
4. Consejo Federal de Inversiones, *La Deserción Escolar en la Argentina*—see also, for a Venezuelan analysis of economic determinants of dropouts, Nancy Velasquez de Rojas, "Relaciones Socioeconomicas en el Problema del Abandono Escolar en Cumana," *Ciencias Sociales*, Vol. 1, No. 2 (June 1964), pp. 168–182.
5. Robert J. Havighurst and collaborators, *La sociedad y la educación en America Latina* (Buenos Aires: Editorial Universitaria de Buenos Aires, 1962).
6. Alvin L. Bertrand, "School Attendance and Attainment: Function and Disfunction of School and Family Social Systems," *Social Forces*, Vol. 40 (1962), pp. 228–233; Robert Jay Thomas, "An Empirical Study of High School Drop-Outs in Regard to Ten Possibly Related Factors," *Journal of Educational Sociology*, Vol. 28 (1954), pp. 11–18; S. M. Miller, Carolyn Comings, and Betty Saleem, "The School Dropout Problem" (Albany, N.Y.: Division for Youth, State of New York, 1963); Jean E. Floud, "Social Class Factors in Educational Achievement," in A. H. Halsey (ed.), *Ability and Educational Opportunity* (Paris: Organization for Economic Cooperation and Development, 1961), pp. 91–112; Glen H. Elder, Jr., *Adolescent Achievement and Mobility Aspirations* (Chapel Hill, N. C.: Institute for Research in Social Science, 1962); John Pierce-Jones, "Vocational Interest Correlates of Socio-Economic Status in Adolescence," *Educational and Psychological Measurement*, Vol. 19 (Spring 1959), pp. 65–71; W. D. Wall, F. J. Schonell, and W. C. Olson, *Failure in School* (Hamburg: UNESCO Institute for Education, 1962).

7. Miller, *et al.*, *The School Dropout Problem*.

8. For example, Miller *et al.*, *The School Dropout Problem*; Elizabeth G. Cohen, "Parental Factors in Educational Mobility" (Unpublished Ph.D. dissertation, Harvard University, Department of Social Relations, 1958); Paul H. Landis, "Teenage Adjustments in Large and Small Families" (Washington: Agricultural Experiment Station, Bulletin 549, April 1954).

9. S. Schachter, "Birth Order, Eminence, and Higher Education," *American Sociological Review*, Vol. 28, No. 5 (October 1963), pp. 757–768.

10. Floud, "Social Class Factors"; Miller *et al.*, *The School Dropout Problem*; Thomas, "An Empirical Study of High School Drop-Outs." This is true at the primary level in Puerto Rico. See Consejo Superior de Ensenanza, *La deserción escolar en Puerto Rico* (Rio Piedras, 1964). In Puerto Rico, girls drop out more frequently than boys in high school.

11. Bertrand, "School Attendance and Attainment"; Elder, *Adolescent Achievement and Mobility Aspirations*; Jean E. Floud (ed.), A. H. Halsey, and F. M. Martin, *Social Class and Educational Opportunity* (London: Heineman, 1956).

12. Lee G. Burchinal, "Differences in Educational and Occupational Aspirations of Farm, Small-Town, and City Boys," *Rural Sociology*, Vol. 26 (1961), pp. 107–121; Lois J. Gill and Bernard Spilka, "Some Non-Intellectual Correlates of Academic Achievement among Mexican-American Secondary School Students," *Journal of Educational Psychology*, Vol. 53 (June 1963), pp. 144–149.

13. Irving Krauss, "Sources of Educational Aspirations among Working Class Youth," *American Sociological Review*, Vol. 29 (December 1964), pp. 867–879.

14. Floud *et al.*, *Social Class and Educational Opportunity*.

15. Allison Davis, "Personality and Social Mobility," *The School Review*, Vol. 65 (1957), p. 137.

16. E. Grant Youmans, "Factors in Educational Attainments," *Rural Sociology*, Vol. 24 (1959), pp. 21–28.

17. Richard L. Simpson, "Parental Influence, Anticipatory Socialization, and Social Mobility," *American Sociological Review*, Vol. 27 (August 1962), pp. 517–522.

18. Floud, *et al.*, *Social Class and Educational Opportunity*.

19. Joseph A. Kahl, "Educational and Occupational Aspirations of 'Common-Man' Boys," *Harvard Educational Review*, Vol. 23 (Summer 1953), pp. 186–203.

20. The economic importance of children is associated with the frequency of marital instability in Venezuela, as in other parts of Latin America. Women must depend on their children, husbands are too unreliable. Male children are preferred because they are more likely to be able to support their mother. The more children a woman has, the more secure she can be that she will be maintained in old age.

21. Floud *et al.*, *Social Class and Educational Opportunity.*
22. Kahl, "Educational and Occupational Aspirations"; Elder, *Adolescent Achievement and Mobility Aspirations.*
23. Glen H. Elder, Jr., "Family Structure and Educational Attainment: A Cross-National Analysis," *American Sociological Review*, Vol. 30 (February 1965), pp. 81–96.
24. William R. Morrow and Robert C. Wilson, "Family Relations of Bright High-Achieving and Under-Achieving High School Boys," *Child Development*, Vol. 32 (1961), pp. 501–510.
25. Wall *et al.*, *Failure in School.*

Chapter 9

1. This group is largely composed of older children from low-income families with a history of not enrolling or not completing school years. As such, it is not a fair representation of all children not enrolling in school in any given year. But it does offer a chance to look at the children and the families who have not "made it," at the group which poses the greatest challenge to the school in terms of universal education. For a discussion of causes of educational attrition in Puerto Rico, see Melvin M. Tumin and Arnold S. Feldman, *Social Class and Social Change in Puerto Rico* (Princeton, N. J.: Princeton University Press, 1961), especially Chapter 6. See Velasquez de Rojas, "Relaciones Socioeconomicas en el Problema del Abandono Escolar en Cumana," for a list of reasons for nonenrollment and nonattendance in another part of Venezuela.
2. No formal research has been carried out on the epidemiology of illnesses in Ciudad Guayana; but informal conversations with personnel of the government's Social Security Hospital in San Félix revealed that most illnesses among children involve either intestinal parasites or bronchitis, both of which could be controlled through a preventive medicine program. In 1965, Ciudad Guayana had forty-five doctors for its 75,000 population, and roughly eighty hospital beds available to the general public.
3. Courtney B. Cazden, "Subcultural Differences in Child Language: An Interdisciplinary Review," *Merrill-Palmer Quarterly of Behavior and Development*, Vol. 12, No. 3 (1966).
4. On the contrary, as indicated in the research by Gladys de Acosta Saignes (*Investigatigación Sobre Materiales de la Escuela Venezolana*), teachers present subject matter supposed to be covered at higher grade levels. Second-grade teachers attempt to train fourth-grade skills without first training in second-grade skills. She concludes that teachers are not following the official curriculum. Further, there is a wide discrepancy between official recommendations with respect to teaching methodology and actual practices. Teachers infrequently give students an opportunity to apply arithmetical skills to practical problems. Writing exercises are usually dictated by the teacher instead of allowing students to compose. Reading is infrequent and seldom designed to whet students' appetites.

5. Research on this topic is voluminous. One source of studies is Dorwin Cartwright and Alvin Zander, *Group Dynamics* (Evanston, Ill.: Row, Peterson and Co., 1953).
6. A. Hugh Livingston, "High School Graduates and Drop-Outs—A New Look at a Persistent Problem," *School Review*, Vol. 66 (1958), pp. 195–203; Thomas, "An Empirical Study of High School Drop-Outs"; Youmans, "Factors in Educational Attainments."
7. Venezuelan law requires attendance at school by all children of school age, but the law is not enforced. It is hard to see how universal compulsory attendance can be realized until sufficient school space has been provided throughout the country.
8. In Venezuela, especially the Guayana, "friendships" may be based on casual acquaintanceships. The data should not be taken to mean that parents have close relationships with teachers, but rather that some consider teachers as friends (47 percent in the sample).

Chapter 14

1. The plan was embodied in several drafts, and ultimately an updated version of it was published as a monograph by the CSED (Noel F. McGinn and Russell G. Davis, "Human Resource Development in Ciudad Guayana, Venezuela"). The first draft of the plan was in English, under the title, "Strategy for Human Resource Development in the Distrito Caroní: A Summary" (Corporación Venezolana de Guayana, Staff Working Paper C-37, December 1964). The second draft of the plan was in Spanish, titled "Estrategia para el Desarrollo de los Recursos Humanos de la Zona de Guayana," and dated 1965. It was this version that was circulated officially to other Venezuelan government agencies.
2. A. O. Hirschman, *Development Projects Observed* (Washington, D.C.: The Brookings Institution, 1967).
3. Edward F. Mackin, "Planning Education in Response to Industrial Requirements: The Organization of a Technical Education Committee, in Ciudad Guayana, Venezuela" (Cambridge, Mass.: Harvard University, 1968). (This was a final analysis presented to the Faculty of the Graduate School of Education of Harvard University in partial fulfillment of the requirements for the degree of Doctor of Education.)
4. Hirschman, *Development Projects Observed*, p. 154.

Appendix A

1. This step was carried out by the Economic Planning Section of the CVG.
2. MacDonald, "Migration and the Population of Ciudad Guayana."
3. For a critique of various methods of estimating future demand on an educational system, see Russell G. Davis, *Planning Human Resource Development. Educational Models and Schemata* (Chicago: Rand-McNally, 1966).
4. Thanks are owed to Evelia Quijada H., Mrs. Maria de Vazquez, Fernando Gonzalez, and Graciela Hernandez of the Oficina de Ejecución y Promoción,

Sector Desarrollo Humano, CVG, located in El Roble, Ciudad Guayana. They gave generously of themselves, believing that the study would benefit the people of Ciudad Guayana.

5. ENCUESTA, C.A., Apartado del Este 4898, Caracas. Ramon Baez and Sergio Sucre did a magnificent job of directing all of the field work.

6. The outstanding character of these women is an encouraging sign for the city's future.

7. The interviewers used the child's name, that of his guardian, and the address to locate the house. On finding the house, they asked to speak with the mother of the child named on the face-sheet. If the child's mother did not live in the house, but the child did, they then spoke with the adult female chiefly responsible for the child's upbringing. In all but a few cases this person was also the *ama de casa*, or female head of the house. The thirteen extra cases interviewed were rejected from use in the sample either because the child no longer lived in the city, or because the adult female caring for the child had lived with the child for only a short period.

On meeting the prospective interviewee, the interviewers said something like,

"Good morning, my name is_____. We are doing a study of families and the future in Ciudad Guayana. We are trying to find out what people around here like yourself think about things. Could I talk with you for awhile?"

8. Sonja Bolling was of great assistance in coding the questionnaires.

9. Mercedes Pulido and Hugo Illarramendy were the testing psychologists.

Appendix C
1. Note that these are indications and *indications only*! The text designates which were tested and the manner of testing.

Index